MAN, MYTH & MAGIC

AN ILLUSTRATED ENCYCLOPEDIA OF THE SUPERNATURAL

VOLUME 20

MAN, MYTH & MAGIC

AN ILLUSTRATED ENCYCLOPEDIA OF THE SUPERNATURAL

EDITOR
Richard Cavendish

**EDITORIAL
ADVISORY BOARD**

C.A. Burland
Glyn Daniel
E.R. Dodds
Mircea Eliade
William Sargant
John Symonds
R.J. Zwi Werblosky
R.C. Zaehner

MARSHALL CAVENDISH CORPORATION / NEW YORK

CONTENTS

© 1970 BPC Publishing Ltd.
Manufactured in Italy.
Library of Congress Catalog No. 70-141143

All of the material contained herein has previously been published
in separate parts under the title Man, Myth & Magic.

SPRING

John Moss

The celebration of returning fertility, and its magical stimulation, is the basis of all spring rituals and festivals, from the Great Dionysia of the ancient Greeks to the Mardi Gras which is still an annual event in modern New Orleans

DRINKING, DANCING, FEASTING, noise-making and love-making have been the usual ways in which men have celebrated occasions of communal happiness; the winning of a war, for instance, or an election, the birth of a royal heir or the death of a tyrant. But ever since prehistoric times man has reserved special celebratory energies for the turning of the seasons, and has reacted with perhaps the strongest surge of emotion to spring, the time when the earth is freed from the shackles of winter.

This emotion was expressed in the form of religious rites, mainly because for ancient man no aspect of life could be kept apart from religion. Modern commentators have seen in the Paleolithic cave paintings of dancing figures in animal masks or disguises a form of hunting magic that itself was probably seasonal; but later ages brought agriculture to mankind, and the seasonal rites became of crucial importance. The celebration of returning fertility along with the magical stimulation of fertility form the basis for all ancient spring rituals and festivals, and so through them for most modern ones.

Something of their essence can be seen in the ancient spring customs of Mesopotamia in which the Babylonians performed

The renewal of life in spring has been celebrated since very early times and some pagan rites blended with the Christian festival of Easter: children dressed as angels, in an Easter procession in Brazil

ritual re-enactments of a Creation myth, reflecting the re-creation of spring. And they staged the sacred intercourse of the king and a priestess in a room set aside for the rite and decorated with leaves and flowers.

Sex and drama also occur in the rituals of the Greeks, a festive people who took every opportunity available for some sort of celebration. And the eastern cults that were introduced during later centuries offered many opportunities. Before that the early Greeks held a spring Festival of Flowers to

The sexual and dramatic aspects of springtime revelry sometimes overlap with another common motif in which the normal order of things is overturned

praise fertility and the god Dionysus (see DIONYSUS), with plenty of sacrificing, feasting and drinking. There was also some placation of the community's dead, the ancestral ghosts, a practice that found its way into many later traditions.

In March, the Great Dionysia was celebrated, which by the 6th century BC had come to be a time not only for general revels of a wildly unrestrained nature, but also for the presentation of drama in Athens. Evolved from older choric hymns and rites of Dionysus, the tragedies of Aeschylus, Sophocles and Euripides developed first, but comedy followed fast. And the latter retained explicit aspects of its fertility rite origins, as in the traditional flaunting of over-size phalluses.

Rome's spring festivals took up many of these older threads and entwined them with new ones. In early Republican days there were minor festivities such as the dancing and processions of the *Salii*, in March (see MARS), or the uninhibited merrymaking of the April *Parilia*, originally a shepherds' rite (see SHEEP). Also in April was a movable feast, the beautiful *Floralia*, which in the true primitive tradition combined vegetation magic and ritual sexuality.

The better known ceremonies of the *Lemuria* in May recall the Greek festival that paid homage to the dead: for the Romans it was also a time for laying restless ancestral spirits, and preventing them from wreaking harm. Something of the same intention functioned in another well-known late Roman festive occasion, the *Lupercalia*, which was held in February, at the very start of the Roman spring. It involved sacrifices, offerings of the first fruits of the previous harvest, and the other usual basic enjoyments. But it also required some ritual flagellation of people, most usually of barren women, to stimulate their fertility and perhaps to drive off whatever evil baulked that fertility. The priests also 'beat the bounds' of the communities, or of the fields, again to set up magical protection against evil for the year to come.

The declining Empire came to know many new cults and their festivals (apart from the novel worship of Christianity). One was the *Bacchanalia*, the frenzied Roman version of the Greek Dionysia, but another more austere festival developed with the cult worship of Attis (see CYBELE).

This was the March celebration called *Hilaria*. It involved processions and sacrifices, followed by abstention from meat, and general restrictions, to accompany the ritual mourning of the god's death. The god's eventual resurrection was followed by ritual joy and festivity. Christians will find the pattern not unfamiliar.

First and Last Flings

From the earliest Christian times, the celebration of spring tended to begin on or shortly after Twelfth Night, but to come to a head especially in the few days before Ash Wednesday and the austerities of Lent. Many pre-Christian festivals were held at this time, and again this is an example of Christianity superimposing itself onto paganism. In fact, the folk festivals, as opposed to the liturgical ones, always tended towards the secular, not to say the profane. Nevertheless, the Church's terminology took over: the final day of the festivals is invariably Shrove Tuesday, presumably so called because it was a day for priests to shrive folk in preparation for Lent. Yet, although the festivals may appear to be in the nature of 'last flings' before Lenten asceticism, they were, and are, also 'first flings', expressing universal joy at the spring renewal. The pre-Lenten festivals were not the sole spring festivities, but for Christian Europe and the Americas, they were the first.

Some motifs are found in most of these early spring celebrations. Feasting is always important, especially for Christians who had to give up meat and any kind of rich delicacy in Lent; but sometimes the feasting is merely symbolized by the eating of some special Shrovetide food. Dancing invariably takes place, as always at times of communal joy; some special dances may be mimetic and dramatic, concerning some suitable springtime theme, while others might be processional, the ancestors of later parades. The modern idea of parades with great decorated 'floats' was foreshadowed in the Germanic rite praising the goddess Nerthus, which involved processions with sacred objects borne on a strange 'boat-on-wheels' called a ship-wagon or ship-cart.

Masks and costumes are always part of the festivities, perhaps recalling the prehistoric dancers in animal head-dresses, and the primitive belief that fearful masks

provided a way of keeping evil spirits at bay. But in more modern times the costumes are worn largely for the sake of competitive splendour, and the masks have always helped the celebrants to shed their inhibitions in relative safety.

The motif of warding off or driving off evil crops up in many places in forms other than masking. Sometimes it is a magical ritual to protect the crops, at other times it appears as a magical destruction or exorcism of the demonic winter or some other appropriate symbol of evil. Noise plays a large part in the expulsion, as it does in many primitive rites; often an effigy figure is burned or suitably destroyed.

Mock battles of one kind or another occur frequently, and are probably linked with the motif of driving off evil. For while they may have taken on special colourations, such as re-enactments of historical combats, or riotous sport, their presence in a spring festival links them with more ancient ritual battles symbolizing the conflict of winter and summer.

Spring festivals all naturally incorporate some form of sexuality – not only private sex activity, which has always accompanied drinking, feasting and dancing, but also ritual sex that long antedates the Christian traditions. Some traditions incorporate variants of the sacred marriage; others merely bring in rude songs, the coarse antics of clowns, and earthy folk drama.

Drama, on any level, is a spring motif of its own. The incomparable Greek drama grew from much older, primitive rites; and the high traditions of English drama had their roots in choric liturgical rites of the Church at Easter which gave rise to later mystery and miracle plays, and the folk dances, mimes and mummery of the people, performed at Shrovetide, which developed the morality thread of the English tradition. Many lands still have special folk dramas and masques which are performed before Lent as they have been for centuries (see DANCE; DRAMA; MYSTERY PLAYS).

The sexual and dramatic aspects of the revelry sometimes overlap with another common motif, in which the normal order of things is overturned. Servants or fools become rulers, Lords of Misrule dominate the festivities of many countries, men dress as women.

It may seem odd that countries of the far

he celebration of fertility, and its magical timulation, form the basis for spring rituals ll over the world *Right* Fertility dance, in a illage on the Ivory Coast *Below right* The naypole with its phallic symbolism is a raditional feature of springtime celebrations, nd the custom of performing a dance around t is widespread: young men raising the naypole in Sweden

Uniphoto

North start their festivities to celebrate spring and fertility at a time when the snow s usually no less deep than at Christmas. Similarly, it may seem strange that customs eft over from Catholic observances of Lent till survive in primarily Protestant countries. The latter fact may be accounted for simply because the old ways die hard, especially when they are enjoyable, and the former may be because the combined pagan and Christian jollity, though perhaps imported to the northern lands, proved able to overcome even the frost and ice of February.

Indeed, a Finnish tradition makes use of the snow: outdoor games are part of the holiday, and old lore says that if the children's sleds can coast long distances on Shrove Tuesday, the year's crops will be bountiful. Elsewhere in Scandinavia, feasting, processions, games and dances are hallmarks of the pre-Lent time as is the custom of playful ritual flagellation with birch or willow switches, recalling the old purification theme, the driving off of winter and evil.

Driving off demons also seems allimportant in Teutonic traditions, especially in the great *Fastnacht* celebrations of Germany, known as *Fasching* in Austria. The Austrian *Schemen*, a wild assortment of masked demonic dancers, which form the centrepiece of the Innsbruck festival the week before Ash Wednesday, are especially notable. Cologne's revelry features a Prince of Fastnacht with a court of fools, while Saxony was given to staging a mock battle between the forces of winter and summer. Munich's gorgeous pageantry is worldfamous, but seems to dwell more on the city's medieval history than on folk custom or ancient rite; the German-speaking Swiss of Zurich have a tradition of killing an effigy of winter in their spring festivities.

British customs generally seem to have missed out the parades and pageantry so favoured in other lands, but some of the old spring motifs make their appearance. Shrove Tuesday is still Pancake Day in Britain, symbolic of the coming abstention from meat. But apart from this special food, Shrovetide for Britons once meant a time for rough games and hooliganism. In the past apprentices were given a holiday on the Tuesday, and showed their appreciation by all kinds of happy rowdiness. A special sort of Shrovetide football was played in many towns and rural villages (see GAMES).

Spectrum Colour Library

The sexuality theme seems to be lacking in the British Shrovetide, though the traditional post-Easter fun, and especially the Maytime delights of the past, tended to make up for this lack (see MAY DAY).

In other countries pancakes are eaten as in Britain, and there are also splendid parades or dances. In Belgium where pancakes and door-to-door begging are both part of the tradition, glorious processions were staged. These were dominated by the Gilles, who wore beautiful costumes of silk embroidered with lace, and ostrich-plume head-dresses, and who used to pelt onlookers with oranges.

Old Russian and eastern European customs included eating special cakes: the Russians called them *blini*, and the time of celebration was known as *Maslenitza*, 'butter week'. Apparently the Soviet Union has retained some of these traditions — especially the blini — though stripped of any religious associations. However, it is unlikely that other Slavic customs have lasted; the eastern European dance where the women had to leap high, so that the crops would grow tall, for instance, or the Bulgarian processions with men, dressed as women, performing mimetic ploughing and sowing dances.

Farther south in Europe, terms meaning 'Shrovetide' are replaced by the word carnival, which has come to mean unrestrained festive gaiety. Italy sometimes begins its *carnevale* in mid-January or earlier, and keeps up the feasting and

In Christian Europe, and later in North and South America, the first celebrations of spring were also in the nature of a 'last fling' before the strict fasting of Lent; the Shrovetide celebrations of Britain were paralleled further south by carnivals, times of unrestrained festivity *Above* and *Left* Scenes from the Mardi Gras held annually in New Orleans; brought to Louisiana by French settlers when the state was a colony of France, it has developed into a major tourist attraction *Above right* Masks are always part of the festivities, possibly recalling the primitive belief that they keep evil spirits at bay: masks for sale in Rio de Janeiro which is the scene of the most famous carnival in South America *Far right* Effigy used in celebrations held in May in Portugal

John Moss

Robert Estall

The spring fiesta in Spain includes many folk dramas on sacred marriage or Resurrection themes, and dramatic dance battles between Moors and Christians

dancing and pageantry until Shrove Tuesday. Venice crowns an overweight effigy, the spirit of fleshly indulgence, as King of Carnival and ritually burns him to bring in Ash Wednesday. Florence, among other centres, is noted for the delightful rudeness of traditional carnival songs.

The Spanish carnival spirit produces most of the usual traditions, especially public dancing and masked processions. In northern Spain, a stuffed effigy again acts as the emblem of carnival licence; it rides in a cart decorated with greenery, reflecting the ancient belief in vegetation magic, and is duly burned. Elsewhere in Spain an effigy representing the King of Evil is ritually buried; and the spring *fiesta* also includes many folk dramas on sacred marriage or

Resurrection themes, or on the symbolic battle theme, which is sometimes in the form of dramatic dance battles between Moors and Christians.

The Spanish concepts of pre-Lent fiesta were widely adopted in Latin and South America, and there too the motif of the mock battle seems to be strong. A Mexican drama ritually depicts the capture of a famous bandit by soldiers, while in southeast Mexico a mock battle dance concerns 'priests' and 'devils'. Throughout Latin America maskers represent devils and the dead, signifying the supernatural forces that are to be warded off.

But the Spanish ex-colonies take fiesta to its heights in their immense variety of special dances, such as the quadrille-type

dance of central Mexico, for instance, in which participants wear medieval garb. Many of the dances incorporate elements of pre-Columbian Indian dances and rites. In Mexico, for instance, the time that is now carnival was once given to revelry in praise of the Aztec god of agriculture.

Portugal's carnival spirit rivals that of Spain. It was once especially famous for the extreme coarseness of the songs, dances and jokes of the masked Fools who dominated it, though this feature has diminished in recent times. The mock battle theme recurs abundantly: in the town of Loulé, for instance, the ritual conflict is fought out with flowers.

Portuguese carnival traditions were naturally exported to Brazil, where in 1840 the urban carnival of Rio de Janeiro began;

it is now regarded as the most lavish on the continent. All the expected features of carnival can be found in costly abundance, especially parades with vast resplendent floats and ornate costuming, in which various societies and clubs ruthlessly compete. Otherwise, besides the street dancing and music, noise and drinking and wild revelry, Rio finds some quiet corners to stage a major song contest, with rich prizes. And the whole festival culminates in a masquerade ball in the Municipal Theatre.

'Fat Tuesday'

The French have always enjoyed many different kinds of carnival, including a now extinct festival of butchers in Paris, which featured Le Boeuf Gras, a fattened ox decorated with ribbons, which was probably another emblem of the indulgence to be forsworn in Lent. But the chief festival is the carnival of Nice, with glorious parades and pageants, dominated by King Carnival and his court of clowns and harlequins, embodying the free wild spirit of the season. This spirit flourished especially in the French colony which is now the American state of Louisiana. There the significant French name for Shrove Tuesday took on new meaning as the general term for the whole festive time. The name is Mardi Gras, 'Fat Tuesday'.

Mardi Gras traditions date from the mid-18th century, in New Orleans, when private masquerade balls often exploded onto the streets to become public, sometimes violent, merrymaking. By the early 19th

century the city's revellers had taken to parading through the streets on horseback or in carriages to display their finery; and tableaux, masques and similar light dramas had become a part of the occasion.

By the mid-19th century, the Creole domination of this essentially French tradition had begun to be eclipsed by the eager 'Saxons'. Then in 1857 a group of the latter formed a theoretically secret society called the 'Mystic Krewe of Comus', and staged a colourful street parade depicting the demons from Milton's *Paradise Lost*. So the modern Mardi Gras was born.

The Civil War interrupted the tradition but the Krewe of Comus formed itself again afterwards and continued its parades, always with a special theme that might be allegorical or sometimes satirical. There was always a torchlit night parade on the Tuesday. The Krewe also staged tableaux, and topped off the night with a grand ball that rapidly became a major social occasion.

The festivities were often marred by Creole-Saxon conflicts and general riotous behaviour, but the protests of some citizens could not stem the Mardi Gras tide. In 1872 the day was declared a legal holiday, though by then the festival had been getting under way much earlier. Indeed, in 1870 a Lord of Misrule figure had briefly appeared, with a parade of his own, on Twelfth Night. But in 1872 he faded out, for Rex, King of Carnival, and his court of Dukes, came into being partly to impress the Russian Tsar's younger son, who was visiting the city. The parades were

enormous that year, the decorations lavish the merriment frenzied. On the Tuesday more than a dozen bands played a song called *If Ever I Cease to Love*, supposedly a favourite of the royal Russian; and though he must have been heartily sick of it by the end of the day it remains a traditional tune of Mardi Gras. That year also there was a Boeuf Gras in the old French tradition Rex, whose parade was at noon on the Tuesday, initiated the now fixed custom of acquiring a Queen, usually a pretty society debutante, and escorting her to the 'court' of Comus at midnight, to pay respects to the first lord of Mardi Gras.

Soon other krewes, as the clubs and societies are still generically known, began to take part. The Knights of Momus led the newcomers, and at first paraded on New Year's Eve, later switching to the Thursday before Fat Tuesday. In 1882 the Knights of Proteus began parading on the Monday the Krewe of Hermes took over the Friday and krewes of Orpheus, Osiris, Mithras Elves of Oberon, the Harlequins, Pierettes Marionettes and dozens of others found room where they could for their own parades and displays.

Some citizens thought it was all getting out of hand. Sometimes the festivities began before Christmas, as they still do: in 1965 the society balls began on 23 December and there had been 62 of them by Fat Tuesday From the start, the inter-krewe rivalry had been lavishly expensive. But there was no stopping the flood. Neighbourhood parades began to spring up, smaller versions

tended to promote fertility and reinvigorate
e year, the *Holi* is celebrated in northern
dia when the crops of the spring harvest are
most ripe; festivities include ritual dramas in
hich women battle with the men, and
nerally culminate in a procession; on the
cond day dust and coloured water are flung
er the spectators *Left* 18th century gouache,
owing men of a village spraying red water
er the women during the spring festival *Right*
es for use in the celebrations, for sale in an
dian market place

the great downtown processions, and on
e Saturday schoolchildren organized
eir own parades. After the First World War
e Negroes of New Orleans introduced a
rade on the Tuesday itself, before Rex's
rade began. The black contribution was
aded by the Zulu King, with a ham-bone
sceptre, who was clearly in the Lord of
isrule tradition of overturning the usual
der of things. He parades still, though black
ilitants deplore his presence.

Others now tend to deplore the New
rleans' Mardi Gras as a whole, feeling that
French antecedents and the pre-Lent
iety have been forced into a back seat
the more modern spirit of public relations.
ardi Gras remains still the high point
the social calendar, with an invitation
the Comus ball being a testimonial to
cial success; otherwise, the ruling theme
not snobbery but civic promotion and
mmercialism. The two may overlap, of
urse, for many of the krewes are somewhat
entified with businessmen's lunch clubs.
Mardi Gras has been taken over by the
omoters because it is a vastly successful
urist attraction. Though the carnival
irit of the citizens is supposed to be
e mainspring of the festivities, the Cham-
r of Commerce is in fact a more likely one,
d the city itself pours hundreds of thou-
nds of dollars into the occasion. Nor are
ivate promoters far behind: the trinkets
aditionally thrown to the crowd from
ex's parade, once considered luck-bringing
uvenirs, now carry advertising matter.

Once again, citizens are calling for the
andonment of the celebration because,
ey say, commercialism and violence have
storted the original 'folk-celebration'
irit of Mardi Gras. But it is doubtful if
at folk spirit truly survived much past the
350s. After all, the originators, with their
lf-conscious title of a Mystic Krewe, their
gh literary themes from Milton, and their
panding sense of their own social cachet,
uld hardly be said to have represented a
irit that had much to do with the simple,
e-old human urge to celebrate the earth's
newal in spring.

DOUGLAS HILL

URTHER READING: E. O. James, *Seasonal
easts and Festivals* (Barnes and Noble,
961); R. Wickiser and others, *Mardi Gras
ay* (Henry Holt, 1948).

Many holy wells were pagan sacred springs which were re-dedicated by Christian missionaries; some were prophetic, others therapeutic, and others again had power to work evil

SPRINGS AND WELLS

THE SACRED character of particular springs and wells, like that of many rivers, lakes and waterfalls (see WATER), is an exceedingly old tradition which has its roots in one of the most ancient and universal forms of worship. Water itself was considered to be essentially holy by primitive peoples because it was a basic necessity of life. It was also mysterious, as its movements were often unpredictable

and beyond man's control, and it could destroy by drowning or by flood.

Where rivers flowed, or springs welled up out of the ground, or waterfalls thundered over rocks, there some divine force was felt to have its abode, and was worshipped in fear and hope by all who approached. To the unseen spirits who dwelt there, prayers and propitiatory sacrifices were offered, that their dangerous anger might be averted and the life-giving waters continue to flow. To them also, men came to be cured of their ills, or to seek answers to their problems, or to call down destruction upon their enemies. Such beliefs and practices were very deep-seated and, in one form or another, they managed to survive all the religious changes of many centuries, including the advent of

Christianity. Even today, their traces a clearly visible in numerous legends of heali or wishing-wells, or life-demanding river and in some wellside ceremonies.

Certain springs and streams were believe to have foreknowledge and, from time time, to predict the future by sudden vari tions in level or colour, or the manner of the flow. The now-vanished Drumming Well Oundle in Northamptonshire gave warnin of coming changes in the state of the natic by sounds resembling the persistent beatin of a drum. In his *Certainty of the World Spirits* (1691), Richard Baxter, who hea it once during the Civil War, said that tl noise continued for several days togethe and was clearly audible some distance awa St Helen's Well at Rushton Spencer Staffordshire dried up before any calamit even in the wettest seasons. Tradition say it did so before the outbreak of the Civ War, before the execution of Charles I, an at the beginning of the Popish Plot terror 1679. Other springs, normally dorman foretold misfortune by suddenly breakir out and flowing very freely for a short tim One such is the intermittent Assende Spring, in Oxfordshire, which traditional runs before a war, and is said to have dor so in 1914, and again in 1939. The uncerta land-springs found in chalk country, whic appear only occasionally and are known a levants, or corn-springs, were believed predict by their sudden uprising a dearth corn, and consequently its high price.

Prophetic waters of this kind seem to hav concerned themselves only with matters national importance or, at least, with comir events likely to affect a fairly wide area. The were other springs which had knowledge of different kind, and to which inquiries of more personal character were often directec The famous Holy Well of Gulval, in Cornwal used to be visited by people anxious about th welfare of absent friends. Kneeling by the we and looking into it so that they could see the faces reflected in its depths, they put the questions to an old woman who acted a guardian of the spring, and the water replied If the friend was well, it bubbled up as if were boiling, if he was ill, it became mudd and discoloured. If he was already dead, remained unchanged.

Many ancient holy or healing wells no associated with particular saints starte life as pagan sacred springs, and were re dedicated and given a new spiritual signifi cance by the Christian missionaries of th early conversion period. It was the wis policy of the Church at that time to trans form and purify, rather than destroy, what ever was innocent and harmless in the olde

Found in parts of Derbyshire, the Christia custom of well-dressing is a survival of th pagan belief that each well had its ow guardian who had to be propitiated ever year if the crops were to grow. Ceremonie usually take place on Ascension Da immediately following the three days on whic God's blessing is asked for the crops *Le* Ceremonial blessing of the Yew Tree Well Tissingdon in Derbyshire *Facing page* Plaque depicting Cain and Abel, and illustrating a te from the book of Isaiah

aith and, by consecrating familiar sanc-
uaries anew to the service of Christ, to
nake the transition from paganism to
Christianity easier. This is why the first
mall churches were often built inside or
near stone circles, or close to heathen holy
prings, and the water of the latter was used
or the baptism of converts. The little wooden
hapel that was the humble predecessor of
York Minster was built over one such spring,
which still exists in the crypt of the present
athedral. The healing virtues of medicinal
wells were no longer attributed to the power
of pagan indwelling spirits, but to the inter-
ession of saints in whose honour the wells
had been re-named; and as new legends
eplaced the old, their very existence was
often thought to be due to the prayers of holy
men or, occasionally, to the blood of martyrs
hed at that place.

Tradition says that St Augustine's Well
t Cerne, in Dorset, came into being when
hat great missionary, finding himself astray
and thirsty in a dry countryside, struck the
ground with his staff. Another version of the
ale says that he performed this kindly
miracle when certain shepherds complained
hat they lacked water for their flocks. At
Binsey, near Oxford, a healing well, into
which coins are still dropped by people
eeking relief from eye ailments, was called
up by the prayers of St Frideswide.

The famous medicinal well at Holywell,
n Wales, had its legendary origin in the
7th century, when St Winifrid was murdered in what was then a waterless valley.
Because she repulsed his advances, Caradoc
of Hawarden killed her by cutting off her
head with a single stroke of his sword. Where
the head fell, a strong spring burst out of
the stony soil, and has run unfailingly ever
since. A further legend relates that St Beuno
reunited the severed head to the body and
restored her to life, and that she lived to
meet a second death long afterwards.

Wells dedicated to St Anne exist in many
parts of Europe. In England they are often
known as granny-wells because, being the
mother of the Virgin Mary, she was the
grandmother of Christ. A Breton legend says
that, in her old age, she made her home in
Brittany, and there, just before she died,
Christ came to visit her. At her request, in
order to help the sick people of the province,
he struck the ground three times with his
staff, and so called into being the spring of
St Anne-de-la-Palue. St Anne's Well at
Buxton in Derbyshire has no such personal
legend attached to it, but there is a tradition
that it is dedicated to her because, in the
Middle Ages, a statue representing her was
found in its depths. A figure of the saint,
enshrined in a wellside chapel, certainly
existed in Henry VIII's reign, for it was
removed then and subsequently destroyed,
but whether this was the one so curiously
discovered is now uncertain. Nor can we
be sure that the original image was in fact
one of St Anne, or any other Christian
saint. The spring was venerated in Roman
times, and perhaps earlier, and the statue
may quite possibly have been that of some
pagan water nymph or goddess. It need
hardly be said that no such idea crossed the
minds of the countless pilgrims who came to
the spring to be cured of their ills, and de-
posited their offerings in the chapel of the
saint by whose intercession they had been
healed. In 1538 the well was arbitrarily
closed by one of Thomas Cromwell's agents,
'for that,' as he said in his report, 'there
should be no more idolatry and superstition
there used'. Some 30 years later, by a curious turn of fortune, it was once again a
centre of healing, though not for religious
reasons. It became one of the main medicinal
wells of the then newly-founded spa at
Buxton, and as such it endures to this day.

A Source of Evil

In some holy wells that were once pagan
springs, the ancient indwellers seem never
to have been altogether forgotten, or perhaps
they raised their hoary heads again as the
saints who replaced them gradually lost their
influence on everyday life. St Nun's (or
Nonna's) spring at Pelynt in Cornwall is
sometimes called the Piskies' Well, and
pins used to be thrown into it to gain the
goodwill of the pixies, rather than that of
St Nun, the mother of St David. Its water
was used for baptisms in the parish church,
but according to a story collected in the late
19th century, it was the fairies who were
blamed for the misfortunes that befell a
farmer after he had rashly tried to steal
its granite basin.

When St Aelian in the 6th century prayed
for water and so called up the Denbighshire
spring named after him, he can hardly have
imagined that it would become notorious,

Because of their mysterious nature, wells are sometimes depicted in legends as being suitable refuges for malevolent beings; in the Persian *Romance of Amir Hamza*, the giant Zamurrad is lured into a well, and beaten by gardeners: 16th century Mogul miniature

and universally dreaded, as a cursing-well. It seems at one time to have been a simple healing spring, like many others, but during the 18th and 19th centuries, it had an extremely evil reputation. People came to it to curse their enemies. They gave money to its guardian, who wrote the victim's name in a book. His initials were then scratched on a slate, or inscribed upon parchment, and thrown into the well. A pin was also thrown in, and some passages from the Bible were read aloud. The seeker was then given water to drink, and some was thrown over his head, while he stated the nature of the evil he wished to inflict. It was widely believed that any person so cursed would become very ill, or would meet with constant misfortune, or that he would die. Exactly how these malevolent powers became attached to this spring is unknown; the well has now been filled up (see also CURSE).

Some venerable holy wells, to which pious Christians once came in true faith and devotion, have degenerated into simple wishing-wells, where secretly-formed wishes have taken the place of prayers, and pins or coins, or occasionally small pebbles, are dropped in. Those who visit such springs today are not actuated by religious motives, and probably they have only a very vague notion of who or what it is they expect to grant their wishes. Yet it can hardly be doubted that this is a curious reversion to heathen beliefs, unrecognized though they may be by those who offer their pins or coins. The wheel has come full cycle, and the pagan spirit, which some saint displaced for a time, has come into his own again.

CHRISTINA HOLE

FURTHER READING: Christina Hole, *English Shrines and Sanctuaries* (Clarke, Irwin, 1954); Francis Jones, *The Holy Wells of Wales* (Univ. of Wales Press, Cardiff, 1964).

STAG

ANIMALS WITH HORNS or antlers are depicted in paintings and carvings executed by men of the Old Stone Age; and the 'Horned Sorcerer', a painting of a man wearing antlers, in the cave of Les Trois Frères in southern France, suggests that such beasts were of ritual importance (see ICONOGRAPHY). Among the Hittites a god whose sacred animal was the stag was worshipped. His cult, which dates back to the third millennium BC, was widespread, and models of stags have been recovered from tombs. A god of the countryside, he is represented standing on a stag, holding a falcon and a hare, and it is possible that, before the Hittite city states arose, he may have presided over the chase.

The Celtic divinity Cernunnos was depicted wearing antlers and, usually, in a squatting posture, as on the Gundestrup cauldron found in Jutland, where he is shown surrounded by animals and may have been regarded as a Lord of Beasts. A rock carving in Val Canonica in northern Italy shows a phallic figure apparently worshipping before a horned god who wears a torque (metal ornament). The god was probably regarded as a source of fertility and power. Evidence from the Near East indicates that horns represented supernatural power (see HORNS).

At Syracuse in Sicily women singers wore garlands, and antlers on their heads, and at a festival in honour of Artemis men were similarly adorned. In another such ritual men postured like women. There was yet another ceremony in which men wore phalluses, and one in which women wore imitations of the male organ. There were evidently ambivalent ideas concerning Artemis, the huntress goddess, who was represented in art with one or more stags. Animals, and even human beings, were sacrificed to her. Actaeon, the young hunter who inadvertently interrupted her bathing, was transformed into a stag and torn to pieces by his own hounds (see DIANA).

There is a curious connection between the stag and precious metals. The hinds captured by Artemis and harnessed to her golden chariot bore horns. Hercules's third labour involved capturing the Ceryneian hind which had brazen hooves and golden horns, and which was sacred to Artemis, and bringing it to Mycene (see HERCULES). The *Rama Yana*, an Indian epic, mentions a golden-antlered stag whose coat was flecked with silver, and in China deer are associated with places where precious metals are mined. Silver models of deer were placed in Christian sanctuaries because the stag was regarded as a symbol of Christ; when confronted with a serpent it represented the Christian overcoming evil.

A ritual stag-hunt took place on Mt Lycaeum at the beginning of the Christian era, and as late as the 5th century AD stag mummers danced in the south of France. In North America deer dances were performed by antlered dancers to increase fertility by causing rain to fall, and to encourage the growth of wild crops. Men wearing antlers still perform a dance in September every year at Abbots Bromley in Staffordshire.

Deer Women

The abundance of legendary lore concerning deer where Celtic culture and languages survive confirms that the stag was regarded as a supernatural animal. In the Scottish Highlands and islands the deer is associated with supernatural beings, always female, and there are many tales of deer-human transformations. These fabulous creatures are seldom malicious, but they are sometimes thought of as being gigantic. There was one, for instance, who was so colossal that when she waded across the Sound of Mull the water came only up to her knees.

A Gaelic tale relates that after a tragedy in which her baby was killed, a woman took to the hills where she lived with the deer and eluded her husband's attempts to capture her. After seven years he decided to marry again, but when the day for the wedding arrived his wife appeared at the church and took her place by his side; she was covered in fine fur like that of a red deer fawn. In other tales a hunter sees a deer turn into a woman and falls in love with her. He arranges to meet her at a church where they are to be married, but their plans are foiled by a witch.

The stag was widely regarded as a supernatural animal; in some areas it was thought to be connected with the underworld, but there are also signs that it was associated with the sun. Carving of a stag and a Viking, on a cross at Middleton in Yorkshire

Axel Poignant

After many adventures they meet on a distant island and marry.

According to another Celtic legend Ossian hurled his spear at, but missed, a beautiful white deer, who turned out to be his mother. She led him to a rock in which a door mysteriously opened, and closed after them, and then revealed herself as a lovely woman. Yet another story describes how a hunter wounded a deer which managed to escape. Later she appeared to him in a dream, in human form, and returned the arrow with which he had shot her.

The ghosts of deer were thought to change into supernatural women. In some areas the lore concerning deer suggests that they were connected with the underworld but there are also signs that they were solar animals; a rock engraving in Scandinavia shows stags drawing the disc of the sun.

Fairies' Cattle

Folklore in Scotland and elsewhere refers so frequently to deer serving mankind in various ways that it has been suspected that red deer were domesticated at some time in the remote past. However, with the exception of the reindeer, there is little firm evidence of their having been tamed in ancient times. In Scotland they were said to be the fairies' cattle, and tales of benevolent deer go back to ancient times. Telephus, Hercules's son by the virgin priestess of Athens, was abandoned in a forest, and was said to have been suckled by a doe. Stories of Christian saints and hermits similarly describe their receiving sustenance from these creatures. Hermits gave sanctuary to hunted deer, who aided them in various ways, by carrying baggage, or providing an antler book rest or antler candlesticks.

The antlers of deer have often been regarded as having special powers, often magical. Picks made from deer-horn, and a chalk phallus, which were found at the end of a worked-out seam in a Neolithic flint mine at Grimes Graves in Norfolk may have been placed there in the hope that the mine could be made more productive. Practically every part of the deer has been believed to have medicinal qualities, in one part of Europe or another, while in China powdered antlers was thought to be an aphrodisiac. In some areas antlers are hung up on buildings to ward off evil influences.

E. A. ARMSTRONG

Left The relationship between stags or deer and human beings is generally a benevolent one; the Roman general Sertorius gained the goodwill of the inhabitants of Spain because he had a pet fawn which they regarded as a sign of divine protection: Sertorius and his fawn, 15th century Italian manuscript *Above right* Horned animals were of ritual importance to primitive man, who regarded them as sources of fertility and power: the Horn Dance, performed in Abbots Bromley every year, is a relic of pagan worship. There are many tales of people being transformed into deer; in Greek mythology Diana turned Actaeon into a stag because he saw her bathing: a 16th century Italian dish *(right)* and a painting by Giuseppe Cesari *(following page)* both depict Actaeon's transformation

Homer Sykes

Victoria & Albert Museum/C. M. Dixon

STARS

Mansell Collection

18th century map of the northern hemisphere: the Mesopotamians regarded the movement of the planets in relation to the fixed stars as the 'writing of heaven'; although Christ was said to have disrupted the planets' courses, and to have broken their control over human destiny, belief in astrology has survived throughout the centuries

WHETHER STARS have ever been worshipped purely as stars is doubtful. For, mysterious though they surely were to ancient man, those remote points of light in the night sky had no obvious effect on his life as, for example, the sun had. However, they have been associated with divine beings from a very early period, often as their place of abode or form of manifestation. The ancient Sumerians identified the planet Venus with an important goddess called Inanna, the 'Lady of Heaven'; the Babylonians knew her as Ishtar (see ISHTAR). Since the planet appears as both the Morning and Evening Star, the two forms under which the goddess was conceived could be conveniently represented: as the goddess of the Morning Star, Ishtar presided over war and carnage; as the Evening Star, she was the fertility goddess, associated with love and luxury. Her symbol was a star of eight or 16 rays, inscribed in a circle. The awful god Nergal, the ruler of the Mesopotamian underworld, who was also associated with war and pestilence, was identified with the red planet Mars.

The locating of the gods in the stars and the origins of astrology are graphically recorded in the famous Babylonian Creation epic, known as the *Enuma elish* (see CREATION MYTHS). It is related of Marduk, the great god of Babylon: 'He constructed stations for the great gods, fixing their astral likenesses as constellations. He determined the year by designating the zones: he set up three constellations for the 12 months.' The movement of the planets in relation to the constellations of the fixed stars was, consequently, regarded by the ancient Mesopotamians as the 'writing of heaven', by which the will of the gods for the state or individual persons was signified. This resulted in the development of astrology as a science of divining what was portended by the stars, and the casting of horoscopes, which

can be traced back to at least 410 BC (see MESOPOTAMIA). The belief that the gods revealed the fates of nations and men through the stars, in which they resided, inevitably led to the idea that human destiny was controlled by the stars or planets. This idea became very influential in the world of Graeco-Roman civilization.

In ancient Egypt, the stars were objects of great significance, although none achieved the status of a major god, apart from the sun (Re), which was worshipped as the chief state deity, and the moon god Chons, the 'lord of time' who counted the years of both kings and men. The Egyptians imagined the stars, which 'grow not weary', as manning the boat in which the sun god journeyed across the night sky. The circumpolar stars, that never set in the west, were seen as 'the imperishable ones', and in the Pyramid Texts the dead kings hope to fly up to heaven and join their company, to be for ever safe from change and decay. The association of the dead with the stars was a long-established tradition in Egypt, which finds expression in the depiction of stars on coffins, often in connection with the protecting image of Nut, the sky goddess.

The Egyptians, like the Mesopotamians, formed pictures in the stars, seeing in the various groups the figures of gods, animals and things. The Plough suggested to them both the implement used in the ceremony known as the 'Opening of the Mouth' in the Osirian mortuary ritual (see MUMMIFICATION), and the thigh of an animal. Because the latter symbolized a sacrificial offering, which in turn was connected with the evil god Seth (see SETH), the Plough was also called the 'thigh of Seth'. The constellation of Orion was held in particular veneration; like many other peoples, the Egyptians saw in it the form of a man, whom they identified with Osiris (see OSIRIS). The equation had a deep significance, in view of the ancient connection of the dead with the stars: for Orion, the 'king of the stars', was also Osiris, the ruler of the dead.

Another star of great significance was Sothis (Sirius, the 'dog star'). Because of its apparent proximity to the constellation of Orion, which represented Osiris, Sothis was identified with the goddess Isis (see ISIS) the wife of Osiris; and because Isis had succoured the dead Osiris and helped him to rise from the dead, Sothis was accordingly deemed to help those who had died. Further, the Egyptian calendar had originally been based upon the fact that Sothis's rising near the sun coincided with the commencement of the annual flooding of the river Nile. Consequently, since the prosperity of Egypt depended upon the fructifying flood waters of the Nile, the equation of Isis with Sothis was endowed with even greater meaning. According to the Greek writer Plutarch (1st century AD), Sirius (Sothis) was the soul of Isis. In iconography Isis is often depicted with a star between the two horns of her crown.

The ancient Egyptians did not come to believe that the stars controlled human destiny until the Hellenistic period (330–30 BC). Then, most probably under the influence of Mesopotamian astral beliefs,

they adopted the idea with enthusiasm and developed a form of astral religion or mystical philosophy which became widely influential in the world of Graeco-Roman culture. Star charts were elaborated, comprising 59 deities who presided over the various time units of the year: months, decades, and supplementary days. Astrological writings were composed c 150 BC, doubtless in Alexandria, and were ascribed to a fictitious king Nechepso and a priest Petosiris, who were associated with the attribution of each day of the week to one of the planets, although the notion probably originated with Chaldean astrologers. The importance of horoscopes became so great in Egypt that they were inscribed on the roofs of tombs. How this astrological lore assumed that the fates of individual persons were decided by the planets is set forth, with pseudoscientific detail, in the *Tetrabiblos* of Ptolemy, who wrote in Egypt in the 2nd century AD. For example, he attributes to each planet a particular form of death: Saturn controls death by pulmonary consumption and rheumatism; Jupiter by apoplexy and cardiac affections; Mars by strokes and kidney diseases. The planets similarly determined the temperament and length of life of each man and woman.

Slaves of the Universe

The idea that mankind was subject to demonic powers, resident in the planets, was elaborated into a complex doctrine of salvation in the *Corpus Hermeticum* (see HERMETICA). This remarkable collection of mystical scriptures purport to be revelations made by Hermes Trismegistus, who was in origin the Egyptian god Thoth. In one of the texts, known as the *Poimandres*, the subjection of mankind to the planets is explained in an esoteric imagery. In the beginning the Primal Being, who is described as Mind, *Nous*, Life, *Zoe*, and Light, *Phos*, generated a second demiurgic Nous, who created the universe. In the course of his creation the demiurge made the seven planets called governors, *dioiketai*, whose cycles envelop the material world, which they govern; their government being called *Heimarmene*, Destiny. Next, the Supreme Nous generated an archetypal man, *Anthropos*, in his own image. This Anthropos, seeing the creation of the demiurge, desired himself to create. Passing through the celestial spheres, he descended to the material world, where he cohabited with Nature, *Phusis*. From their union mankind was born, having a dual nature: their mortal bodies derived from Nature, and their immortal souls from divine Man. But owing to their situation in this material world, human beings are subject to the planetary powers, who control their destiny. It was the purpose of the *Poimandres* to show how the human soul could be saved from this fatal enslavement to the planets, and ascend through the spheres to the highest heaven from which its divine progenitor had come.

This explanation of the human situation, variously adapted, constituted the basic doctrine of the many forms of Gnosticism which flourished in the Graeco-Roman world (see GNOSTICISM). Its ideology ppears in many writings of St Paul and it obviously influenced his doctrine of salvation (see PAUL). He uses a number of terms which relate to this astral doctrine: he reminds the Galatian Christians that before their conversion they 'were slaves to the elemental spirits of the universe' (Galatians 4.3); he explains that God misled the 'rulers of this age' into crucifying Christ, which enabled mankind to be delivered from their power (1 Corinthians 2.6–8); he tells how Christ, through his crucifixion, 'disarmed the principalities and powers' (Colossians 2.15); and he asks the Christians of Galatia whether they desire to return to their bondage to the planets, because they 'observe days, and months, and seasons, and years' (Galatians 4.10).

In Christian Gnosticism these ideas were further developed. It was maintained that Christ had broken the control of the planets over human destiny by disrupting their courses. The star which announced his birth to the Magi (Matthew, chapter 2) was explained as a new star that changed the old inevitable astral order to one that was providential. This subjection of the planetary powers is dramatically symbolized in the book of Revelation (1.16), where Christ as the Cosmocrator, ruler of the world, appears holding the seven stars in his right hand.

Although Christ was deemed to have delivered mankind from the dominion of the stars, Christians continued to regard them with awe. Astrology survived the downfall of paganism, and its practice continued on through the Middle Ages with even popes consulting the prognostications of the stars. The planets still remained associated with the pagan deities, and their depiction in medieval manuscripts reveals that they were still conceived of in personified forms. (See also ASTROLOGY.)

S. G. F. BRANDON

FURTHER READING: S. G. F. Brandon, *History, Time and Deity* (Barnes and Noble, 1965); F. Cumont, *Astrology and Religion Among the Greeks and Romans* (G. Putnam, 1912); J. Doresse, *The Secret Books of the Gnostics* (Viking Press, 1960); J. Seznec, *The Survival of the Pagan Gods* (Harper and Row, 1961).

Axel Poignant

Stations of the Cross

A series of paintings or sculptures representing the 14 stages of Christ's Passion; usually ranged round the walls of a church, they depict scenes, from the condemnation of Jesus by Pilate and his reception of the cross, to the crucifixion, descent from the cross and burial; in the Roman Catholic Church a form of devotion is to pray before each station in turn

The extraordinary originality of Rudolf Steiner's mind led him to a philosophy which linked up the world of natural science with the world of Spirit; his revolutionary ideas took form in a number of enterprises, ranging from art and architecture to education and farming

RUDOLF STEINER

THE SON of a minor official on the Southern Austrian Railway, Rudolf Steiner was born on 27 February 1861 at Kraljevic, then on the borders of Austria and Hungary, now in Yugoslavia. The modest schooling available made little impression on him but he was intensely awake to Nature, and to the personalities with whom he came into contact. A conviction as to the reality of the inner life, 'a soul space in man' as he called it, which manifested itself in some clairvoyant experiences and was strengthened by a delighted discovery of the world of pure ideas in geometry, gave the first promise of his future activity. At his secondary school he studied science but taught himself the classics, and even tutored other pupils in the humanities. He continued this practice when he entered the Technical College of the University of Vienna, and laid the foundation of the extraordinarily wide-ranging knowledge for which he was so remarkable. Outside his official science course, philosophy was his principal interest, but he was keenly interested in literature and the arts.

The unusual combination of scientific and artistic interests led him to Goethe, and at the age of 23 he edited Goethe's scientific works for an edition of *Deutsche National-literatur*. The connection with Goethe was later to take him to Weimar to work at the Goethe Archives on the scientific side of another edition of Goethe's works. One special activity he undertook in Vienna was the tutoring of a backward boy, an experience of great importance for his later work. Meanwhile, however, he was elaborating his own philosophy in *Truth and Science* (for which he received a Ph.D. from the University of Rostock) and *The Philosophy of Freedom*, in which he argued that thought can become an organ to perceive a spiritual world. He was attracted to the mystics but differed from them in wanting to experience the sources of human wisdom through ideas – 'a mystical experience of thoughts'.

The work in the Goethe Archives at Weimar, begun when he was 29 years old, was Steiner's first settled job. His elucidation of Goethe's *Theory of Colour* later deeply influenced Kandinsky, the Russian painter. Nor did Steiner confine himself to Goethe. He also edited the works of Schopenhauer, and concerned himself with the Nietzsche archives.

Weimar, however, gave him no opportunity for the expression of his own growing spiritual experience, and in 1897 he accepted an invitation to go to Berlin to edit the *Magazine for Literature* which was associated with a stage society which produced 'modern' plays that were not likely to reach the ordinary theatre. Here Steiner, always devoted to drama, had his first experience of stage management. In Berlin he also joined the staff of a working men's college, which gave him a deep insight into prevailing social conditions. In the magazine he could only express his ideas exoterically, in a form adapted to its readers.

Meditation, however, had become a necessity to him – that 'experience of the whole man through which he reaches the actual spiritual world far more than through ideas'. His first opportunity to speak to an audience esoterically was when a certain Count Brockdorff, having read an article of Steiner's on Goethe's esoteric fairy tale, *The Green Snake and the Beautiful Lily*, invited him to lecture to a theosophical circle.

This led to a ten-year connection with the Theosophical Society, to visits to London where he met Annie Besant, Colonel Olcott and other leaders of the movement (see BESANT; THEOSOPHY), and to his accepting the position of General Secretary to the German branch of the Society. He reserved the right, however, to speak only of his own spiritual investigation. He was already lecturing on 'An Anthroposophy' and in 1909, being totally opposed to the declaration of a further incarnation of Christ and other theosophical trends, he broke with that society and founded the Anthroposophical Society (from the Greek words *anthropos* and *sophia*, 'man' and 'wisdom'). Speaking of the Anthroposophical movement in a letter written the year before his death, Steiner said: 'Anthroposophy has its roots in the perceptions – already gained – into the spiritual world. Yet these are no more than its roots. The branches, leaves, blossoms and fruits of Anthroposophy grow into all the fields of human life and action.'

Earth-Memory

From the beginning of his theosophical connections, Steiner had given independent lectures in many places, helped by Marie von Sivers (whom he subsequently married), and had produced the monthly magazine *Lucifer* ('light-bearer'). In this he published his first two anthroposophical works, *Knowledge of the Higher Worlds* and *From the Akashic Chronicle*. The former contains his description of the path of initiation for modern Western man, with exercises leading to successive stages of development. Characteristic of the book is the recognition of the dangers as well as the difficulties of initiation, and the need to take three steps in morality for every one in higher knowledge. The second begins the teaching about Universe, Earth and Man which he was to elaborate during the next 20 years. For Steiner claimed that there is such a thing as an earth-memory, written in the earth aura, and that this memory, accessible to a trained and conscious clairvoyance, is valid for a new interpretation of human and geological history. This interpretation must, however, take fully into account all the discoveries (not necessarily the theories) of modern scientific investigators.

During this early period of his theosophical or anthroposophical activity, Steiner lectured widely on the gospels. He had never been able to accept Christianity as a religion 'revealed from without'. It was his own inner experience of the event of Golgotha that led him to see it as the fulfilment of what had been presented in the ancient Mysteries. He had expressed all this in his book *Christianity as Mystical Fact* (1902). He now expounded the gospels as esoteric documents, that is documents meant only for the initiated. The 'Mystery of Golgotha' became central to his teaching of the evolution of world and man.

To this period also belongs *Occult Science – An Outline*, a compendium of 'spiritual science' (as he often called Anthroposophy) dealing with the four 'bodies' of man, his soul members, and his spiritual principles; with life in the spiritual worlds between death and a new birth; with the evolution of the earth through the four embodiments as Saturn (warmth), Sun (air), Moon (water), and Earth (mineral). In Steiner's monism (the position opposed to dualism) even physical substance had its origin in living spirit, and man himself – the last to appear in evolution – was the first in conception, though indeed as macrocosmic man. The section on Earth evolution introduces the seven epochs and the seven historical civilizations, developed in great detail in later lectures, and the two opponents of human evolution, Ahriman and Lucifer, fundamental to Steiner's teaching on ethics, psychology, history, and all his 'science of man'. The book ends with a chapter on initiation, complementary to *Knowledge of the Higher Worlds*.

During the years of his association

Rudolf Steiner: founder of the Anthroposophical Society, and a prolific teacher and author, in the last years before his death in 1925 he 'developed with special intensity the subject of karma and reincarnation (the latter in a new and Christian form), which he considered vital for the modern age'

with the Theosophical Society, between 1902 and 1912, Steiner travelled on lecture tours with Marie von Sivers over almost the whole of Europe, also studying the art and architecture in all the places he visited. He wanted to express his spiritual vision in the form of art. With the help of Marie von Sivers, who was a trained actress, he first produced Eduard Schuré's *Drama of Eleusis* at a congress in Munich in 1907, after which he wrote, in successive years, four mystery plays dealing with the karmic connections of a group of people in successive incarnations, with scenes in the soul and spiritual worlds as well as on earth. He was also developing eurythmy, an art of movement to speech and music, based on the gestures latent in the sounds of speech and in the tones and intervals of music. This new art is used effectively in representing the soul and spiritual scenes in Steiner's mystery plays.

All this artistic activity, together with Steiner's conviction that a new spiritual impulse demanded a new form of architecture, led to the building of the first Goetheanum, at Dornach near Basle in Switzerland, as the headquarters of the Anthroposophical Society, which had been founded in 1912. It was built largely of wood and consisted of two intersecting domes, the smaller over the stage, and the larger (bigger than the dome of St Paul's in London) over the auditorium. Notable features in it were the interior columns made from different woods, the change of form in their capitals and bases, the windows of sculptured glass (since copied in many places) and the painting of the dome.

During the First World War men and women from all combatant nations worked on its construction. It was burnt down on the night of 31 December 1922, only the great sculpture of the 'Representative of Man between Lucifer and Ahriman' surviving: it had been carved by Steiner with the help of an English sculptress. Steiner immediately designed the second Goetheanum in a completely different and equally original style of moulded concrete.

At the end of the First World War Steiner won much support for his suggestion of a threefold commonwealth to solve the tangled problems of central Europe. This arose out of a view which he had developed in great detail, over many years, according to which the whole physiology (not the brain and nerves alone) is related to the psyche. Steiner maintained that thinking finds its physical basis in brain and nerves, feeling in the rhythmical processes of heart and lungs, and willing in the system of limbs and metabolism. He now extended this threefold conception into social life, which he saw as three spheres of human activity, each of which should have its own suitable organization: a cultural sphere with the ideal of liberty, a political or 'rights' sphere with the ideal of equality, and an economic or production sphere with the ideal of fraternity. Rightly conducted, these spheres would find a natural harmony (comparable to that of head, heart and hand), but these spheres of operation would by no means necessarily coincide.

The Waldorf Schools

An example of an institution free from political control within the cultural sphere was the Waldorf School in Stuttgart, originally founded in 1919 for the employees of a local factory. As its educational director, Steiner gathered teachers from all walks of life, and lectured to them on the three great psychological and physiological periods of childhood, on the temperaments, on the curriculum, and so on, as well as discussing with them the problems of individual children. This educational work roused particular interest in England, where he was invited to the 'New Ideals' educational conference in Stratford-on-Avon, and in the same year to a summer school in Oxford under the patronage of H. A. L. Fisher, Professor L. P. Jacks, and other well-known educators. At this time he also met Margaret McMillan, pioneer of the nursery school movement, who became his fervent admirer. The Waldorf School movement has now extended itself over most of Europe and the English-speaking world.

Among other groups who approached Steiner at this time for help and guidance in their special tasks were teachers of backward children, farmers, actors, doctors and a circle of ministers and others concerned with religion who wished to work for religious renewal. The lectures and practical advice which Steiner gave to these groups led to a widespread movement in curative education, to the biodynamic method of agriculture (in which soil, plant and animal live in a healthy and natural relationship), to stage productions at the Goetheanum and other teiner's conviction that a new spiritual impulse demands a new form of architecture led to the building of the first Goetheanum in Dornach, Switzerland *(right)* as the headquarters of the Anthroposophical Society; constructed largely of wood, it was burnt down on the night of 31 December 1922; the second Goetheanum which replaced it *(below right)* is made of moulded concrete. Both buildings were designed by Steiner, who believed that their form should correspond, to the smallest detail, with the activities that would take place within them

places, to a school of medicine centred on a clinic near Basle (founded in conjunction with a Dutch doctor, Dr I. Wegman) and to an independent religious body known as the Christian Community.

In the years before his death Steiner's lecturing activity was of immense range, embracing mathematics, astronomy, science, medicine, theology, philosophy, drama, education, economics and many other subjects. Many lectures were for specialists who were astounded at his knowledge in their special fields. But he continued to foster the esoteric character of the Anthroposophical Society, believing that esotercism should become an open secret for all who have eyes to read. In his last years he developed with special intensity the subject of karma and reincarnation (the latter in a new and Christian form), which he considered vital for the modern age. And in 1923 he founded the Anthroposophical Society anew, placing at its centre the 'School of Spiritual Science' for those who wished to follow a path of self-development. He died two years later, on 30 March 1925.

A. C. HARWOOD

FURTHER READING: Rudolf Steiner, *The Philosophy of Spiritual Activity* (1963), *Knowledge of the Higher Worlds and its Attainment* (1969), *The Threefold Commonwealth* (1966), *The Course of My Life* (1970), *Occult Science — An Outline* (1969), *Christianity as Mystical Fact* (1947), are all published by the Rudolf Steiner Press. Books on Steiner include: A. P. Shepherd, *A Scientist of the Invisible* (Musson, 1954); H. Poppelbaum, *Man and Animal* (Anthroposophical Publishing Co., London, 1960).

Amulets representing ladders, the means by which a king was thought to ascend to the sky after death, have been found in Egyptian tombs; and in the Mithraic Mysteries, the worshipper climbed the seven steps of initiation, symbolized by a ladder with seven rungs

STEPS AND LADDERS

IN THE GAME of Snakes and Ladders the snakes, being betraying and evil creatures, lead downwards. The ladders lead up, which is perhaps a reflection of the main role of ladders, steps and stairs in symbolism, as means of ascent. They lead up from the earth into the sky and to climb them is to rise above the human condition to a higher plane. St John Climacus (from *klimax*, the Greek for 'ladder'), a monk of Mount Sinai in the 7th century, wrote a book called *Ladder to Paradise*, which helped to bring into Christian iconography the picture of the souls of the dead climbing the rungs of a ladder towards heaven, with the unrighteous being snatched off it by demons (see JUDGEMENT OF THE DEAD). There is a tradition that Mohammed saw a ladder rising into the sky from Jerusalem, on which the souls of the just ascended to God.

We connect height with spiritual superiority and power, and when the source of ultimate power or the final home of the blessed is located in the sky, kings, heroes, shamans and the souls of the good are naturally thought of as rising into it (see SKY). Among the methods of ascent, besides ladders and stairs, are climbing a mountain, a tree, a rope, the rainbow or a spider's web, or being carried up by angels or in a chariot. The Tree of Life in the Cabala (see CABALA) and the idea of rising through its spheres to God is an example of the same underlying idea. A Maori hero reached the sky by climbing a vine and the folktale hero Jack by shinning up a beanstalk (see JACK). There is a widespread myth in the Pacific in which the hero fires an arrow into the air, then a second arrow which transfixes it, then a third, and so on until he can climb into the sky on a chain made of arrows.

The Pyramid Texts of ancient Egypt (see

means of ascent or descent, a ladder can symbolize the path from heaven to earth: *God's Covenant with Abraham*; in this 11th century Anglo-Saxon manuscript Abraham is shown lying on the ground while God, descending from heaven on a ladder, promises that he will make him 'the father of a multitude of nations'

BOOK OF THE DEAD), in spells meant to enable a dead king to ascend to the sky, speak of him climbing a ladder or staircase, as well as flying like a bird, leaping like a grasshopper or using other methods. He 'flies as a cloud to the sky' or 'kisses the sky like a falcon'. He 'goes to the sky on the wind' or 'stairs are laid for him' or he ascends upon the ladder' which the sun god made for him. Amulets representing ladders have been found in Egyptian tombs, and the Egyptians saw in the rays of the sun shining through a gap in the clouds a pathway to the sky, the radiant stair which the king ascends.

The Romans sometimes placed a miniature ladder, made of bronze, in a tomb, and in the Mithraic Mysteries of Roman imperial times the worshipper rose to divine status by climbing the seven steps or grades of initiation, symbolized by a ladder of seven rungs, one for each of the planets (see MITHRAS). The staircase, with its steps corresponding to planets and metals and stages in the spiritual process, appears frequently in alchemical symbolism. The stairs lead to the summit of a mountain or to the gateway of the celestial city, and to climb them is again to transcend the ordinary human state and attain perfection and the divine.

The Ladder of Bethel

The golden ladder which Dante describes rising to the highest heaven (in *Paradiso*, cantos 21 and 22) he identifies with the most celebrated of all symbolic ladders, the one which Jacob saw in a dream at what is now the village of Beitin, some ten miles north of Jerusalem. He went to sleep with his head on a stone: 'And he dreamed that there was a ladder set up on the earth, and the top of it reached to heaven; and behold, the angels of God were ascending and descending on it!' When Jacob woke up, he said, 'How awesome is this place! This is none other than the house of God, and this is the gate of heaven' (Genesis, chapter 28). He named the place Bethel, 'house of God', and later the ark of the covenant was kept there and God was consulted there in time of stress (Judges, chapter 20). According to cabalistic commentators, the ladder had 72 rungs, corresponding to the 72 syllables of the great mystic name of God (see NAMES).

Christians interpreted the ladder of Jacob's dream as a sign that the righteous will attain salvation (and Bethel became a general term for a Nonconformist meeting-house). St Benedict in a vision saw his monks rising to heaven on a ladder, and in the 11th century St Romuald, founding a monastery at Camaldoli in Italy, dreamed of men in white robes ascending a ladder to the sky, and decided that he would dress his monks in white.

The ladder or stair leads down as well as up, of course, and the Pythagoreans saw the particles of dust which swirl and dance in a sunbeam as souls or life-sparks descending to the earth on wings of light. The Jewish author Philo in the 1st century AD and the Christian author Origen in the 3rd century both interpreted Jacob's ladder as the air through which souls descend and ascend before birth and after death.

Walking Under Ladders

Disinclination to walk under a ladder, even at the cost of stepping out into traffic on the street, is very common. The simplest explanation of it is that it is based on a sensible reluctance to risk something falling on your head. Another possible explanation is that to walk under a ladder is to break through the triangle formed by the ladder, the wall and the ground, and that this is dangerous because the triangle is a symbol of good luck in general and of the Trinity in particular.

In folk tradition, a dream of going up a ladder is a beneficent dream of good omen, and a dream of going down one is the reverse. A more modern interpretation, by Freud, is that dreams of going up or down ladders, stairs or slopes are symbolic representations of sexual intercourse.
(See also HOUSE; SUPERSTITIONS.)

'physical phenomena have appeared in holy men and women for which no 'natural' cause has so far been found; it may be, however, that profoundly religious temperaments may be correlated . . . with metabolic effects in which biochemical and psychosomatic factors participate'

STIGMATA

'WOUNDS', MARKS OR POINTS of bleeding which simulate the injuries of Christ are known as stigmata. Stigmatics (those who receive stigmata) can develop marks corresponding to any or all of the piercing of hands and feet, the *ferita* or lance-wound in the side, the bruise on the shoulder caused by the weight of the cross, chafing of wrists and ankles, weals of scourging and a coronet on the brow (Crown of Thorns). Allied to the stigmata is the mystic ring, a modification of the skin or flesh of the ring-finger of the right hand, appropriate to a nun's 'bethrothal'.

If healing miracles are omitted as essentially psychological (see MIRACLES), the curious physical phenomena reported variously of some mystics include: stigmatization, *incendium amoris* ('flames of love'), incombustibility, fragrance, bodily elongation, and *inedia*, the ability to survive without food. Physiological peculiarities alleged of the mystic's mortal remains comprise the ability to bleed, incorruptibility and absence of rigor mortis. Levitation, irradiance, telekinesis and 'miracles of abundance' may also be classified as physical phenomena.

It is difficult to reject all the alleged physiological and physical phenomena as frauds or fictions. Admittedly we can have little confidence in many of the reports, particularly concerning the elder saints, where hagiographers (writers of saints' lives) have been over-zealous. But the position has improved of late as a result of modern critical hagiography and the principles established by Pope Benedict XIV (1675–1758), who stressed that nothing should be ascribed to the supernatural if a natural explanation is possible. Extraordinary phenomena (other than posthumous miracles of healing) are not nowadays required in proof of holiness of life; and this diminishes the motive for ascribing wonders to the virtuous departed.

The tests of evidence in this field are the same as those in psychical research or in historical studies. Eyewitness depositions are preferred to hearsay evidence, and should be recorded soon after the event with circumstantial detail. The value of depositions made at processes for beatification or canonization is often, but not always, reduced by the lapse of time between the death of the candidate and the inquiry. Because of these or other uncertainties we cannot readily form a judgement concerning the status of fragrance, *incendium amoris*, bodily incorruption and so on, telekinesis or miracles of abundance. But with levitation, irradiance and stigmatization the evidential position is distinctly better.

A Kind of Trance

Little is known with any certainty of mystic phenomena in the orient, in Islam or in the Orthodox Churches; Protestants, it seems, incline neither to mysticism nor phenomena. Almost all the material worthy of study occurs in the Roman Catholic sphere. Non-Catholic students (including the present writer) have to overcome a lofty barrier of initial scepticism. But it is wrong to suppose that intelligent Catholics (to whom we are indebted for searching factual and critical studies) have all been gullible. Even in the 13th century, many ecclesiastical authorities would bear heavily on mystics suspected of fraud or love of notoriety.

In the present context 'mysticism' means 'mystical prayer' ('contemplation'). It is not given to all to graduate from ordinary prayer to any or all of the three stages of mystical prayer. At the first level the mystic concentrates his mind, by conscious effort, on divine themes. If the state of 'full union' supervenes, he enjoys a sense of divine presence but is still capable of voluntary withdrawal, unless the state of 'rapture' or 'ecstasy' has been attained. Ecstasy is, broadly speaking, a kind of trance in which the mind is cut off from the environment unless aroused by some drastic intervention such as a blow or an imperative command. Sometimes, when overtaken by ecstasy, the mystic continues in automatic fashion with his present occupation which may be preaching or saying Mass.

Attempts have been made to equate ecstasy with other forms of trance; hysterical catalepsy, somnambulism, hypnotism, the mediumistic trance or drug-induced states; but it is unsafe to suppose that these conditions are identical either to one another or to ecstasy, though as pointed out by St Teresa of Avila (see TERESA OF AVILA), distinguishing between 'natural' and mystic ecstasies, a hysterical trance can be confused with ecstasy. Religious mystics normally interpret ecstasy in terms of real contact with God. This is debatable in cases where they receive demonstrably false revelations concerning matters of fact. But in other cases the belief cannot be contradicted, though equally it cannot be logically proved true. Judgement has therefore to be suspended in the face of an important empirical fact; the majority of the alleged physical phenomena occur in persons who engage in mystical prayer and experience ecstasies. This goes some way to explain why, if the phenomena are not fraudulent or illusory, they belong only to religions where mystical prayer is practised. The link between ecstasies and phenomena does not, of course, prejudge the issue as to whether the latter are supernatural or due to obscure natural causes.

Few stigmatizations, if any, can be dated earlier than 1224 when, it is said, St Francis of Assisi (see FRANCIS OF ASSISI) received wounds in hands and feet after a vision of a seraph received during ecstasy. His stigmata were described as fleshy excrescences resembling the curved-over point of a nail on the palm, and a nail-head on the back of the hand. But examination of portraits of the saint and evidence from modern cases suggest that the excrescences were merely raised scar tissue, so that the problem is reduced to how the wounds originated. As many as 300 subsequent instances of stigmatization have been alleged but only a few provide data of value.

Bleeding Through the Skin

Elena Ajello (born in 1901 in Montalto Uffugo, Calabria, Italy) was especially devoted to St Rita of Cascia (1386–1457), who was said to have had an evil-smelling stigmatic wound which remained unhealed in her forehead. In 1923 Elena experienced a vision in which Christ injured her brow with his own Crown of Thorns. Some hours later, while she was still in an ecstatic state, a physician was called to her because blood was flowing copiously from her forehead. Dr Turano wiped away the blood and found that at intervals she would contract her brow in a painful spasm and blood would then exude from the pores. Similarly, when Dr Gerald Molloy wiped the blood from the backs and palms of the hands of the famous stigmatic Louise Lateau (1850–1883) of Bois D'Haine, Belgium, he found oval marks of a bright red hue about one inch long by half an inch wide. The blood forced its way through unbroken skin in sufficient quantity for visiting pilgrims to soak it up in their handkerchiefs several times in an hour. Dr Warloment of the Belgian Medical Academy enclosed Louise's arm in a special glass apparatus and showed that the bleeding was spontaneous and not due to prior irritation of the skin by Louise. Anne

Catherine Emmerich (1774–1824) of Coesfeld, Rhineland, besides other stigmata, had the lance-wound on her right side and a Y-shaped cross on her chest, both of which were areas from which the blood exuded at certain times.

Bleeding through the skin is indeed an exceptional occurrence but would seem to lie within the limits of what is naturally possible. Various facts weaken the case for supernatural causation. On the supernatural hypothesis it is odd that 12 centuries elapsed without stigmatics. The historical facts of the Crucifixion are not made plain by the stigmata. Was Jesus pierced in the left side (Louise Lateau) or the right (Catherine Emmerich)? The shape of the stigmata vary between stigmatics and from time to time in the same person; the marks on the hands of Teresa Neumann (1898–1962; see NEUMANN) of Konnersreuth, Bavaria were sometimes square and sometimes round. Elena Ajello was devoted to St Rita. Catherine Emmerich's Y-shaped cross was unique to her, but resembled the unusual Y-shaped cross in the church of St Lambert at Coesfeld where Catherine had spent long hours in prayer. These oddities are suggestive of the influence not of the supernatural but of ideas that have become lodged in the mind of the stigmatic.

Indeed, if supernatural intervention be discounted, stigmatization cannot be explained naturalistically in purely organic terms such as haemophiliac bleeding because of the specific location of the stigmata. Analysis shows that in stigmatic

'Drink of My Chalice!'

Day after day (Passitea) lay there upon her bed, motionless, and, as all believed, at death's door. Good Friday came, when suddenly between two and three o'clock she rose up on her knees with outstretched arms, a dazzling ray like lightning flashed through the room, a sharp loud clap as if of thunder was heard, and with a piercing cry, Passitea, her face radiant with some unearthly glow, fell swooning in utter collapse. Her two sisters who were in the room, alarmed, ran to lift her up when to their astonishment they saw that blood was pouring from her hands, her feet, and her head, whilst her white night-rail was crimsoned all down the left side with blood welling through as if from a deep wound. As quickly as they could they mopped up the stains with towels and ewers of fresh water; they changed the coverlets which were all spotted with blood, and even scoured the floor round the bed . . . a priest of much experience in mysticism was urgently sent for. Upon his arrival he at once recognized that Passitea had received the stigmata. In reply to his questions . . . Passitea under obedience described that she had seen as it were in a vision, Christ crucified, livid and bruised, and covered with wounds streaming with red blood. She heard the words "Daughter, drink of My Chalice", whereupon there darted out rays of transparent glory which struck her hands, her feet, and for a second's space encircled her head. The pain was so acute that she lost all consciousness.

Montague Summers *The Physical Phenomena of Mysticism*

bleeding actual blood is exuded, which further distinguishes the condition from haemathidrosis, which is characterized by red perspiration due to the presence of the bacterium *micrococcus prodigiosus*. The naturalistic explanation of stigmatization therefore sees the stigmata as the result of auto-suggestion on the part of the stigmatics who, almost without exception, have been given to brooding intensely on the sufferings of Christ.

This theory is well supported by the fact that many stigmatics show undoubted signs of having suffered from hysteria at some time in their lives. 'Hysteria' is employed in the technical sense to designate an illness that can take a bewildering variety of forms: temporary blindness, deafness, paralysis, losses of sensibility in the skin, or excessive sensibility; comas, fainting fits, spasms; miscellaneous aches and pains, and so on. Some stigmatics like Elena Ajello are described as manifesting hysterical symptoms. Others like Teresa Neumann and Berthe Mrazek (a friend of Nurse Edith Cavell who was shot by the Germans in 1915) suffer from mysterious paralyses of sudden onset, relieved by equally mysterious cures, which almost infallibly may be ascribed to hysteria.

A hysterical illness has no organic cause, and is psychological in origin (see FAITH HEALING). But the patient is not shamming; he is really ill and is the victim of a complex and mainly unconscious process of auto-suggestion. When hysteria is found in a stigmatic it is a good indication of a high degree of auto-suggestibility. The naturalistic theory of stigmatization ascribes it to auto-suggestion affecting blood flow and tissues in persons endowed with unusual suggestibility and an obsession with the sufferings of Jesus. This is not quite the same as ascribing stigmatization directly to hysteria, which would go beyond the facts, as there are stigmatics like Father Pio Forgione (1887–1968), of the Capuchin monastery of San Rotundo near Foggia in Italy, who cannot at the present time be classified as hysterical. The link between hysteria and stigmatization is merely that each is a possible result, in appropriate conditions, of a temperament potentially auto-suggestible in certain ways.

Wounds that Open and Close

Advocates of the supernatural origin of stigmata have stressed the rather minor character of the effects such as blisters, rashes and eczemas, produced on the skin by suggestion under hypnotism. But this does not do full justice to Dr Adolph Lechler's results with 'Elizabeth', an Austrian peasant girl who was both very devout and under treatment for hysteria. On Good Friday 1932 she was deeply affected by seeing a film of the suffering and death of Christ, and (significantly) complained of pain in feet and hands. That evening Dr Lechler gave her the hypnotic suggestion that wounds would develop at the site of the pains. Moist wounds appeared during the night. Further suggestion deepened them, and resulted also in tears of blood, the Crown of Thorns and inflammation and sagging of the shoulder. Dr Lechler substantiated his claim with

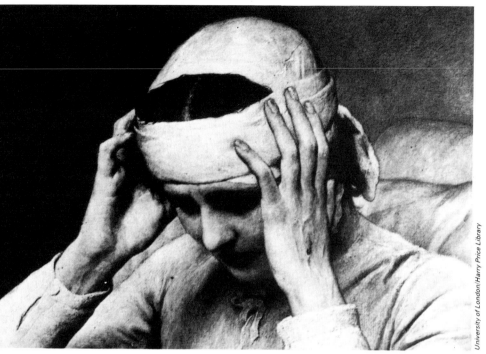

University of London/Harry Price Library

A naturalistic explanation of stigmatization is that the stigmata are the result of auto-suggestion on the part of the stigmatics who, almost without exception, have brooded intensely on Christ's sufferings *Left* Anne Catherine Emmerich: besides the stigmata shown in this picture, she also had the lance-wound on her right side, and a cross on her chest *Below left* St Catherine of Siena: she was said to have suffered the pain of the stigmata while undergoing a mystical experience at Pisa; painting by Sodoma

photographs taken before restoring normality by counter-suggestion.

In the light of Lechler's achievement it would be daring to say that stigmata are supernatural, and in modern canonization processes such as that of St Gemma Galgani (1878–1903) of Lucca the Church abstains from doing so. On the other hand, we cannot assert that stigmata have yet been proved entirely natural. Difficulty may rationally be felt concerning a naturalistic interpretation of St Gemma's stigmata. A beautiful Italian girl with a disposition of great sweetness, Gemma often had ecstasies each Thursday evening (a common pattern to which many stigmatics conform) when red marks showed on the backs and palms of the hands. A rent in the flesh opened by degrees, sometimes becoming very deep, the openings on each side almost reaching each other so far as could be ascertained without painful probing. The cavities were full of blood. On the Friday the flow would cease and the wounds close and heal with astonishing rapidity, usually leaving very little trace except sometimes a raised scar.

St Gemma's case lends credibility to the accounts of deep wounds in some of the older stigmatics such as St Mary Frances of the Five Wounds (1715–91). Extraordinary as these deep stigmata are, they do not decisively contradict the naturalistic hypothesis. 'Elizabeth's' wounds deepened under suggestion and we cannot say to what depth they might not have proceeded had Dr Lechler persisted with suggestion beyond the point that was medically ethical.

The genesis of the mystic ring is akin to that of stigmata. Marie-Julie Jahenny (1850–1941), a somewhat exhibitionistic stigmatic of La Faudrais in Brittany, was in the habit of announcing the particular stigmata she would receive some time before they appeared; a fact strongly in favour of the auto-suggestion hypothesis. In an ecstasy in January 1874 she predicted that she would plight her troth to her heavenly spouse on 20 February. On the predicted day in the presence of 14 witnesses the ring-finger of the right hand became swollen and red beneath the skin. Shortly afterwards it bled. Within 30 minutes a ring shaped formation appeared. There is evidence that Marie-Julie retained it for at least 20 years as a ring of fleshy tissue resembling a hoop which had sunk into the skin.

The tears of blood shed by St Gemma and others were observed by the French physician Dr Parrott in the last century in a patient (presumably hysterical) who shed them while affected by violent grief. She bled also from the breast, hands and knees.

Scala

It is a curious fact that apart from St Francis only three cases of conditions akin to stigmatization have been reliably reported as occurring in men, and these all in the present century. At first sight it might seem to follow from the correlation between hysteria and stigmatization, in view of the old belief in masculine immunity to hysteria. But this comfortable premise was shattered in the last century. Present estimates differ but it seems that hysteria, in one form or another, occurs in men at least half as frequently as in women. Retaining the naturalistic viewpoint there is no reason, however, either to deny the indirect link with hysteria or to suppose that the male stigmata are not produced by the same auto-suggestive mechanism that operates in women. The low incidence in men may be explicable in terms of biological or hormonal differences between the sexes, or by a lesser proclivity to brood on physical aspects of the Crucifixion.

Flames of Divine Love

Some very famous saints such as Catherine of Genoa (1447–1510) and Mary Magdalen of Pazzi (1566–1607) were reputedly sufferers from *incendium amoris*, ascribed to the warmth of their love of God, so that even in winter they sought for cooling winds and cold compresses. In the case of the boy saint Stanislaus Kostka (1550–68) who died during his novitiate we may suspect an actual infection. In other cases we might suppose the ardours to have been subjective. But Cardinal Crescenzi said of St Philip Neri (1515–95) that the touch of his hand was as from one in a raging fever, and the attendants of St Catherine in her last illness deposed that the blood she discharged was exceptionally hot, even for a patient in fever. At the beatification process of Serafino of Dio (d. 1699), nuns affirmed that it scorched them if they touched her.

Fever of hysterical rather than organic origin has been alleged to occur as a medical condition, but would appear to be extremely rare. But it seems that a restricted region can have its temperature raised by hysterical mechanisms. (The left arm of a poltergeist girl, Angélique Cottin, investigated in Paris in 1846 gave off a gentle heat.) St Philip Neri was neither stigmatized nor hysterical, but Mary Villani, St Catherine and Mary Magdalen were stigmatics, which may be relevant. We would however tend to disregard the whole problem were it not for Father Pio Forgione whose stigmata, received first in 1915, were declared in 1923 by the Holy Office not to have been proved to be supernatural. Father Pio was something of a latter-day Curé of Ars (see CURÉ OF ARS), because, though very reserved and retiring like St Jean Vianney, he was also a great confessor and was said to have the same gift of telepathy or 'reading of hearts', as well as other psychic abilities. It is said that as a novice at Benevento he occasionally ran a fever with a temperature so high as to break the clinical thermometer. Special measurements showed a blood heat of 112°F (45°C).

It would be unwise to speculate overmuch on incombustibility or immunity to fire

Abresch Federico

ecause little of this nature has been
sserted since the 16th century, when it was
aid that Venerable Domenica del Paradiso
(1473–1553) could carry live charcoal in
er hands. Numerous incidents of this sort
ere reported of St Francis of Paola (1416–
507), such as putting his hands into boil-
g oil or mending hot lime-kilns. St
atherine of Siena (1347–1389) and her
othes are said to have been miraculously
reserved from scorching when she lay for an
ppreciable time in contact with the kitchen
re, in an ecstasy. Father Thurston has
ttempted to erect some parallels between
ystic incombustibility and the practice of
re-walking, as well as the feats of the 19th
ntury medium Daniel Dunglas Home
ee HOME), but the subject seems at
resent beyond the reach of critical analysis.

Because of the opportunity for fraud in
arkened seance rooms, it is hard to attach
uch significance to the fragrances (usually
f known species such as rose, verbena or
andalwood) common at Spiritualist seance
ooms in the last century. Peculiar smells,
ften unpleasant, reported in contemporary
oltergeist cases are also difficult to assess.
ut stories concerning the 'odour of sanctity',
erfumes manifesting in the vicinity of
ersons of holy life, are numerous. There
as abundant testimony regarding the
ragrance which clung to everything touched
y St Mary Francis of the Five Wounds,
nd to the scent of a species of violet that

was associated with St Catherine of Ricci (1522–29). These saints were stigmatics, as was Sister Mary of Jesus Crucified (d. 1878), who was similarly favoured according to her Carmelite companions. The nuns at Reckshill in New York state claimed that a wonderful fragrance persisted in their chapel after a visit by the stigmatic Margaret Reilly (d. 1937). In the case of St Veronica Giuliani (1676–1727) it was definitely believed that the scent proceeded from her stigmata. The same was said of Father Pio Forgione, and there appears to be competent medical testimony as to the objective reality of the scent which was variously compared to roses, violets or incense.

It is not clear whether these fragrances are invariably associated with stigmata. No chemical analysis of stigmatic blood yet published has claimed to find aromatic substances therein. The door is by no means closed to a naturalistic explanation. Agreeable odours are occasionally reported by physicians in connection with various maladies; and it is not inconceivable that profoundly religious temperaments may be correlated in some degree with metabolic effects in which both biochemical and psychosomatic factors participate.

Allegations of distortion or elongation of the mystic's person would seem on the face of it to be too grotesque for pious hagiographers to insert them into the record as conventional indications of sanctity. But there are no recent instances. Also, even if the veracity of the witnesses is accepted, there is in some cases a doubt as to whether the more understandable and better authenticated phenomenon of levitation has not been mistaken for elongation. Thus the fellow nuns of Sister Veronica Laparelli (1537–1620) measured her height with a yardstick and found that during her prolonged ecstasies she seemed to be some 10 inches taller than usual. But on one occasion Mother Plautilla Semboli put her hand under Veronica's robe and 'found she was lifted up above the ground'.

Other cases can in principle be explained as being hallucinatory, like the occasion in about 1700 when a single witness saw Sister Maria Constante Castreca 'grow a considerable height from the ground'. More puzzling, was the affidavit signed by 21 ecclesiastics and notables to the effect that both arms of Blessed Stefana Quinzani (1457–1530) appeared to their view to be stretched some inches during her Friday ecstasies. There was muscular tension, swelling of the veins and blackening of the hands. But a careful reading suggests that the elongation may well have been within the limits of natural stretching possible in some individuals. Dr Imbert-Gourbeyre described some remarkable distensions, contractions and distortions exhibited by Marie-Julie Jahenny in 1880. Though he was a professor of medicine and believed the contortions to be inexplicable by natural means we are entitled to reserve our opinion, particularly in view of the fact that the stigmatic had previously announced that her body would be compressed and her limbs shortened in expiation of the sins of mankind.

Living with very little food, *inedia*, varies

from instances like that of the Curé of Ars, where great activity is maintained on a very light diet, to cases often hailed as miraculous where the individual, almost invariably a woman, apparently survives for months and years on no food and little drink. Many attempts have been made to prove by observation that fasting is complete, and occasionally they end tragically in the subject's death, which suggests that the inedic does in fact take a little nourishment when unsupervised. Inedics are not always Roman Catholics or even particularly religious. Usually there is evidence of nervous disorder; they are bedridden with a mysterious illness, or given to fits or trances. Hysteria inedia or anorexia is a very well-known disorder, and can end in death. The anorexic is often literally incapable of accepting solid food and rejects it by automatic choking or vomiting outside of conscious control. It is not fully understood why inedics can survive for such long periods and it would be foolish to underestimate residual difficulties of naturalistic explanation. But there is no obvious feature by which inedia in the devout differs from anorexia in hysterical persons. Religious inedics usually show other signs of hysteria; female stigmatics are almost invariably inedics also.

As pointed out by Father Thurston, a surprisingly high proportion of saints have been exhumed *after* beatification and their bodies discovered to be in a remarkably good state of preservation. In only a few cases has beatification or canonization been authorized on the basis of apparent incorruptibility of the remains. The body of St Bernadette of Lourdes (1844–79; see LOURDES) was found to be incorrupt in 1909, though the face was brown and the eyes sunken, but only bones were revealed when St Thérèse of Lisieu (1863–97) was disinterred.

If there is no circulation of air the decay of a corpse can be hindered. Dry conditions favour mummification even if there has been no embalmment. Moisture sometimes produces saponification, in which the internal tissues are converted into a kind of ammoniacal soap, called *adipocere*, or *gras de cadavre,* and the skin becomes like that of a mummy. The body of Blessed Marie Pelletier was found in this condition in 1903 when exhumed 35 years after death. But when Blessed Anna Maria Taigi (1769–1837) was exhumed in 1868, the surgeon reported that the corpse resembled that of a person only three days dead. The skin was soft and discharged an inoffensive somewhat aromatic fluid, recalling the balsam or oil which have been reported of the bodies of holy persons on other occasions. The absence of rigor mortis has often been commented upon, but might just possibly occur naturally in aged inedics who have had a tranquil death. Liquidity of the blood and bleeding from incisions long after death have also been alleged. At present it seems impossible to say whether or not naturalistic explanations are potentially available, or whether attitudes of mind during life can bequeath unusual biochemical features to the remains.

Detail from *Christ in the House of His Parent* in this romantic painting, by Millais, Jesus depicted showing the stigmata in anticipati of the wounds that he later received on t Cross; many people regarded the picture blasphemous when it was first exhibited

The heaps of corn in the granary of t 'Filles de la Croix' at La Poye, Poitou, France, were mysteriously replenish over a continuing period around 182 after St Andrew Fournet (1752–183 had prayed over them. But one wonde whether the supplies were put there stealth by an unknown well-wisher. One is at a lo to comment on St John Bosco's basket whi contained initially only a score of rolls, b which in 1860 provided, it seems, enou bread for his 300 students. Interesting enough no other marvels are narrated 'Don Bosco' (1815–88), not even ecstasie

Levitation is alleged of comparative few saints; which suggests it is not a hagi graphic commonplace. Professor Leroy scholarly review lists 50 traditions ancient (before 1500), 85 cases as mode (1500 to 1800), and 20 cases as rece (since 1800). In the ancient traditions, with St Dunstan (918–988) and St Franc we encounter the difficulty that their le tations are mentioned by their later bi graphers but not their earliest ones. Sor modern critics have taken the view th levitation is purely a subjective feeli experienced by ecstatic persons, many whom have certainly spoken of a sense lightness and of being lifted up. But tl case of St Joseph Mary Desu (Joseph Copertino, 1603–63) is adequate by itse to prove the occurrence of levitation as objective physical happening. Very slow wit, he nevertheless gained such fame in tl district of Copertino in southern Italy f his goodwill, piety and holiness that he w examined by the Inquisition of Napl but acquitted of the charge of deceiving tl populace by false miracles. Subsequently tl authorities, rendered even more suspicio by his levitations, transferred him to Assi Urbino, Fossombrone and Osimo, but each place he attracted a pilgrimage.

Joseph's levitations occurred durir joyous raptures which could easily l triggered off by music or the sight of sacred image or a beautiful leaf or twi Sometimes they were simple suspensio in the air as happened in Rome before Po Urban VIII; to which the Holy Fath testified. At Copertino alone, no less than 7 levitations are alleged. Some were comic rather than edifying. The wife of the Hig Admiral of Castile fainted when she an her husband saw Joseph fly a distance of 1 paces over their heads. The Lutheran Du of Brunswick, and his chaplain, saw Josep at Mass transported in the air about five pac from the altar while still in a kneeling postur and return in similar fashion. They becan Roman Catholics.

Joseph's flights are exceptional amor levitators. The majority of eyewitne accounts concerning other mystics (ar there are many relating to widely differe times and places) affirm that the mystic suspended about six inches above the grour

Lifted Up by Ecstasy

Psychokinesis is the name given in parapsychology to the movement of objects by means unknown to physics (see PSYCHOKINESIS). It occurs in poltergeist outbreaks (see POLTERGEISTS) and is alleged to happen in seance rooms. Catholic writers recognize 'diabolical assaults' on the religious, which to the non-Catholic bear a considerable resemblance to poltergeist phenomena. Psychokinesis is rarely alleged of the more recent saints. However the term telekinesis is applied to the spontaneous flight of the host (the wafer of consecrated bread in the Mass) to the mouth of a divinely-favoured recipient. An aspirant to a reputation for sanctity might fraudulently conceal a wafer in his mouth prior to announcing the

miracle, as seems to have been done by Vittoria Bondi in the 18th century. However when the Curé of Ars said that the host once detached itself from his fingers and placed itself upon the tongue of a communicant we cannot doubt his veracity, although the possibility of a hallucination or a false memory remains. It is also possible that the Curé produced the 'miracle' himself by unconscious psychokinesis, having been for many years the centre of poltergeist activity.

Teleportation or apportation, the mysterious conveyance of objects into closed rooms, is alleged both of poltergeist cases and the mediumistic seance. The only phenomena at all analogous to teleportation met with in connection with latter-day saints are alleged miracles of abundance.

while in ecstasy and at length makes a gentle landing. The levitating mystic may be preaching like St Alphonsus Liguori (1696–1787) and St Andrew Fournet or praying like St Teresa of Avila and the great theologian Francis Suarez (1548–1617). The evidence is not conclusive but it strongly suggests that levitation occurs only in ecstasy. In 24 cases out of the 155 listed by Leroy the face or figure of the levitating ecstatic have been said to give off or be bathed in a mysterious radiance. Sometimes this light is said to emanate from a sacred image or crucifix, but in other cases there is no obvious source. Puzzling as this may be, it does not weaken the evidence for levitation which rests on non-irradiated cases like St Joseph's. Levitation (including

radiance) is the one mystic phenomenon requiring us to postulate either a supernatural explanation or the existence of natural forces unknown to physics.

On a naturalistic view such forces are possibly the same as those released in poltergeist outbreaks, but with a different 'style' of operation corresponding to a radically different psychological situation. The contrast between the wilder transportations of St Joseph and the gentler levitations of most mystics so favoured also points to psychological factors. Accounts of radiance are not easily equated to the 'aura' as described in occultist literature. Scientists have tended to discount the observation by the reputable 19th century French physician Charles Féré of orange-coloured light

surrounding the head and hands of two hysterical patients.

A. R. G. OWEN

FURTHER READING: Fr. Amadeo, *Blessed Gemma Galgani* (Burns and Oates, London, 1935); Charles M. Carty, *The Two Stigmatists: Padre Pio and Teresa Neumann* (Radio Replies Press, 1956); O. Leroy, *Levitation* (Burns and Oates, London, 1928); Paul Siwek, S.J. *The Riddle of Konnersreuth* (Bruce Publishing Co., 1954); Robert D. Smith, *Comparative Miracles* (Herder, 1965); Montague Summers, *The Physical Phenomena of Mysticism* (Barnes and Noble, 1950); Herbert Thurston, S.J., *The Physical Phenomena of Mysticism* (Regnery, 1952).

Mansell Collection

Stockings

It is often considered lucky to put on the left stocking before the right, or by mistake to wear odd stockings, or put them on inside out: to correct the mistake is to change the luck; a pair of stockings fixed crosswise at the head and foot of the bed was thought to banish nightmares; to hang up an empty stocking at Christmas is to invite Father Christmas to fill it with gifts.

Archeology has shown that Stonehenge was not built by the Druids, as was sometimes supposed, but existed at a far earlier period. As to whether it served as a temple, observatory or political centre, opinion is still divided

STONEHENGE

FEW PEOPLE would disagree that Stonehenge is an unnerving place, rising out of the empty Salisbury plain, with a quality of immensity and stillness and awesome age seldom conveyed by anything man-made. And no one would dispute that it consists of a number of giant standing stones, some in pairs with lintel stones across their tops, and also many fallen stones – all placed with sufficient symmetry to indicate that what we now see may not have been the whole of the construction in its original state. But people disagree about who built Stonehenge, when, and for what purpose, and even how it was built. The best we can do is to hint at the immense range of theories, and to sketch broadly some of the more cogent conceptions and some of the more fanciful, including some of the best-known legends.

The most persistent of these legends describes it as a monument erected in memory of a number of ancient British nobles, murdered by the treachery of Hengist, the Saxon, during a supposed truce. The king of the Britons sought the advice of Merlin on a suitable memorial; and the magician recommended the use of

vast stones brought from a structure he called the Giant's Dance, in Ireland (see MERLIN). These stones were especially rich in magical force. But it required Merlin's powers to convey them to England, once the Britons had routed the Irish who defended them. It is an interestingly tangled legend, containing elements of Arthurian myth, the age-old belief in the magic of stones (see STONES), and possibly some kind of folk memory of the actual transporting of the stones to Salisbury Plain.

The main source for this tale is the 12th century chronicler Geoffrey of Monmouth. Another story is that the Devil built Stonehenge for the malicious pleasure of puzzling everyone in years to come. A friar spied upon him and ran to reveal all, but the Devil flung one of the great stones and pinned the friar by his heel. Hence the stone standing alone to the north-east of the main structure is called the Heel Stone. (Its name has been otherwise derived from the Anglo-Saxon *helan*, to hide – but no one knows what it hides, if anything.) Finally, a variant tale combines the two: the Devil is said to have built Stonehenge on Merlin's instructions, for the memorial purpose mentioned, having bought the stones cheaply by trickery from an old Irishwoman.

Today, it is still commonly thought that the Druids built the place as a sun-worshipping temple and site for human sacrifice. Many 18th and 19th century authors produced lengthy proofs of the Druid involvement, and many 20th century authors

(not to mention newspapers) continue to accept this explanation. In fact, all the archeological evidence makes it clear that the structure had existed for over 1000 years before the arrival of Druidic cults and practices in Britain.

It was the 17th century antiquary John Aubrey who first suggested the connection with the Druids and the idea has persisted, particularly as the self-styled Druid sects of today have tended to gather at Stonehenge for midsummer observances (see DRUIDS). It is possible that the ancient Druids might have used Stonehenge now and then for ceremonies, but normally they preferred forest groves. The modern sect seems to have been drawn to Stonehenge because of Aubrey's idle suggestion, and the later credit given to it.

These romantic Druid links led to the silly but lasting names of two of the great prostrate stones – the so-called Altar Stone, near the centre of the structure, and the Slaughter Stone lying out near the Heel Stone. Both are now thought to have once been standing, and to have had nothing at all to do with any kind of sacrifice.

There has been no lack of other notions about the builders, if none so popular as the Druidic one. Inigo Jones, the 17th century architect, rejected the Druid theory (on the sound grounds that the Druids were not noted for architectural achievement), but thought Stonehenge to be a Roman edifice in the Tuscan manner. Others have ascribed it to invading Belgae from north-eastern Gaul, or even Phoenicians. And because in

Celtic lore the Little People are traditionally thought to have put up dolmens and cromlechs (megalithic tombs), they have been credited with Stonehenge too.

Present-day archeology has managed to sort out fairly clearly who the builders were. In doing so it has also managed to deduce a general dating of the construction, which apparently went on for some centuries. It was built in three stages, corresponding to stages in the cultural development of ancient Britain.

The first builders, it is thought, were a Neolithic people who moved into Britain before 3000 BC, bringing with them a penchant for circular earthworks. They also buried their dead in vast barrows, 100 feet or more in length, many of which are in the vicinity of Stonehenge. The tribes of this period left many enclosures surrounded by circular banks and ditches, and are usually thought to have made the ditch and inner embankment around Stonehenge, now mostly filled in by wind and time. They may also have set up the Heel Stone.

The next stage, from about 1800 BC, saw the arrival of the 'Beaker' people, who are known for their pottery and who buried their dead in individual tombs; they are also known for setting up many circular arrangements of standing stones along with 'henge' enclosures – like that at Avebury near Stonehenge. These were the people who brought the bluestones to Stonehenge from – it is now generally agreed – the Prescelly Hills in Wales.

The Beaker folk were a highly developed late Stone Age and early Bronze Age people. The ensuing stage introduced an even higher Bronze Age culture, the 'Wessex' people – workers in metal ruled by warrior chiefs, with direct trade links to Europe reaching perhaps as far as the Mediterranean. It was once thought that there might be Mycenean influence in the architecture of Stonehenge, but it is now known that Stonehenge was completed before Mycene. In their time, the mighty project became mightier. The older bluestones were uprooted and the huge inner 'trilithons' (structures formed of three stones), of sarsen sandstone from some 20 miles away, went up. Then followed the outer circle of uprights and lintels, also sarsen, and some crucial single stones including the Slaughter Stone.

So ended the construction of Stonehenge, somewhere about 1400 BC. Apart from the structures so far mentioned, there are various holes where no stones stand – like the 'Aubrey holes', named after the antiquary and surmised later to be pits dug for some sepulchral or chthonic rites.

A Prehistoric Computer

People have believed that Stonehenge was either a temple or a place of worship, or a vastly important meeting place for chiefs and kings, or a structure for observing and

predicting the movement of heavenly bodies mainly the sun and moon. This last idea based on the belief that the sun rises, at the summer solstice, directly over the Heel Stone as seen from the centre of Stonehenge And so, apparently, it does – depending on what spot you call the centre, what precise line you take to be the much sought-after axis of Stonehenge, what precise moment you take to be true sunrise, and how much margin of error you allow for erosion, cosmic adjustments over the millennia, and so on

R. J. C. Atkinson, archeologist and leading authority on Stonehenge, insists that the midsummer sunrise alignment was only approximate, and that the reasons for it remain unknown. Nor does he accept the dating of the structure that is based on the alignment. But more recently G.S. Hawkins an astronomer, turned to a computer and announced that he had 'decoded' the place He found quantities of astronomical alignments, involving the Heel Stone, the outer 'Station' stones (from which diagonals give a putative centre), the Aubrey holes and much else. By his account Stonehenge was no less than a prehistoric computer, a device for making highly intricate astronomical calculations, including predictions of equinoctial sunrises and sunsets, moonrises and moonsets, and eclipses. But these findings are still very much in dispute.

FURTHER READING: R. J. C. Atkinson, *Stonehenge* (Collins, Toronto, 1956); Gerald S. Hawkins, *Stonehenge Decoded* (Dell, 1966).

Stonehenge silhouetted against the sunset: its quality of awesomeness, and its antiquity, have made it the focus of romantic legends; modern Druids gather there to celebrate the midsummer solstice

British Museum

MAN MYTH & MAGIC · 7

Even before man sculpted representations of his gods, he recognized in stones and pebbles a supernatural power to be venerated and, on occasions, tapped

STONES

THE PRESENCE of pebbles, ordinary stones and chunks of unhewn rock in so much mythical and magical lore reflects mankind's willingness to find the supernatural in anything and everything. Demons in wild animals, gods in trees, magical power in lightning or eclipses are readily comprehensible. But it must be an overwhelming, all-consuming myth-making urge that puts spirits in mossy old boulders, magical power in a handful of gravel.

In man's earliest myth-making days the stone would often be worshipped directly as a god in itself. Usually the object of such worship inspired awe because of its size, its odd shape or its colour. Pre-biblical Semitic peoples apparently possessed stone-worshipping cults, as did tribes in parts of pre-Hellenic Greece, Crete and Thessaly. Stones have also been worshipped as gods in parts of Africa, and widely in India.

But sophistication of a sort usually overtook these cults fairly soon, and the stone ceased to be a god, becoming instead the abode of a god. The god in the stone, the natural stone, not the sculpted, is a worldwide phenomenon. The ancient Greeks devoted much of their religious attention to such stones, including those that were vaguely phallic in shape and associated with Apollo. The Greeks also set up their famous *hermae*, cairns or heaps of stones ascribed to Hermes (see HERMES), which partook of some of his divinity as god of travellers. These were placed on roadsides, on boundaries, and in later days on street corners and outside houses. And though they eventually developed into carved representations of the god, erect phallus and all, many were originally plain, unwrought, columnar rocks.

The boundary stones of the Babylonians were often also plain, columnar rocks, though the boundary-makers carved inscriptions on them, mostly warning anyone who might dare to shift a particular stone that an awful curse would descend from the god to whom it was dedicated. In much the same

Previous page Deucalion and his wife Pyrrha, according to Greek legend the only survivors of a universal flood, created mankind anew by casting stones behind them: as they struck the ground, the stones thrown by Deucalion became men, while those thrown by Pyrrha turned into women: illustration from a 15th century Flemish edition of *The Romance of the Rose*
Below left Stone dolmen in County Donegal: these constructions of flat, unhewn stones resting horizontally across stone uprights are numerous in Celtic regions
Below right Formation in Cornwall dating from **1600–1000** BC; stones with natural holes were taken to represent the female principle, and sick persons or barren women might be passed through the hole in a symbolic rebirth

way, the Celts scraped semi-abstract representations of gods onto tall, upright monumental stones known as menhirs. But the Celts, along with many other peoples, also made much use of unadorned, natural standing stones, sometimes in groups, as at Stonehenge, or as in the great dolmens of Celtic regions, flat, unhewn stones which rest horizontally across upright stones. Stones were also used singly, frequently as grave markers. The idea of erecting a tombstone over a grave may possibly have arisen from the belief that the spirit of the dead person would inhabit the stone. What is now a memorial may have once been a spiritual abode (see BRITTANY; CULT OF THE DEAD; STONEHENGE).

The Jungian psychologist Marie-Louise von Franz has written that ancient Germanic peoples believed in this role of the tombstone, adding that the belief may spring from 'the symbolic idea that something eternal of the dead person remains, which can be most fittingly represented by a stone'. This may explain much of the general mythological role of unwrought stone: its eternality symbolizes and magically confers spiritual eternality.

The most primitive form of boundary or marker stone, still widely in use, was the cairn, which was built up at holy places and to which each traveller added another stone. The practice is found throughout Celtic regions of Europe, including Britain, in the Middle East and Asia, and among Australian aborigines. The Celts dedicated many cairns to mountain gods on peaks and

Ianthe Ruthven

mmits, believing that adding a stone magically swept away the traveller's weariss. Hikers and mountain-climbers still rry on the practice today, but as a pleant tradition rather than a piece of magic worship.

The 'god-in-the-stone' motif also occurs nong North American Indians. Vast stones re worshipped by Plains tribes like the oux, Ojibwa and Canadian Cree, to whom, viously, a solitary huge boulder on the npty face of the prairie would seem pecially awesome. In the myths of these ibes, the great stones seem to be both welling places for special gods and almost ncestral spirit beings in their own right, if they had not quite completed the transion from 'god-as-the-stone' to 'god-in-e-stone'.

The spirits in stones can often be lesser vinities, not much more than imps. Many d Irish and Welsh tales tell of stones that eak or move, usually on especially supertural occasions, like Midsummer Eve; d there are moving stones in the folklore France, Borneo, Central America and sewhere. The Central American stones e on a mountain and are shaped rather ke jaguars; they are believed to transrm themselves into these animals at will. he Chukchansi Indians of California had legend of a rock, about five feet high, that uld grow, if anyone tried to jump it, just ough to scrape the jumper's backside. he belief that all stones increase in size is mmon to many peoples. According to an d American superstition, lightning aids is growing process.

oronation Stones

many parts of the world the concepts of e god-as-the-stone and the god-in-theone frequently develop into the belief that particular stone is a sacred object merely ecause of some mythic association with pernatural powers. Perhaps the most mous example is the Black Stone of Islam, the Kaaba at Mecca (see MECCA). It es not contain a god, but has traditional ssociations with God. Of course, as a eteorite it would be doubly venerable, as eteorites are considered to be extremely cred in almost every mythology.

The Old Testament contains its share of acred stones, like the one set up and anoined by Jacob at Bethel, after his dream of e ladder to heaven (Genesis, chapter 28). nd Joshua set up a great stone to mark e covenant he made with the people of rael that they would forsake 'foreign gods' nd serve the Lord (Joshua, chapter 24).

According to a Greek legend, the centre f the world was found by Zeus to be at elphi, and was marked by the conical avel stone' called *omphalos* (see NAVEL). s shape and site undoubtedly made it acred to Apollo; and a variant of the myth tates that the omphalos marked the grave f the sacred snake of an older religion, upplanted by the worship of Apollo.

With the movement away from the conept of the god-in-the-stone to that of the ss divine sacred stone, men developed the dea of the altar-stone: a sacred stone that till provided a way of access to the god,

even if he no longer lived in it (see ALTAR). For instance, some tribes in Annam, now part of Vietnam, would wash natural, unwrought stones and place food and drink on them for the gods. The Aztecs and Maya used vast stones, partly hewn, and grooved to catch blood, as altars for human sacrifice; and Norse saga mentions Thor's stone, a sacred rock on which men being sacrificed to the god had their backs broken.

Another famous stone, which is not strictly an altar but which nevertheless is a feature of holy occasions, is the Stone of Scone, on which the kings of Scotland were once crowned. Edward I took it to Westminster Abbey in the 13th century, where it forms part of the throne occupied by British monarchs at their coronation. It was stolen by Scottish nationalists in 1950, but was recovered and returned to London the next year. A legend identifies the Stone of Scone with the coronation stone of the old kings of Ireland. Known as the Lia-fail, it was said to shriek aloud whenever the rightful heir to the throne stepped on it. The Anglo-Saxon tribes crowned their kings on a sacred stone at the present site of Kingston-on-Thames in England. The name Kingston is in fact derived from King's Stone.

Most sacred stones were believed to possess inherent magical powers and this is especially true of the chipped-flint tools of the Stone Age, when they were found in the fields of later peoples. Throughout Europe and much of the rest of the world these flint axes and arrowheads were thought to have dropped from the sky, or to have been hurled by the gods, and were called thunderbolts or thunderstones. Naturally they were associated with Zeus or Jupiter in the

Gravestones near Lake Awusa in Ethiopia, thought to belong to Arussi chiefs: 'the idea of erecting a tombstone over a grave may possibly have arisen from the belief that the spirit of the dead person would inhabit the stone'

Graeco-Roman world, and with Thor in Scandinavia, although some ancient Scandinavians apparently worshipped them directly, almost as household gods in their own right.

Fire and Magic-Maker

In North and South America the Indians venerated flint. The Cherokee, for instance, regarded this kind of stone as a god, as did the Quiché of Guatemala, for whom it was the fire god, because of its ability to create fire. The Pueblo Indians had flint societies among their numerous clans and secret cults; predictably, these groups were concerned with weather control and magicmaking.

Throughout Europe, the old popular superstitions give a protective role to the Stone Age implements, which were thought to protect against lightning, disease, witches or (in France) difficult childbirth. Many Asians considered the sacred flints to be lucky charms, and also aids in searching for buried gold. In Britain the prehistoric axes and arrowheads were sometimes called elf-bolts, or fairy-shot, for they were said to have been fired by the little people at humans, to bewitch them. By reverse magic, it was said that carrying such a flint ensured safety from fairy-shot, an idea once also current in Sweden.

Europeans took these ideas about flint to the United States, where rural superstition says that a clean white flint will keep witches from a house, or hawks from the chickens. And rubbing with a flint cures goitre, if the flint is returned to the exact spot where it was found.

Apart from flints, everything from vast granite blocks to plain pebbles can contain magical virtue. The Irish Blarney Stone confers eloquence on those who kiss it; a sacred stone in British Columbia needs only to be struck to cause rain for nearby Indian tribes; special stones in Scotland, Fiji,

John Moss

Greece and elsewhere bring storms if they are turned or set upright. In India standing stones with their phallic associations can be ritually used to cure barrenness in women, or to ensure easy childbirth; and another ritual widespread in India employs a sacred stone to keep evil spirits at bay during funerals.

Stones with natural holes (the female symbol) tend to be as prominent in magical lore as the upright phallic kind. Barren women, or any ill person, would be passed through the holes of large specimens, to undergo the curative power of a symbolic birth or rebirth. Pledges may be sealed with such stones when the participants clasp hands through the hole, as with Scotland's 'Plichtin (plighting) Stane o' Lairg'. Small stones with natural holes are worn as amulets the world over, on pendants or necklaces.

An old American superstition suggests hanging such an amulet over the bed of a woman in labour, or over a door to fend off witches. From similar backwoods American sources come many uses of plain pebbles,

Mohammed, chosen by lot for this sacred task, reverently replaces the Black Stone in the repaired Kaaba: from a 14th century Arabic MS

without holes or any other unusual features, for minor magic-making such as curing warts. For instance, take as many pebbles as you have warts, spit on them (or rub them on the warts, or prick the warts and smear the blood on the pebbles), then throw the pebbles over your left shoulder and walk away without looking back. This cure was also said to work for freckles.

Round white or black pebbles from a beach are supposed to be lucky in American lore. And it is unlucky to trip over a stone, unless you go back and touch it. This idea parallels the bad luck omen of stumbling, which crops up in an old Hawaiian tale of a man who kicked a stone that was, unknown to him, sacred to a god. His sleep was plagued with dreams of being struck by the stone, and they stopped only when he went back and replaced the stone exactly as it had been.

In the southern states of America it was

once believed that snakes, and sometime toads, could be made to excrete a miracu lous stone that could extract poison fro a snakebite; and elsewhere the toad-ston was credited with magically protectiv powers (see JEWELS; TOAD). In Nort Carolina a fish called a sheepshead wa believed to have a magical stone in its hea small and white and marked with an 'L presumably because of the good luck would bring to its finder. And in the Nort of England miners used to believe in the pr tective magic of a hard, black, compacte stone called a 'coal nut', occasionally foun in a vein of coal.

The ancient Japanese used sacred stone in a method of divination, based on the apparent weights when lifted in the hand And some Central American Indians looke for the future in the face of smooth an naturally polished stones. This was a early form of mirror divination, and wa used mainly for death omens, as the ston was said to show the face of Death to anyon fated to die in the near future.

DOUGLAS HIL

Himself a model of domestic virtue, the stork is best known in folklore today as the bringer of new life to human households

STORK

TWO SPECIES of stork, the white and the black, breed in Europe, but folklore is concerned mainly with the white species, which is more conspicuous and bolder. In many parts of Europe, and in North Africa, it has adapted itself to living in close proximity to man and chooses to nest on houses, church towers and, in some places, cart-wheels that have been fixed on tall poles or heavily pruned tree trunks. Although the white

stork is practically voiceless, the clatterin of its mandibles as it arches its neck over it back attracts attention. Ovid, Petronius an Dante are among the writers who mentio this characteristic. The regularity of th bird's appearance in spring was noted i ancient times. Jeremiah commented: 'Eve the stork in the heavens knows her time (Jeremiah 8.7); while the Roman write Pliny remarked that the birds' comings an goings were mysterious.

Legends tell of storks being transforme into human beings, possibly because th large size and upright posture suggest a affinity with mankind. Typical version occur in Germany, where it is also sai that a wounded stork weeps human tear and there are modern Greek and Ara tories relating that in the distant lands to which the birds go in autumn they live as men. As early as the 13th century, Gervase of Tilbury mentioned people who at times became transformed into storks. There is an Eastern legend of a man who managed to turn himself into a stork, and who found the birds' conversation so amusing that he forgot the formula by which to regain human form.

Filial Duty

During the Middle Ages writers quoted Aristotle to the effect that the male stork kills his mate if she is unfaithful, and Chaucer referred to it as 'the avenger of adultery'. In the 3rd century AD Aelian embroidered on this belief in a story about a stork who blinded a human adulterer in gratitude to the husband who had allowed it to nest on his house. From classical times the stork has had a reputation for filial piety. The young were said to care for their parents in old age. The English poet Michael Drayton (1563–1631) referred to the 'careful stork . . . in filial duty as instructing man'. In a Russian folktale an old man pleads with a stork to be his son.

The fable that the stork brings babies seems to be a fairly recent one and is most detailed in Germany. Bavarians say that baby boys of good disposition ride on the bird's back while naughty boys are carried in its bill. In some localities, if a Christmas mummer dressed as a stork nudges a woman or girl it is said that she will soon be pregnant. In Holland and Germany children

sing to the stork to bring them a little brother or sister.

A number of ancient ideas may have contributed to the development of the baby-bringing theme. Its association with water connects the stork with fertility, it was the messenger of Athene, who in some places was associated with childbirth, and its old Germanic name, *Adebar*, means 'luck-bringer'.

The stork's bill is red and, in common with a number of other birds with red markings, it is associated with fire. A stork's nest on the house protects it from fire, although if its young are stolen it may set the building on fire. Although it is generally regarded as a bringer of good fortune, there are localities where it is held to be an evil portent if a stork alights on a house. In other regions a wedding may be expected if this occurs.

A Welcome Guest

As an ambassador of spring the stork's arrival is greeted with a great variety of welcoming calls and songs. Predictions may be made from the bird's behaviour, for example, that when they arrive late in spring the season will be unfavourable. To see a white stork foretells a dry year, whereas a black one indicates that the coming months will be wet. An exceptional saying is that if storks circle over a group of people one of them will die shortly.

The kindliness with which the bird is generally viewed is probably due in part to the fact that certain types of storks kill

small snakes. This is given as the reason why it was held in such great honour in ancient Thessaly that a man who killed a stork was treated as a murderer.

The stork has long been regarded as possessing valuable medicinal qualities. The bird's stomach was a remedy against murrain, an infectious disease in cattle. Its sinews were used to bind up a foot afflicted with gout, on the principle that a bird with legs as long and healthy as those of the stork must be capable of alleviating pain in human limbs. According to Jewish folk traditions, its gall may be used to cure scorpion stings.

The stork appears in Aesop's *Fables*, where we are told that the wolf swallowed a bone which stuck in its throat. He roamed around howling with pain and offering a generous reward to anyone who would help him. At last the stork undertook the task. Poking his long bill into the wolf's throat he extracted the bone. When he asked for the promised reward the wolf laughed and said: 'You should count yourself lucky that I did not bite your head off when it was in my mouth.' The moral is that kindness is not always requited.

In another fable a farmer catches a stork in a net with cranes and geese. The stork pleads that he only happened to be in the company of the other birds and was not stealing grain as they were, but the farmer tells him that as he was with thieves he must suffer the same punishment. In other words, be careful what company you keep.

E. A. ARMSTRONG

Storm

Frequently regarded as an expression of the anger of the sky god, whose voice is the thunder and whose weapon is lightning: Yahweh, Zeus and Jupiter were all storm gods as well as supreme gods, but storm may also be the preserve of a lesser deity; the analogy between storm and war is frequently drawn; in parts of Europe church bells are rung to ward off storm damage, and various plants traditionally give protection against lightning. See SKY.

Mary Evans Picture Library

A length of string can serve as a link, while the function of a knot is to impede or make fast; man's ability to see occult meaning in everyday objects is typified by the symbolic importance of cord and knots in witchcraft, medicine and magic ancient and modern

STRING

THE NEED TO BIND and connect, to fasten and make secure, must have led man in very early times to produce forms of twine, thread and cord, which could be made firm by knotting. He needed line for fishing, thread for stitching and cord for rudimentary construction work, such as bridge-building,

or lashing together the framework of log huts. And taking into account man's tendency to invest the familiar natural objects of the world around him with supernatural qualities, it is fairly easy to understand how thread, string and knots came to acquire their present symbolic meanings.

Thread is regarded as the connecting link between two separate planes of existence, and it is also connected with fate, as the thread of life. In classical mythology Clotho spins man's destiny, Lachesis weaves the web of luck or chance which sustains his life, and Atropos severs the thread when death comes (see FATE). Thread was also linked with fate in Finno-Ugrian folklore, and it was the means by which the dead ascended to the otherworld; thread was at

one time placed in coffins for this purpose. There was also a custom in which the mourners participated in a kind of lottery of death, each picking a single thread. The one who drew the shortest was fated to die next.

In the interpretation of dreams, a tangled thread is said to represent trouble, and a broken one disaster. Some actors believe that it is very lucky to pick up a long thread from the floor of a theatre, as this promises a long and successful production.

String possesses symbolic qualities closely akin to those of thread. It represents the line of continuity and is used when making a magic circle, and to bind individuals with unbreakable spells. As a medical amulet it protects against sterility and death.

Making string figures (such as 'cat's cradles') is a popular game among children, and in primitive communities all over the world, and these pastimes often possess magical overtones. In the Far East, ghost traps made from string are sometimes set on the outskirts of villages to ensnare prowling spectres.

The Power to Bind

The bulk of the lore relating to string and thread is concerned with knots, which represent tightly closed links, and have many psychic implications that arise from the fact that, in magic, that which has the power to bind the body can also be used to confine the spirit. The knot is also the symbol of the sealed bargain. The continuous knot in the form of a horizontal figure eight represents infinity.

The Gordian knot which was wrought so intricately that no one could undo it — until Alexander cut it with his sword (see SWORD) and thus became conqueror of the East — also had an occult significance. It stood as a symbol of the labyrinth, and it was said that to untie the knot to its heart was equivalent to finding the centre which formed such an important part of mystic thought. In certain religious orders and secret societies, ceremonies involving knotting and binding take place during the initiation of a new member, as in the case of high-caste Brahmins and, in the past, the Knights Templar. Modern witches use cords and knots in many rituals: for example, cord of a given planetary colour may bind an image in a restraining spell, or a knot may be tied as a focus of concentrated will in a healing spell.

Closely associated with the knotting of cords or garments, are a number of religious taboos. The *flamen Dialis*, the Roman priest of Jupiter (see JUPITER), was forbidden to have a single knot in his clothing; and Moslem pilgrims to Mecca are prohibited from wearing knots and rings. It has been suggested that the origin of the phrase 'the bonds of matrimony' is the custom of draping the priest's stole over the clasped hands of the bride and groom to form a symbolic knot. In former times, knotted ribbons were often worn at weddings to symbolize the binding effect of the marriage ceremony as well as for their decorative value.

Love, Birth and Death

A girl who used illicit love magic in an attempt to lure a reluctant lover into her clutches would tie knots in lengths of thread or wool, at the same time chanting:

> This knot I knit,
> This knot I tie,
> To see my lover as he goes by,
> In his apparel and array,
> As he walks in every day.

The symbol of fidelity and love, the love-knot, is a double knot of ribbon with two bows, and two ends.

One of the arts of the Age of Chivalry was point-tying, a method of inhibiting the sexual prowess of a husband on his wedding night by artfully tying a knot in his points,

the tagged lace or cord that attached his hose to his doublet. Similarly, tying a knot in a length of thread or string was popularly supposed to render a man sexually incapable. If the knot were not discovered, the condition of impotence could be permanent. This practice, which savoured of black magic, was greatly frowned upon by the Church.

Tying knots to avoid an unwanted pregnancy was at one time practised by both men and women. A Moroccan husband would knot and then swallow the oviduct of a hen, while in eastern Europe a woman would tie ten knots in a length of flax which she would wear for nine successive days and nights before burying it.

During the Renaissance churchmen were

often horrified by the superstitious practices associated with childbirth; in 1584, for instance, in Shropshire, the prevailing custom of unlocking all the doors and loosening every knot in the house in order to ease the mother's labour was roundly condemned. This curious custom persisted in some rural districts of Britain until less than a century ago.

Because untying knots was supposed to facilitate childbirth it seemed perfectly logical to ascribe difficult births to the malicious tying of knots by an enemy of the mother concerned. As a result of this reasoning, a great number of so-called witches ended their lives on the gallows or at the stake, having 'freely' confessed under torture to the crime of inhibiting childbirth.

Tate Gallery/John Webb

Clotho spins the thread of human life, Lachesis measures its length and Atropos waits to cut it at the last: the three Fates, in a detail from a painting by John Melhuish Strudwick, *The Golden Thread*

Knots have been used in the magical treatment of disease from ancient times to the middle years of the 19th century. A well-known country remedy for nose bleeding was to tie a skein of red silk, which had previously been knotted by nine maidens, around the neck of the sufferer. The mystical number nine occurs yet again in the once popular cure for whooping cough, in which a string with nine knots was worn as a neckband. A well-known treatment for warts was to knot a piece of string and then bury it in the earth. It was said that the wart would disappear as the string rotted. In ancient Babylon, 4000 years ago, a three-fold cord with twice seven knots was said to cure headaches if it was tied round the brow.

Before the development of sedative drugs a protracted death could impose an intolerable burden upon both the dying person and his family and, understandably, every legitimate method of hastening the inevitable end was explored. Every door in the house was unlocked, all windows were opened and all knots loosened to clear a way of exit for the departing soul. The relief that members of a family felt when death had finally claimed its victim often resulted in agonies of guilt, and these led, perhaps inevitably, to a growing fear that the angry ghost would return. To insure against this happening, a piece of knotted thread or string would be carried in a pocket to serve as an antidote. A holed stone suspended from the ceiling by a thread with nine knots was said to give protection against nightmares.

In Scotland, fishermen use knotted thread and string, in various different colours, as charms. Red thread is said to be the most effective, particularly when used in conjunction with a piece of rowan or mountain ash (see RED; ROWAN). There was an old saying:

Rowan tree and red thread
Will put the witches to their speed.

This charm was believed to be effective only if the thread had been knotted by an

C. M. Dixon

Axel Poignant

Above 'The continuous knot in the form of a horizontal figure eight represents infinity' magical knot inscribed with the name of Pharaoh Tuthmosis III, dated c 1450 BC
Below Games with string are popular all over the world, sometimes carrying magical or religious overtones: a Maori woman teaches her grandsons how to make the two volcanoes of the central highlands of North Island

individual 'having the knowledge'.

Even the most innocent forms of magical knot-tying could involve great dangers in 17th century Scotland, where all supernatural practices were constantly scrutinized by the clergy. Margaret Barclay, one of the witches of the town of Irvine in Ayrshire, was put to torture solely on the evidence provided by a length of knotted red thread and a twig of rowan which she carried as a protective charm. Witches were said to be able to steal the milk of cows, from a distance, by plaiting, or tying magical knots, and Isabel Gowdie (see GOWDIE), the Scottish witch, confessed to this crime. She declared: 'We plait the rope the wrong way (widdershins) in the Devil's name and thereby take with us the cow's milk.'

As recently as the 1870s Scottish farmers attempted to protect their stock against bewitchment by threading red cord through one of the ears of each new cow when it first entered the byre.

At a Rate of Knots

One of the best-known arts of the sea witches of Finland, the Orkneys and the Isle of Man was that of controlling the wind by means of magical knots. Three knots were to be tied in a length of string, and as each was undone the power of the wind increased. It was said of the women of the Isle of Man, especially those on the coast, that they would 'selle to shipmen wynde so it were closed under three knotes of thread, so that the more wynde he would have the more knotes he must undo'.

The last surviving relic of the ritual tying of knots is possibly the ornamental intertwining of cords known as knotwork, an art which was popular in Britain towards the end of the last century, and which under the name of Macramé is currently enjoying a revival of popularity in the United States.

ERIC MAPLE

SUBTERRANEAN RACE

AN ANCIENT PERUVIAN legend relates that four brothers and four sisters emerged from the cavern of Pacari-Tambo, east of Cuzco, the ancient city that became the capital of the Inca Empire. The eldest brother climbed a mountain and, throwing stones to the four cardinal points, took possession of the land. The youngest brother, Ayar Uchu Topa, contrived to dispose of his elders, married the sisters, and subdued the surrounding peoples. He founded Cuzco and many other cities.

The great Mammoth Cave in Edmondson County, Kentucky, in the United States,

was discovered only in 1809. Bodies of an unknown race reputed to antedate the Indians were found in its recesses with reed torches beside them, but all crumbled to powder when touched.

There is a belief that a low type of subterranean being sometimes appears in astral form on the earth's surface, and that it is somehow attracted by manifestations of human sex-force. For example, in *Real Ghost Stories*, W. T. Stead tells of an apparition seen by a woman in an English suburb: 'I saw this light develop into a head and face of yellowish-green light, with a mass of matted hair above it. The face was very wide and broad, larger than ours in all respects, very large eyes of green which, not

being distinctly outlined, appeared to merge into the yellow of the cheeks; no hair whatever on the lower part of the face. The expression was diabolically malignant.'

One of the most interesting accounts of the subterranean people, which purports in one sense to be factual, is by the Theosophist C. W. Leadbeater. Although he claims elsewhere to have up-to-date confirmation of some of the facts, his story is alleged to be a report of an experience undergone by two Indian youths, which took place in 10,402 BC and was recovered from the 'memory of Nature' (the record of history supposed to exist on the astral plane).

Both young men had some psychic faculty, and one heard a voice, from time to time, hich guided him and suggested interesting nterprises. On the instructions of this nvisible guide, who demanded a pledge of ecrecy, they set out on the pretext of a ilgrimage to a certain mountain area where ey ultimately found a cave entrance. hey prepared food packages to last several eeks and bundles of torches, and with some eluctance entered the depths of the cave.

After a long, fairly level, penetration into e mountain, they reached a sloping rugged ownward fissure, which they descended erilously for some days. Finally they eached an immense cavity in the earth. heir torches were unnecessary there, ecause the air overhead and around them as charged with a strange luminosity.

They found underground rivers, several arieties of vegetation (which lacked the reen of the upper earth), semi-reptilian nimals and, to their astonishment, naked umans. These were of less than normal tature, but broad and stocky, and their kin had a repulsive leaden hue. The people ad no culture and no shelters, and merely aught the reptiles and ate them raw. They lso fed on an abundant huge toadstool-ke fungus.

The youths declined the reptile flesh, but ound the fungus quite good and invigo-ating. After a week or so their unseen uide directed them to walk in a straight ne away from the wall where they had ntered. Having done this for some hours, hey came upon a different type of people, f higher intelligence. Although they were gnorant of fire, like the primitives already

seen, they availed themselves of hot springs or geysers to cook the flesh of turtles and goat-like animals that they kept, and they drank the animals' milk. They lived in chambers hollowed out in the rock, and wove a kind of matting and string from reeds. Some of the women wore coloured stones, and both sexes smeared themselves with rose, green and yellow mud from the edges of the hot springs.

They were able to draw, and incised meaningful sets of marks on the rocks. These were mainly cup-markings, rounded hollows ground on the surface and arranged in patterns, each pattern having a meaning.

'Mysterious race in the earth's interior': illustration from *The Occult Gazette*

In other words they were not letters but ideographs, symbols in picture-writing. A certain number of these in a straight line had one meaning, a set making an angle had another. The two young explorers eventually found their way back to the entrance of the cave, as they had carried their primitive fire-making equipment with them, and could relight their torches.

A Scientific Possibility?

The existence of an underground race, or races, presupposes that there are great cavities in the rocks deep inside the earth. Surprisingly enough, there seems to be a possibility that these races could exist. Although the core of the earth is a molten ball, the mantle or overlying mass of rock must have two distinct zones, one nearer the core where heat and pressure put the solid rock in a state of 'flowage', and an upper zone where 'fracture' can occur. The depth of this upper zone is the crucial point. Professor Frank D. Adams of Montreal has shown by actual experiment that empty cavities might exist in granite at a depth of at least 11 miles, and his conclusions were supported by the mathematician Louis V. King, who calculated that, at normal temperature, a cavity could exist at depths down to between 17.2 and 20.9 miles. The newly-discovered 16 Rouse Belts, which give planes of fracture completely penetrating the globe, give additional support to the possibility.
(See also LYTTON.)

C. NELSON STEWART

Succubus

Female counterpart of the incubus: a demon in female form which makes love to men while they sleep; the Devil himself was said to serve his worshippers as incubus or succubus and the children of such a union were expected to be deformed and demonic; belief in these demons is often attributed to exotic dreams and nightmares.
See INCUBUS AND SUCCUBUS.

Sufism is a concentrated essence which for the majority needs diluting'; yet paradoxically, its most remarkable quality is a universality which bridges East and West

SUFIS

JUST AS the Cabalists are the mystics of Judaism, the Sufis are the mystics of Islam. The Sufi orders fulfil in Islam something of the same function as that of the monastic orders in Christianity. They differ from the Christian orders in not being celibate, in not being under the control of any outside authority, and in not being so highly

organized. They nevertheless have a certain organization, and many of them have accumulated rich endowments with the passage of the centuries, nearly always including a mosque which has in it the tomb of the saint who founded the order.

As in other religions, the mystical orders of Islam appear to have originated in groups which gathered spontaneously round some person of outstanding spirituality. One of the earliest of these guides was the Prophet Mohammed's cousin and son-in-law, Ali (d. 661), the fourth caliph. All the orders trace their spiritual ancestry back to Mohammed himself, and in most of these 'chains' Ali is the ultimate link, though one or two orders are descended from the Prophet

through Abu Bakr, the first caliph (d. 634). By the end of the 9th century some of these groups had become organized brotherhoods, and the term 'Sufi', which was not used at the beginning of Islam, had become current. Junayd of Baghdad (d. 910) is something of a landmark in this early period, and most of the Sufi masters are his spiritual descendants, whence his title 'the Sheikh of the Sheikhs'.

Sufi means literally 'wearer of wool', and long before the beginning of Islam woollen dress had been traditionally associated with the spiritual life. But the Sufis have not made a speciality of wearing wool. The term, which has profoundly venerable implications, was no doubt first applied to a particular group, spreading subsequently into a more general use.

The Sufis refer to themselves however as *fuqara*, 'poor (in Spirit)', plural of *faqir*, in Persian *darvish*, whence the English words 'fakir' and 'dervish' (see FAKIR; DERVISH).

The Koran affirms that the community of Mohammed is 'a middle people' and it is, above all, in its mysticism that his religion shows itself as a bridge between East and West. A Vedantist, a Taoist or a Buddhist can find, in many aspects of Islamic mysticism, 'a home from home', such as he could less easily find in Christianity or Judaism. Prince Dara Shikoh (d. 1659), the Sufi son of the Mogul Emperor Shah Jahan, was able to affirm that the only difference between Sufism and Advaita Vedantism is one of terminology. But this universality of Sufism cannot be attributed to any influences outside Islam. The foundations of Islamic mysticism were laid, and its subsequent course irrevocably fixed, long before it would have been possible for any farther Eastern or even Neoplatonic influences to have introduced non-Islamic elements, and when such influences came they touched no more than the surface. The universality of Sufism must be attributed in a large measure to the fact that in Islam, from the very beginning, a clear distinction is made between exoterism and esoterism. The majority are provided for by a well defined legal minimum, and esoterism is left free to devote itself to the needs of the few, absolved from any duty to stretch beyond measure the mystical net in order to find room for as many adherents as possible. The Sufis have always concentrated on the highest doctrinal truths and on the practices which correspond to them; and what is highest in religion is at the same time what is most universal.

Flash of Absolute Truth

The doctrine of Sufism, like that of Islam as a whole, is summed up in the formula of testification 'there is no god but God' which every entrant into Islam must pronounce. The Supreme Name *Allah*, 'God', is not to be separated from the Name *Haqq*, 'Truth, Reality', so that the above formula means also 'there is no reality but Reality'. Every Moslem must believe this, but only the Sufis take this belief to its ultimate conclusion. Reality, according to them, is that which *is*, and if only God is absolutely Real, only God *is*, whence the term 'oneness of being' by which the doctrine of Sufism is known and which is none other than the *Advaita* (nonduality) of Hinduism.

This does not mean that God is made up of parts, but that the whole created universe in all its seemingly incalculable multiplicity is mysteriously one substance with the Transcendent Infinite. The Sufi Abd al-Karim al-Jili (d. c 1428) used the image of ice and water to denote respectively the illusory world of coagulated forms and the Reality which is its Origin and End. Other Sufis use the image of the waves of the ocean which symbolize form and vicissitude while never being really separate from the ocean into which they are bound to subside.

The Koran formulates this doctrine as follows, indicating at the same time that it is not within the scope of everyone: 'Verily We created the heavens and the earth with naught but Truth, yet most men know not' (Sura 44.39). On other occasions also the Absolute Truth suddenly flashes out of the Koranic text, as for example in the verses: 'Wheresoe'er ye turn, there is the Face of God' (Sura 2.115); and 'He (God) is the First and the Last and the Outwardly Manifest and the Inwardly Hidden' (Sura 57.3); and 'We (God) are nearer to him (man) than his jugular vein' (Sura 50.16). In connection with this last verse we may quote the saying of the Prophet: 'Who knoweth himself knoweth his Lord'. Also relevant is another of his sayings, of the kind that is known as a 'Holy Tradition', because in it God speaks in the first person: 'I was a Hidden Treasure and I wished to be known and so I created the world'. These two Traditions form the basis of some of the profoundest writing of Ibn Arabi (see IBN ARABI).

The Sufis are unanimous in considering the Prophet Mohammed to have been not only the first Sufi (in all but name) but also the first and incomparably the greatest master of Sufism. The main practices of the Sufis were all instituted by him; the differences between the orders are for the most part differences of choice, by the founders of the orders, from the wide range of possibilities offered by his own example. The whole of Sufism – its means and its end – is summed up in another Tradition: 'Nothing is more pleasing to Me, as a means for my slave to draw near unto Me, than the worship that I have made binding upon him; and My slave ceaseth not to draw near unto Me by devotions of his free will until I love him; and when I love him I am the hearing whereby he heareth and the sight whereby he seeth and the hand wherewith he smiteth and the foot whereon he walketh.'

The opening part of this Tradition refers to practices that are often called the 'five pillars of Islam' (see ISLAM). The voluntary practices referred to in the second part are drawn from what was recommended by the Prophet and they consist of reciting the Koran, extra prayers, fasts and pilgrimages, litanies, vigils, spiritual retreats and, as a complement to these solitudes, organized gatherings for the purpose of communal glorification and invocation. It is at these gatherings that in some Sufi orders a sacred dance is performed, as a means of inducing concentration, the most elaborate and celebrated of these being that of 'the whirling dervishes' originated by Rumi, the founder of the Mevlevi Order (see RUMI).

The most basic rite of Sufism is the invocation of the name Allah, which was enjoined upon the Prophet in one of the first Koranic revelations. There might seem to be a contradiction between the opening of the last quoted Tradition, which sets the obligatory before the voluntary, and a verse of the Koran (Sura 29.45) exalting the invocation of Allah, which is voluntary, above the five daily prayers, which are obligatory. The question is resolved for the Sufis on the understanding that the invocation, in itself

the most powerful of all rites, is only acce[p]table to God on the basis of the invoker having performed what is obligatory.

The first thing done with a novice in a Su[fi] order is to make sure that he is regular i[n] his practice of what is binding on all Moslem[s.] In this connection it may be remarked th[at] the Sufis altogether disown those pseud[o-]Sufi movements in the modern world whic[h] profess to have made Sufism independe[nt] of Islam. The claim to be a Sufi witho[ut] being a Moslem is on a level with claimi[ng] to be a Franciscan or a Dominican witho[ut] being a Christian.

In the Sight of God

The dimension of depth which Sufism re[p]resents in Islam was indicated by the Proph[et] in his definition of the religion as a who[le] when, in addition to what must be believe[d] and what ritually accomplished, he me[n]tioned a third aspect of the religion whic[h,] by its very nature, is beyond the reach [of] the majority, namely, being an adept [as] regards faith and practice: 'Excellence [is] that thou shouldst worship God as if tho[u] sawest Him; and if thou seest Him no[t] He seeth thee.' This definition, which is on[e] of the foundation stones of Sufism, ha[s] always marked an ideal for the Sufis and [is] quoted again and again in their writings.

The difference between the Sufis and th[e] majority of Moslems is not so much in wha[t] they do but how they do it. The prostratio[n] for example, which is a gesture of humilit[y] before God, means for the Sufi no less tha[n] extinction, a ritual affirmation that ther[e] is no room in the Divine Presence for mo[re] than the One. The fast is another mode [of] extinction, 'abstaining from other than God[';] the ablution yet another, for it enacts th[e] washing away of the impurity of the illusio[n] that one exists apart from God. In thi[s] connection we may quote the saying [of] Rabiah (d. 801), one of the greatest wome[n] saints of Islam, who replied to a man wh[o] asked for her spiritual advice, saying tha[t] he had not sinned for 20 years: 'Alas, m[y] son, thine existence is a sin wherewith n[o] other sin may be compared.' It is onl[y] through extinction that the end of the pat[h] can be reached; in other words, it is onl[y] through emptiness that the receptacle ca[n] be flooded with the Divine Consciousne[ss,] in the sense of the words: 'I am the hearin[g] wherewith he heareth and the sight where[with] with he seeth.' The Sufi does not conceiv[e] of the beatific vision as anything other tha[n] vision of God by God.

Sufism is a concentrated essence whic[h] for the majority needs diluting – hence th[e] Koranic distinction between 'the slaves [of] God' (the word slave here implies extinc[c]tion) and 'the righteous'. The slaves drin[k] directly from the fountains of Paradise whereas the righteous drink a draught whic[h] is flavoured at those fountains. Sufism[,] like all mysticisms, is both dangerous an[d] necessary – as necessary to its religion a[s] the heart is to the body. It is both close[d] and open; the Sufis are continually cleavin[g] chasms, as it were, between themselves an[d] the rest of the community, and buildin[g] bridges. The relationship between Islami[c] esoterism and exoterism is both comple[x]

British Museum

nd delicate, for if the Sufi orders are losed, requiring a rite of initiation for ntry, their practices are in principle open the community as a whole, even those hich, in consequence of their power, are irtually dangerous.

But the power – and therefore the danger of mystical practices depends partly on heir methodical performance with the nplacable regularity of a drumbeat, whence he insistence of the Sheikhs on patience nd perseverance to a degree which far urpasses the average conception of these irtues. An unqualified person is normally rotected from danger by the mediocrity of is practice, the danger in question being hat a psychic substance which is caught up n the hook of some hidden or half-hidden goism will be ruptured by a pull that is too udden or too sharp. It is part of the function f a Sheikh to protect his disciples in this espect. A true master will know how much train each soul is capable of taking.

The Wings of Poetry

Heralding as it were the exclusive aspect f Sufism, Abu Hurayrah (d. 678), one of he Companions of the Prophet, said: 'I lave treasured in my memory two stores of knowledge which I had from the Messenger f God. One I have divulged; but if I divulged he other ye would cut my throat.' In connecion with this aspect of Sufism, mention nust be made of the inspired ejaculations vhich have always been characteristic of he Sufis such as the 'Glory be to Me!' of Abu Yazid al-Bistami (d. 874), sword hrusts which may bring about a sudden ppening up of new horizons in the intelliences not only of disciples but also of those learers who, unknown to themselves, have a vocation for the mystic path. But for those vho have not, namely the vast majority, such ejaculations are liable to cause scandal, especially when repeated out of context and in cold blood'. No doubt the most famous of

A Sufi saint, refused a passage on the ferry, calmly seated himself upon his prayer-mat and floated across the river in the boat's wake: a Persian miniature depicts the incident

them is Hallaj's 'I am the Truth', for which, in 922, he was put to death.

Apart from such ejaculations and kindred aphorisms, many of the most profound formulations of the Sufis are in their poetry. Rumi is generally recognized as the greatest of Persian poets, and his contemporary, the Egyptian Umar ibn al-Farid (d. 1235) is certainly one of the greatest of the Arab poets. For the more uncompromising of their utterances formal beauty serves as a cloak and also lends wings to bridge chasms which could not otherwise be crossed. It is unlikely that Hallaj would have been put to death for his poem which begins:

I saw my Lord with the eye of the heart.
I said: Who art Thou? He answered:
    Thou.

Many of the Sufi poems take the form of love lyrics. Sometimes God is addressed directly, but often the Divinity is personified by a woman, usually named Laila which, in addition to being the name of the heroine of the best-known love story of the Near East, has the meaning of 'night', indicating that it is the holiest and most secret inwardness of God, the Divine Essence Itself, which marks the end of the Sufi path.

Of the Sufi treatises, some are written by the Sheikhs exclusively for their most intimate disciples, while others are written for a much wider circle of readers; and this brings us to what might be called the inclusive aspect of Sufism, the overflow of which into the outer domains of Islam is especially incarnated in Sufis who, in addition to their esoteric function, have been eminent exoteric authorities in ritual law or dogmatic theology. Amongst the most famous of these is Ghazali (see GHAZALI). In response to this 'overflow',

almost every great order has at its fringe a multitude of men and women who would not be capable of following the Sufi path but who seek blessings from the Sheikh and also his guidance as regards voluntary worship. Such guidance often takes the form of a litany, long or short as the case may be, to be recited once or twice a day; but from humbler aspirants a Sheikh may simply demand that they make a solemn pact with him to perform regularly, until their dying day, all their ritual obligations.

Sufism Today

In connection with this aspect of Sufism it must be remembered also that visits to the tombs of saints play a large part in the spiritual life of the Islamic community as a whole, and apart from the tombs of the Prophet, his close companions, and some of his family, by far the most venerated tombs in Islam are those of the Sufi Sheikhs. In fact almost every community in the Islamic world has as its patron saint a Sufi who lies buried in its midst.

It is partly because of this that Sufism is banned by the puritanical Wahhabi sect which rules Saudi Arabia. Even prolonged visits to the tomb of the Prophet at Medina are frowned on, for fear lest some element of worship might be given to other than God. They cannot, however, prevent Sufis from making the pilgrimage, and in consequence Mecca and Medina are meeting places for Sufis from all over the world. Sufism is also officially banned in Turkey, but for very different reasons. It was in the Sufi orders, as the most conservative element in Islam, that the revolutionary statesman Kemal Ataturk (1881–1938) met with the sharpest resistance to his secularizing aims. Consequently, heads of orders were put to death and the orders themselves made illegal and thus driven underground. In other Islamic countries, however, the Sufi orders are a recognized part of the community –

a 'backward' part, no doubt, in the eyes of the majority for, like all mysticisms, Sufism would be untrue to itself if it subscribed to any of those aspirations and ideals which dominate the modern world.

The orders differ considerably from each other. The Tijani Order which is fairly widespread in north-west Africa and particularly so in West Africa (Senegal and Nigeria, for example), and throughout the Sudan is not well disposed to other orders, which it claims to have superseded. It is less aloof and more proselytizing than they are. Some of the other orders, the Isawi and the Rifai, for example, have degenerated in certain of their branches to the point of being dominated by snake-charming and fire-eating, practices which

originated as subsidiary tests of faith and of reliance upon God. But the main body of Sufism can be said to be still true to its medieval heritage.

In India the Chishti Order is of considerable importance, and so throughout the East is the Naqshabandi Order; but the most widespread in both East and West are the great Qadiri and Shadhili Orders, founded respectively by Abd al-Qadir al-Jilani (d. 1166), and Abu 'l-Hasan ash-Shadhili (d. 1258), who imposed on his disciples an intellectual approach which still characterizes the Shadhili Order in its

Dancing dervishes of the Mevlevi Order, one of the numerous Sufi sects: illustration from a Persian *Lives of the Mystics*

many branches. One of the most emine[n] of these is the Darqawi Order, with i[ts] Alawi sub-branch, founded respectively [by] Arabi ad-Darqawi (d. 1823) and Ahma[d] al-Alawi (d. 1934), both outstandin[g] amongst the Sheikhs of more recent times.

MARTIN LING[S]

FURTHER READING: Martin Lings, *A Su[fi] Saint of the Twentieth Century, Shaik[h] Ahmad al-Alawi* (Allen and Unwin, Londo[n] 1971); Shaikh ad-Darqawi, *Letters of a Su[fi] Master* (Weiser, 1970); Frithjof Schuo[n] *Understanding Islam* (Roy, 1963); Titu[s] Burckhardt, *Introduction to Sufi Doctrin[e]* (Weiser); A. J. Arberry, *Sufism* (Hillar[y] House, 1956).

Sulphur

According to early alchemists, the element in a substance which enables it to burn: regarded as one of the basic components of all matter, the others being mercury and salt; in man's constitution, identified with the emotions and passions, the 'fiery' part of the personality; associated with hell-fire and the Devil because of its fiery stench.

See ALCHEMY; MERCURY.

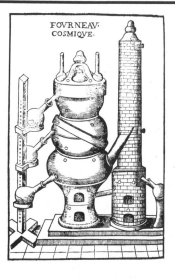

FOVRNEAV·
COSMIQVE·

Sumerians

Early inhabitants of Mesopotamia: they had settled in Babylonia by 3500 BC and 'initiated a cultural revolution which gave the world writing, cities, and a corpus of religious practices and concepts'; each early settlement had its own local deity, so that there was a large pantheon of gods and goddesses, and a complex web of relationships between them.

See MESOPOTAMIA.

SUN

Orthodox Hindus begin the working day with an invocation of the sun: 'We meditate on the lovely light of the god, Savitri; may he inspire our thoughts'

ON THE FACE of it, there is no more obvious recipient of divine honours than the sun: visible and yet mysterious, beneficent and yet thoroughly dangerous, it is the giver of life and yet the most potent of destructive forces. In fact it can be regarded as summing up most of the characteristics which mankind has always attributed to its gods and goddesses, not least the characteristic of awesome remoteness. In the 6th century BC the Ionic philosopher Anaximander announced that the sun was not a deity, but merely a circle of fire. That he also

said that it was only 28 times larger than the earth seems little more than curious; the denial of deity was the more important thing. To Anaximander's contemporaries, and the majority of his successors the world over, however, the sun was surely a deity, impinging upon the life of man at every point, measuring the rhythm of the days and the seasons, giving and withholding life, warming and burning by turns.

Nevertheless, the study of sun worship is by no means as straightforward as might at first sight appear. The simple adoration of the sun in its daily march, or ride, across the heavens can be observed and documented. But connected with this are a host of kindred notions. For instance, there is the matter of the daily and seasonal cycles

which the sun establishes. Does the sun in fact establish the sacred rhythms, or is the sun itself subservient to a greater and more divine order, within which it acts essentially in the role, not of master, but of servant? Ancient Indian speculation spoke of a natural order, *rita,* of which the High Gods Varuna and Mitra (a sun god) were the guardians; but it certainly seems that they were not held to be the originators of this order. And from the other side of the world, Garcilaso de la Vega recorded the story of the Inca who was puzzled by the thought that if, as was supposed, the sun was the Supreme God, then why did he have to follow precisely the same path across the heavens every day? Was he not free to wander like the other planets? The Inca in

Corvina, Budapest

estion is said to have concluded that
ere must be a god greater than the sun
nom the sun was forced to obey, and to
ve set up an altar to that unknown deity.
The problem here is to know what is (or
as) the relationship between the sun god
d the High God of the sky. Other prob-
ms concern the relationship between the
n god and the world of men as reflected,
r instance, in astrology; and the sun god's
le in determining man's destiny after death.
When evaluating the mythology of sun
orship, a great deal obviously depends on
e geographical location of myth and cult.
tropical and sub-tropical areas, where
e pattern of the seasons is not as clear-
t as it is in Europe, and where the omni-
esence of the sun is taken for granted

for the greater part of the year, particular
importance is attached to the daily cycle
of the sun's rising and setting; in temperate
zones and in the Arctic, the seasonal cycle
is by far the more important. It is significant
that the nearest approach to a solar mono-
theism in the history of religion comes from
ancient Egypt; such a belief would have
been virtually impossible in northern
Europe, where the sun emerged in the spring
only after a bitter struggle with dark powers.

Explanatory Myths
The so-called primitive peoples of the
world possess a vast store of myths concerning the sun, often coupled with moon
myths, since sun and moon are frequently
regarded as being related in some way.

Previous page **The rising sun brings light into
darkness, a symbol of inward and spiritual
illumination: from *Splendor Solis*, an alchemical
work of the 15th century *Above* As Phoebus
Apollo, 'bright Apollo', the Greeks identified
the god of prophecy, healing and the arts with
the sun: in a painting from the studio of Rosso
Fiorentino, the sun god escorts the four
seasons of the year**

The sun is sometimes male, sometimes
female. Among certain Australian aboriginal
tribes, for instance, it is personified as a
woman who has a lover under the earth,
among the dead. Every night she enters
the underworld to be with him, and every
morning ascends once more dressed in her
lover's present, a red kangaroo skin. Another

Giraudon

C. M. Dixon

Left Helios, a Greek solar deity sometime confused with Apollo, rises from his palace i the east in readiness to drive his chariot acros the heavens: chariots were also associate with the sun in Denmark and India *Below le* 'It has been said that solar worship is the rea religion of India': Surya holds in each hand lotus, symbol of divine light, immortal life an fertility *Below right* Pyramid to the sun Teotihuacan, a centre of Mexican civilizatio of the 1st millennium AD: the similaritie between sun worship in America and in ancien Egypt have led some scholars to believe tha Egyptian culture must have crossed the Atlant

tribe is said to have had a myth to the effec that every day the sun burns up her stock fuel, and has to descend into the underworl each night for fresh supplies of firewoo Stories of the sun entering the underworld night and emerging afresh every morning ar legion, the sun having walked, ridden, been carried from west to east.

Its daily course is similarly surrounde with stories and explanations. Ancier Indo-European myths usually picture th sun as driving across the sky in a golde chariot, drawn by horses, a belief whic led to the horse being regarded as especiall sacred. From Peru comes a variant, accor ing to which the sun is tethered like a llam by an invisible cord to the pole of the sk and driven round and round it by the powe of the Universal Spirit. There are man such examples.

Another type of myth told of the su concerns the need to 'tame' its power in som way. A Mexican legend tells that the su was once a man who, to show his devotio immolated himself in a sacrificial fire; i reward the Supreme Being conveyed hi to heaven. He burned so fiercely, howeve that the world was endangered by his ver ardour, and arrows had to be shot at hi to persuade him to temper his rays.

Myths concerning the relationship of th sun and moon explain why the two nev meet in heaven. Usually it is held that su and moon are brother and sister, but that f some reason they have become enemies, an the male partner, who can be either the su or the moon, pursues the female for a eternity. There is a Masai legend to th effect that sun and moon were marrie but fell out; in shame, the sun becam bright in order that men might not loo at him. From the Paiute Indians of Cal fornia this is recorded: 'The sun is th father and ruler of the heavens. He is the b chief. The moon is his wife and the sta are their children. The sun eats his childre whenever he can catch them. They fle before him, and are all the time afraid whe he is passing through the heavens. Whe he appears in the morning, you see all th stars, his children, fly out of sight . . . an they do not wake to be seen again until h their father, is about to go to his bed.'

These naïve explanatory myths take on much more serious tone in Scandinavia mythology. There the daily rising and settir

Ancient Indo-European myths usually picture the sun as driving across the sky in a golden chariot, drawn by horses

of the sun was of less importance than the sun's battle with the powers that threatened to destroy her (once again, the sun is female). In Snorri Sturluson's *Edda* the question is posed: 'Swiftly rides the sun; it is almost as though she were afraid, and she would surely not fly faster, though she were pursued by death.' The questioner is told that the sun is indeed pursued, by two wolves, the offspring of giants. 'And it is said that one of that breed will be stronger than all others . . . He feeds on the blood of all those who die, and he pours blood over the air and the sky, so that the sun ceases to shine . . .' This is not only the vision of winter, but also the vision of the end of the world, heralded, among other things, by the howling of the Fenris wolf (see END OF THE WORLD; SCANDINAVIA).

To relate stories of the sun is not necessarily to worship it; but the power of the sun was in fact an object of active worship among many archaic peoples. Once more, though, elements other than 'pure' sun worship were frequently involved. The famous Sun Dance of the Great Plains Indians of North America, for example, was part of a major act of worship that lasted for eight days, and took place every summer after the buffalo hunt (see GREAT PLAINS INDIANS). On arrival at the place of meeting, the participating tribes formed a circle, leaving an opening to the east, the direction of the rising sun. A vast lodge, which might in some cases be open to the sky, was erected and an altar was placed to the west of the site. The dance itself lasted from two to four days, during which the dancers kept their gaze fixed on the sun or on the lodge's centre pole, which symbolized the cosmic tree. Self-torture was sometimes practised as an act of dedication and sacrifice, and as a means of obtaining that vision without which the Sun Dance was held to be incomplete.

It is perhaps justifiable to see in the Sun Dance an elaborate form of a type of sun ritual that was once found in many parts of the world, and which aimed at the annual renewal of the cosmic order by means of participation in the divine power of the sun, the greatest of the Great Spirit's manifestations.

Modern Sun Worship

Our civilization is almost wholly secularized, having lost its symbolic dimension and its guiding myths. That was the meaning of Nietzsche's cry 'God is dead'...

Instead we find our apparently secular substitutes. The cult of the sun is certainly one of the more important. Millions of men, women and children of all classes and many types go to places, usually the edge of the sea, held suitable for their secular rites. They buy vast quantities of oils, greases and lotions to anoint, not as of old the *benben* or other sacred images, but their own bodies. They don strange dark spectacles and strip off their clothes. No less than former worshippers, they are prepared to suffer. Strong men make themselves ill, women ruin their complexions, children get sunstroke. Since the cult began acres of skin must have crusted and peeled, exposing areas of pink and white ruin surely as painful as the gashes of the Aztecs. Yet day after day they return to worship, determined to gain the tan which is the proof of salvation.

Among all these millions there must be many who could say with Julian the Apostate, 'From my childhood an extraordinary longing for the rays of the god penetrated deep into my soul.' I do not doubt that there is an element of mysticism in all these practices... Nudists, presumably, must share in it. And it is there because the sun in our skies has always been able to invoke such feeling in the bodies and minds it has created out of rock and water. Quite simply, the sun has been the agent of our long creation, and we know it.

Meanwhile the travel agencies, far more cynical than any priesthood, pile up their gold. They cover their pamphlets with sun images bright with rays and happy-faced. And when the worshippers reach the beaches and the gardens do they not place themselves under huge, many-quartered umbrellas? Perhaps they, too, are solar symbols — sun wheels, mandalas....

Jacquetta Hawkes *Man and the Sun*

The Maker of Light

It has been said that solar worship was the real religion of India, and to this day the orthodox Hindu begins his working day with this invocation of the sun: 'We meditate on the lovely light of the god, Savitri; may he inspire our thoughts.' Another hymn to the sun, this time from the *Ramayana*, reads in part: 'Adore the Sun rising with all his rays, receiving the obeisance of gods and demons, the shining maker of light... He is indeed the embodiment of all gods... He who with his rays consumes, produces, propels; who traverses the skies like a bird, shines like gold, makes the days and is the golden seminator of the universe. The hot, tawny disc, he burns everything and is indeed death; he is also the universal creator, greatly effulgent, loving and the source of all good...'

The Hindu scriptures contain references to the sun under many names and in many aspects, three of the best known being Savitri, Surya and Mitra. In classical times there were several distinct sects of sun worshippers in India, one of which was responsible for building what must be one of the most spectacular pieces of religious architecture anywhere in the world, the sun temple at Konarak. Built in the form of a temple car, with huge stone wheels, and drawn by horses, this is a tangible reminder of the mythical form in which the sun presented itself to the Indian mind. The close link between sun cult and fertility cult is attested by the erotic nature of many of the sculptures with which the temple is adorned.

An interesting parallel to the Konarak symbolism is provided by the Trundholm sun chariot, excavated in 1902 in Denmark. This is also in the form of a wheeled car drawn by horses, although in this case the centrepiece of the car is a model of the disc of the sun. It has been supposed that the chariot is an actual cult object, carried around the fields at certain times of the year, particularly in spring or at the time of sowing, in order to ensure a fruitful year.

The Indian god Mitra is better known in his Persian form as Mithra, although in this case the sun was only one of his aspects. From Persia the cult of Mithra (see MITHRAS) passed into the Hellenistic world and the Roman Empire, where elements of solar symbolism were combined into the cult of *Sol Invictus,* the unconquered sun, by the Emperor Heliogabalus (3rd century AD). In 274 AD the Emperor Aurelian built a magnificent temple in Rome to Sol Invictus.

Sun Worshippers of Egypt

One of the impulses which helped to establish the solar cult in Rome certainly came from Egypt, where sun worship had been established for many centuries. Its undisputed preeminence in Egypt is one of the factors that has led some scholars to postulate the diffusion of this type of religion from Egypt westward to the Americas, eastward into India and northward into Europe. Certainly, all the nations which went to make up the Near Eastern cultural cauldron in ancient times were sun worshippers to some extent. The sun god, who was always male, had a variety of names: in Sumeria he was Babbar or Utu, in Babylon Shamash, in Ugarit Shapshu. Among the Israelites the worship of the sun was officially forbidden, since it was merely a created agent of God: 'And God said, "Let there be lights in the firmament of the heavens to separate the day from the night..."' (Genesis 1.14). In Deuteronomy

Left On reaching puberty, young girls of the Caraja tribe in Brazil perform a traditional dance in honour of the sun **Above right** Painting from the coffin of a Theban priest, Besenmut, dating from c 600 BC: it shows the dead man receiving life and warmth from the rays of the sun. In Egypt the sun god, Re, was the giver of life and the bringer of light out of darkness

John Moss

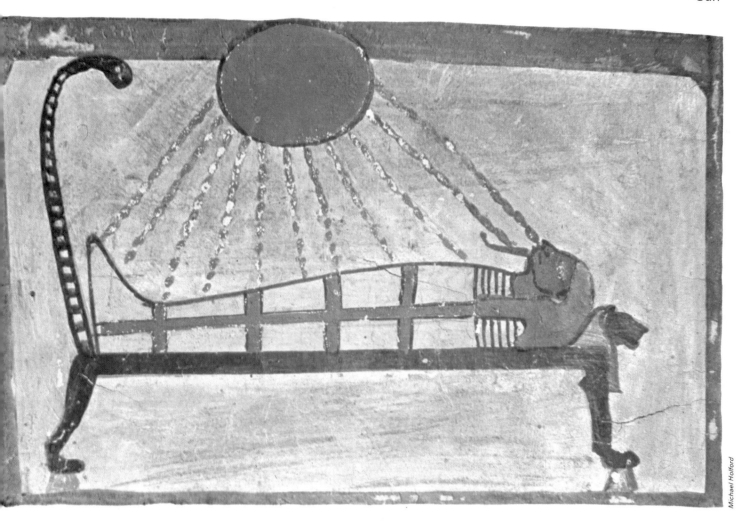

Michael Holford

It became customary to refer to the pharaoh as 'son of the sun', a feature of royal houses from India to the Americas

4.19) the Israelites are warned to 'beware lest . . . when you see the sun and the moon and the stars, all the host of heaven, you be drawn away and worship them and serve them . . .' Such prohibitions were never placed on hypothetical dangers. King Josiah of Judah, in the course of his reforms, '. . . removed the horses that the kings of Judah had dedicated to the sun, at the entrance to the house of the Lord . . . and he burned the chariots of the sun with fire' (2 Kings 23.11). Solomon's Temple, from which these images were removed, was in all probability oriented in such a way that the rays of the rising sun shone into the sanctuary at the autumnal equinox, a common feature of temples throughout the ancient Near East.

In Egypt itself, sun symbolism is so pervasive that it is difficult to disentangle separate elements within it. However, the most widely recognized name of the sun god was Re (or Ra), and the centre of his worship was at Heliopolis, in Lower Egypt (see EGYPT). He is a typical, perhaps *the* typical, sun god: a giver of life, and creator of the balance between light and darkness which is typified by his regular rising and setting. He traverses heaven, not in a chariot, but in a boat, and during the night he sails in another boat through the underworld. Every morning he conquers the dragon Apophis, who lies in wait for him (and, on the occasion of infrequent eclipses, catches him temporarily). This daily battle reflects the struggle which took place at the beginning of time when, in the form of the Creator god Atum, he

created light and order out of darkness and chaos. Re is also identified with other deities, notably with the sky god Horus (see HORUS).

In the Pyramid Texts (see BOOK OF THE DEAD) the pharaoh is already regarded as passing into the sphere of Re after death; later he became identified with the living Horus. After the 5th Dynasty, it became customary to refer to the pharaoh as 'son of the sun', a feature of royal houses from India to the Americas. The greatest of Egypt's sun kings was Amenhotep IV, also known as Akhenaten (see IKHNATEN), who attempted, partly no doubt for political reasons, to create a solar universalism out of elements of the Heliopolitan tradition.

The possibility that at various times in

the remote past, adventurers, merchants or missionaries might have communicated something of Egypt's devotion to the sun god to other lands and races is an intriguing one. Unfortunately it is only a possibility, and one which archeology is very far indeed from having confirmed. There are two entirely independent lines along which a few scholars have believed this influence to have been transmitted. One leads from the eastern Mediterranean westward and northward into Spain, France, the west of Britain and Ireland, north Germany, Denmark and southern Sweden. Its evidence consists in the trail of vast stone structures, megaliths, in which the dead were buried, and in the stone circles and alignments, of which the best known are

Stonehenge and Carnac in Brittany, at which the sun may have been worshipped. Unfortunately, speculation has tended to run riot as soon as this subject has been broached; but it seems to have been established that the megalith-builders were sun worshippers.

The second line leads directly westward, out across the Atlantic to the Americas. The most recent advocate of this theory is the Norwegian explorer Thor Heyerdahl, whose two voyages in the papyrus boats *Ra I* and *Ra II* aimed at demonstrating that such a culture-contact would have been possible. But the theory was expressed forcefully in the 1920s by a British scholar, W. J. Perry, who pointed out that the Peruvian royal family, like that of Egypt,

mummified their dead, practised marriage of near relatives, built pyramids, and called themselves 'children of the sun'.

Writing about the megalith-builders in *The Growth of Civilization* (1924) he noted that: 'The presence of vast graves undoubtedly means the coming to Europe of members of a ruling family, for no one else could build them. The use of solar symbols suggests that the people responsible for these graves were sun-worshippers. Since, the world over, the sun-cult has been an ancestor cult in the family of the Children of the Sun, who ruled Egypt . . . for thousands of years, it would seem that these facts, when put together, mean that the Children of the Sun had begun to move out from Egypt, and had founded kingdoms in

The possibility of the withdrawal of the light was always present: it happened every winter in the North

Jeffrey Craig

left The legendary inventor Daedalus made wings for himself and his son Icarus, but when the boy presumed to fly too near the sun the heat melted the wax, and he fell into the Aegean Sea and was drowned: *The Fall of Icarus* by Petrus Stevens and Joos de Momper *above right* Embroidery representing the sun, from Isfahan, Iran

various parts of Europe, just as they had done when moving out to America.'

No doubt Perry's theories went too far; but the fact, not of sun worship, which needs no diffusionist excuse, but of certain forms of sun worship in various parts of the world, calls for explanation in terms of more than mere chance.

Warnings of Misrule

One other general feature of sun worship is the association of the sun with other heavenly bodies in patterns of astrological prediction. The sun was never isolated in the heavens. Subservient to the High God, linked in various mythical ways to the moon and the stars, maintaining the fabric of the universe by means of its regular rhythm, the sun served in many cultures as a pattern of natural order backed by divine favour. To be sure, sacrifices were always necessary, often, particularly in the Americas, blood sacrifices, in order to mark man's acknowledgement of his dependence; but the possibility of the withdrawal of the light was always present. It happened every winter in the North. And on rare occasions it would happen without warning, in which

case it was taken as an omen of dire events to come (see ECLIPSE).

This extract is from an edict of the Chinese Emperor Ming Ti, consequent upon the solar eclipse of 233 AD: 'We have heard that if a sovereign is remiss in government, God terrifies him by calamities and portents. These are divine reprimands sent to recall him to a sense of duty. Thus, eclipses of the sun and moon are manifest warnings that the rod of empire is not wielded aright. Ever since we ascended the throne, our inability to continue the glorious traditions of our departed ancestors and carry on the great work of civilization has now culminated in a warning message from on high. It therefore behoves us to issue commands for personal reformation, in order to avert impending calamity.' There may be more spectacular, more bloody and evocative forms of sun worship in the history of religion; but there is none more moral.
(See also ALCHEMY; AZTECS; INCAS.)

ERIC J. SHARPE

The Sun in Astrology

As the most important of the heavenly bodies, the Sun naturally plays a dominating role in the interpretation of a horoscope, and is said to be the most powerful single factor in the chart. In popular astrology columns in newspapers and magazines, you will find yourself classified under your Sun sign, the sign of the zodiac which the Sun was 'in' at the moment of your birth, with the implication that this is the major general key to analysis

of your character and fortunes. More sophisticated interpretation tends to give great weight to the Ascendant, where the Sun rises, and the Mid-heaven, where it is at its peak of power, and both the sign and the house occupied by the Sun are taken as influential factors (see ASTROLOGY).

Since the Sun is the world's natural powerhouse of light and heat, it is believed to affect the creative abilities, vitality, ambition and will-power of human beings. Its position in the sky is generally said to indicate your basic temperament, the type of person you are, and sometimes your physical appearance. Some astrologers stress its role in influencing the conscious or 'lighted' part of your mind (with the unconscious mind being the domain of the Moon). If the Sun is favourably placed in the horoscope, especially if it is in its own sign, Leo, it is said to produce a commanding and kingly personality – powerful, proud, dignified, impressive, generous, faithful and affectionate. This symbolic link between the Sun and kingship is very old, and the good humour often associated with the Sun follows from the cheerfulness which its radiant appearance in the sky tends to promote in northern countries.

FURTHER READING: Glyn Daniel, *The Idea of Prehistory* (C. A. Watts, London, 1962); Jacquetta Hawkes, *Man and the Sun* (Random House, 1962); W. J. Perry, *The Children of the Sun* (Scholarly Press, 1968 reprint); G. van der Leeuw, *Religion in Essence and Manifestation* (Peter Smith).

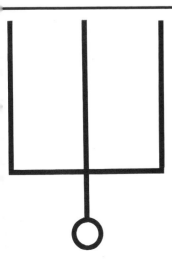

Sunday

The Christian sabbath, the day of rest, set aside for the worship of God in the tradition of the Jewish sabbath, and believed to be the day of the week on which Christ rose from the dead: named for the sun, with which the first day of the week was associated in the Roman Empire; a fortunate day to be born on, but unfortunate for any other secular activity.
See DAYS AND HOURS.

Sunnites

Members of the main branch of Islam, to which the majority of Moslems belong: they hold the Koran to be infallible, as the eternal word of God, and also place reliance on Tradition, originally transmitted orally and stemming from Mohammed or his Companions; the Shiites, the second principal branch, differ from them over the question of imams, over free will, and over other matters of doctrine, tradition and ritual.
See ISLAM.

SUNYAVADA

GAUTAMA, the Buddha, taught that the soul is a temporary combination of transient entities called *skandhas* (see BUDDHISM). Mahayana Buddhism, which arose about four centuries after the death of Buddha (c 483 BC), developed this doctrine more fully, and several of its early literary works, called Sutras, proclaimed the doctrine of emptiness, Sunyavada.

Whereas in early Buddhism wisdom is insight into impermanence, suffering and no-self, in Sunyavada the perfection of wisdom is the realization that all *dharmas* (doctrines or laws of life) are 'empty'. Transmigration and Nirvana (see NIRVANA) are both empty. The saviours are empty, and the beings whom they save are empty. From the absolute viewpoint, there is no difference whatsoever between the relative and the absolute, between *samsara*, the world of change and transmigration, and Nirvana, the perfect state beyond change. Emptiness, though, is not non-being, and Sunyavada is not nihilism, no matter how readily the charge springs to the lips of those bewildered and frightened by this doctrine. Emptiness is just that Middle Path between being and non-being that Gautama had declared. Things do not have being, because they are mutable and impermanent, and what is truly real does not change or perish. Things do not have non-being, because they arise and function, and whatever appears and acts is relatively real. That things are empty means that they lack own-being (*svabhava*), that is, they exist through the power of another rather than through their own power, they do not possess an inalienable set of marks, and they have no immutable essence.

The Hinayana Sutras say that all the skandhas, sense-spheres and elements are impermanent and devoid of self, which is tantamount to saying they are empty. However, the Abhidharma schools, especially the Sarvastivadins, drew up lists of 70 or so conditioned dharmas (force-factors), including all the skandhas, which they treated as realities. The Sarvastivadin doctrine that not only present but past and future dharmas are real comes perilously close to the theory that coming-to-be is just manifestation of what was already there in a latent state. Sunyavada was a reaction against this tendency in Abhidharma. Mahayana, charging that the Abhidharmists denied an *atman* (soul) in the person but admitted one in the dharmas, declared that both person and dharmas are empty of atman.

The Sunyavadin polemic against the Abhidharmists, and against Samkhya and Vaisesika (the two major Hindu philosophies at the time), was prosecuted most brilliantly by Nagarjuna (c 150–250 AD), founder of the Madhyamika school of Mahayana Buddhism. Born a South Indian Brahmin and well educated in Sanskrit and the Hindu philosophies, he became a Buddhist and proceeded to defend Mahayana principles using the logic and debating techniques of the Hindus. He reduces to absurdity all propositions that assume the existence of an own-being. This is not too hard, since the concept is self-contradictory as Nagarjuna defines it. Own-being exists and is immutable. But to exist means to change.

A sample of Nagarjuna's dialectic is his critique of causation. He says that a thing cannot arise from itself, since that would be the arising of the already arisen, an absurdity as great as the second cutting off of a head. A thing cannot arise from another thing, since that which is non-existent cannot be the agent of the action 'arising' or the object of the action 'production'; real action requires that both agent and object be real, too. Nor can a thing arise from a combination of other things (the Abhidharma and Vaisesika position), since the effect does not exist in the separate causes before they are combined.

The Empty-ists introduced a whole new epistemology (theory of the grounds of knowledge) to the Buddhist tradition. Ordinary cognition is essentially deceptive, they held, because it involves thought construction (*vikalpa*). What is changing is grasped as something persisting, class properties are superimposed on events that are really unique particulars, and consequently the imagination, like a magician, figments the ordinary world which is really an illusion or phantom. Ordinary language carries with it the acceptance of vikalpa, and consequently the belief in the own-being of things. Nagarjuna's dialectic aims to purge thought and language by the use of thought and language, just as the physician uses poison to cure poison.

Man resorts to irrational beliefs whenever his faith wilts and he becomes afraid; superstition is a form of personal magic which is used for coming to terms with the unknown

SUPERSTITIONS

IT HAS been said that man is a religious animal, but it could equally be averred that he is a superstitious one. Throughout the whole of man's history an elaborate system of apparently irrational safeguards, often barbaric in character, has provided a foundation for much of his ritual life. The minor ceremonies which survive today in the form of superstitions, are a constant reminder of the fact that man's mind has probably changed but little from that of his primitive ancestors.

Many of these superstitions are apparently outward manifestations of deeply-seated anxieties, the precise character of which remains as yet relatively unexplored territory. Their very existence implies an unquestioning assumption that there is some power (or powers) external to man himself, which is capricious, tyrannical and highly dangerous, a force that must be cajoled and won over to one's side, or, if it is hostile, kept at bay.

The word superstition is related to the Latin *superstes*, a word which includes among its meanings that of outliving or surviving. Used in this sense, superstition

Radio Times Hulton Picture Library

Most superstitions involve a simple, if unscientific, logic *Above* **An eggshell stuffed with horsehair was rubbed on a patient's body and then thrown into the street, transferring the disease to whoever trod on it**
Right **Reversed symbols, the cat and the colour black belong to the Devil as the principle of rebellion, abnormality and darkness**

became a useful term for the description of religious ideas which lived on when the religion from which they sprang had died. For this reason superstitions have usually been condemned as relics of outmoded ways of thinking, rather than as living expressions. More commonly the term has been used to denigrate forms of faith which disagree with one's own. In the 16th century 'Popish superstitions' were roundly condemned by Protestants, and in the 19th century pious missionaries risked their lives to rescue pagan savages from 'superstitious barbarism'.

Yet however superficially absurd their character, unvarying features of behaviour deserve to be treated seriously. Any examination of contemporary superstitious beliefs indicates that these should not necessarily be written off as the result of errors of observation or reasoning, but should be considered as permanent traits of mind.

The thought-processes of pre-scientific man can be observed in the widespread and still current superstition that breaking a mirror (see MIRROR) brings seven years' bad luck. The reflected image was originally regarded as the *alter ego*, or other soul, and damaging it was supposed to cause an injury to the person who had broken the mirror. Fear of walking under a ladder (see STEPS) may be partly derived from the terror once felt at the sight of the gallows, which was often merely a ladder propped against a tree.

The Philosophy of Magic

All superstitions seem to have the dual purpose of attracting favourable influences and warding off unfavourable ones. The name we give to these influences may be good luck and bad luck but they correspond too closely to the good and evil spirits of our primitive ancestors to be dismissed as

Unforeseen effects of observing popular superstitions: 'at the root of every type of superstition lies a belief in magic'

A corpse's eyes will be closed, sometimes by weighting them with coins: superstitious fears still govern our attitude to death

illogical fantasies. The curious predisposition of civilized man to revert in times of crisis to an archetypal mode of thought was noted by Paul Bauer in *Christianity and Superstition,* and he added that whereas the primitive man was perfectly at home in his superstitious environment, the civilized man most certainly is not.

It can therefore be argued that at the root of every type of superstition lies a belief in magic, which is a philosophy to which man resorts again and again whenever his modern gods fail him; in short, when his faith wilts and he becomes afraid. Superstition offers the comforting assurance that it is possible to influence one's fate for good and evil by will-power reinforced with ritual. There is obviously only a difference in degree between the act of worshipping a sacred tree and that of 'touching wood'. By physical contact with a piece of the magically charged wood one summons the power of the tree-spirit to one's aid. This magic is of the defensive type, however, for although the wood may hold bad luck at bay, it has no power to attract good luck.

More positive luck-bringing measures are the various uses of charms and talismans. Although to most people nowadays such objects have little real significance, the modern charm bracelet, first introduced about a century ago, has found ready acceptance as a luck-bringer. The symbolic meaning of the particular charms – the horseshoes, lucky pigs, and nowadays miniature golf clubs and cars – is quite lost upon the wearer, who is conscious only of the fact that they are supposed to exercise a collective power to attract good fortune. To an earlier generation, each particular charm would have had its clearly defined function; the pig, for instance, representing the Scandinavian Sun Boar, protected its domestic counterpart from evil; while the horseshoe, having the shape of a crescent moon, provided a safeguard against witches (see BOAR; HORSESHOE).

The most important characteristic of a luck-bringer is the source of the power with which it is endowed. How does a piece of wood or metal acquire its status as a charm, and what are the channels by which superstitions are transmitted? One of the ways in which an object may acquire supernatural power is through association; thus a toy animal given to a child by its grandmother is regarded as an embodiment of her love and is a powerful luck-bringer. In a series of experiments carried out among London children by the present writer, it became clear that superstitions are mainly communicated to the child by his mother or grandmother, and only occasionally by his father. In an almost literal as well as a figurative sense, they are 'taken in with the mother's milk'. The superstitious routines or lucky charms made their appearance at times of crisis, such as an examination. The particular type of charm employed included objects such as a lump of coal or a bent nail, the one originally representing the power of

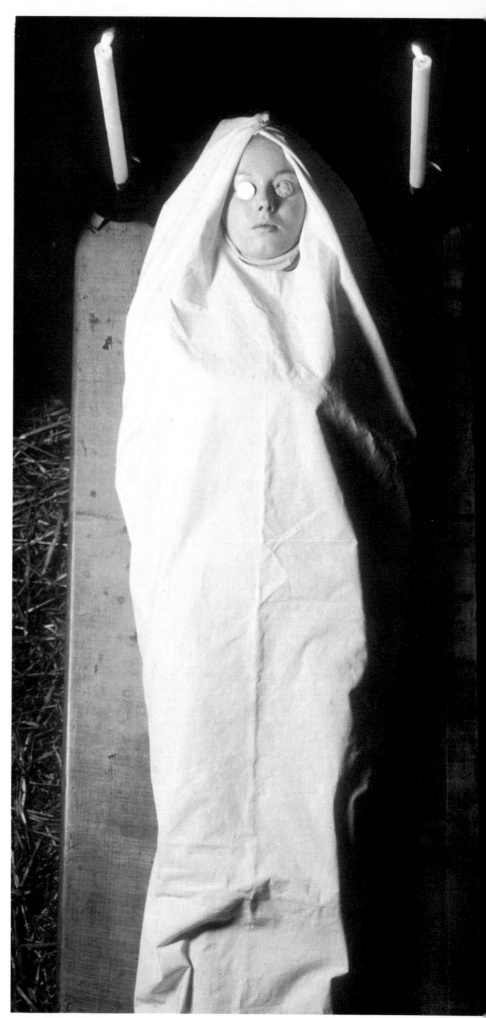

e and the other that of iron (see FIRE; ON). Charms that have failed to produce e desired results are rarely discarded but stead are hidden from sight in a desk or awer. Luck-bringers are traditionally pt secret except in times of crisis, since scussing them is supposed to exhaust eir powers. Protective charms, on the her hand, are more openly displayed nce their function is to keep bad luck at y, in other words to warn off evil spirits.

tages in the Life Cycle

wo human fears may be found at the root a vast number of widely differing super- itions: firstly, fear in the face of change the various crises of life, and secondly, ar of presuming upon the future, thus viting the anger of the gods.

Of the two, perhaps the most dominant that aroused by the prospect of change. was for this reason that new objects and currences were in the past greeted with aborate ceremonies designed to ward off e hostility of the supernatural powers.

Among primitive peoples, the various ages of development in each individual om birth to death were always associated ith protective devices, the vestiges of hich survived until recently in the form superstitions. With today's safer child- earing, many of the old birth taboos have isappeared, but some mothers-to-be ontinue to observe superstitious rites, ich as those calculated to produce a child the desired sex. A mother who wants a oy, for example, will wear a blue dress, nd when hoping for a girl, she may still ear pink. A relic of the old uncertainty ssociated with birth survives in the belief iat it is unlucky to take the pram into the ouse until after the baby has been born; n example of the superstitious fear of resuming upon the future (see BIRTH).

The onset of puberty was originally ccompanied by magic rites designed to give rotection against the hostility of evil pirits who were supposed to be particularly ggressive at this important period of one's fe (see INITIATION; MENSTRUATION; RITES F PASSAGE). The time has long since assed when menstrual blood was con- idered so threatening that a butcher would ot permit his daughter to enter his shop uring her periods, but it is still possible find individuals who retain the belief that he sexual act carried out with a woman at uch times can result in venereal disease.

With marriage comes a complete change f direction in the lives of both partners, nd the marriage ceremony is a veritable useum of old superstitions (see MARRI- GE). Again out of fear of anticipating he future, the bride is careful not to see er image as a completely wedded woman the mirror. If she has to take a last look efore leaving for the church, she is careful take off her glove. For the same reason, he will take care to avoid being seen by he groom before the actual ceremony. very feature of this important magical ccasion has its particular superstitions; ven the dressmaker who inserts the first titch into the wedding dress can expect be a bride herself before the year is out.

Should the wedding ring, which is in effect a magic circle, be removed or broken it becomes ominous for the marriage prospects.

Many primitive sexual superstitions have passed down the generations. Because the heat of the sun was once thought to be the source of life on earth, we continue to regard Mediterranean men as sexual athletes and Negroes as sexual dynamos (see RACE MYTHS). Because sexual activity was once regarded as a magical act, the seed or semen became sacrosanct; hence the long-standing myth that masturbation leads inevitably to a weakening of the physical powers, madness or even death. This may fairly rank as superstition.

Sickness and ill health, once the most feared of life's crises since they could lead to financial ruin, have lost some of their superstitious associations, thanks to modern medicine and welfare systems. Even so, to boast of excellent health is regarded as inviting psychic reprisals. The permanent fear of creating a situation by the mere act of referring to it by name is the real reason why certain diseases are mentioned only in hushed tones. For the same reason, the word death itself is often avoided.

The onset of death is even today associ- ated with natural occurrences, prophetic visions and mystical utterances. Here, at the grand climacteric, superstition reaches its peak. The moment of death itself is signalled by stopping of clocks, and pious drawing of curtains and the covering of mirrors. The mourner, as Geoffrey Gorer has pointed out, has entered 'a special state of mind'. It is in the funeral ceremony that one observes an intensity of superstitious awe that no longer survives in the other departments of life. If the wreath has ceased to be regarded as a magic circle to contain the soul and prevent its return to haunt the living, it remains none the less obligatory even in cremations (see BURIAL).

War and Peace
A crisis in the life of a nation, as in the life-cycle of an individual, is the focus of superstition, and it is traditionally the onset of war which raises the tempo and intensity of irrational belief. During the First and Second World Wars a number of superstitions which were centuries old suddenly received a new lease of life. To paint the portrait of a battleship now became, to the seaman's mind, the equiva- lent of a sentence of death upon her. The jinx ship which is a commonplace of nautical life was discussed with even greater anxiety than previously. Sailors when about to embark upon a voyage considered it danger- ous if a menstruating woman sewed a badge of rank onto a uniform. In 1914 German prisoners-of-war bore ancient amulets offering protection against death from bullets. In 1942 American servicemen carried iron-bound Bibles in their breast pockets for exactly the same reason.

Aircrews tended to resort under danger to a variety of death-defying fetishes, including amulets, mascots and lucky silk stockings, while their planes were invaded by those latter-day familiars, the

gremlins. The belief in lucky and unlucky days was revived and one and all displayed a reluctance to presume upon the future.

In peacetime, the degree of superstition which a man is likely to display is usually related to the riskiness of his occupation. Stockbrokers, whose financial lives are so often balanced upon a knife's edge of chance, have a strong tendency to consult clair- voyants, and American bankers are reputed to derive a sense of security from furtively touching the backs of passing hunchbacks. Out-and-out gamblers, whether at the roulette or card table, wear their super- stitions almost as badges, displaying a fervent belief in lucky seats and hunches. But the perfect example of a truly super- stitious profession is the theatre. The life of an actor is extremely insecure, and every theatrical production is a hazardous venture. In these circumstances many actors have a complete philosophy of superstitious prac- tices, some of which must be as old as the profession itself. To stumble is an omen of forgetting one's lines. The final line of the play is never spoken in rehearsal as any anticipation of completion is an invitation to disaster. If a long thread of cotton is found on an actor's back, it means that a contract is on the way. An actor will fre- quently treasure some little object associated with a successful first night's performance, regarding it as a form of magical insurance.

Another trade which was originally en- crusted with superstitious usages is that of the seaman. In the hazardous days of sail, the men on the big ships surrounded their lives with a complicated system of rituals and taboos (see SEA; SHIP). Today the situation has changed radically as the direct result of a century-long revolution in shipping. Long sea voyages are now relatively safe and in consequence deep-sea super- stitions of all kinds have dwindled. On the other hand, among fishermen, whose lives continue to be at risk and whose incomes are precarious, the majority of the older sea superstitions retain much of their original force. A skipper will frequently refuse to put to sea should he discover his hatch upside down on boarding his craft; a bucket lost overboard is still interpreted as a sign from the fates that the ship is doomed.

Sporting Chance
It would appear to be the rule that if the stock of superstitious beliefs remains un- diminished, the point of emphasis is con- tinually shifting from one situation to another in accordance with the amount of anxiety experienced at any particular time. Today at the factory bench, for example, a threat of unemployment at once brings all the old wives' tales to the fore. Placing a pair of new shoes on a bench is now seen as a threat to one's job, whereas in more settled times it was interpreted as an omen of death, the shoes being required for that long journey to the underworld.

All competitive situations, whether at work or at play, tend to create anxiety and therefore provide a solid foundation for the growth of superstition. In sport this principle is often paramount. The traditional belief that there is luck in odd numbers

Harry Price Library

Radio Times Hulton Picture Library

Left A variety of superstitions illustrated: it lucky to hear a goblin sneeze, unlucky to wa under a ladder or to be the third to share lighted match *Below* Members of th Eccentric Club defy the omens of bad luck a luncheon held on Friday the 13th

prompts punters to place their bets o threes, sevens and nines. Jockeys hav their lucky caps, cricketers their lucky ba and boots, and some footballers not onl touch the goal-posts at the commencemer of a match but have been known to prever their wives from looking at the game o television. In most cases a lucky obje acquires its supernatural reputatio because of its association in the player mind with some important success in th field. The cricketer who makes his centur while wearing a particular shirt will ofte go on wearing it until it is almost reduced t tatters. Luck by association is the rule i sport as in all other kinds of activity.

Any survey of the superstitious scer makes it clear that superstitions posses a powerful tendency to move with the time changing in outward form although never i essence. Motorists advance down the moto ways protected by lucky key-fobs, an automobile salesmen display a noticeab aversion to dealing in cars that have bee involved in fatal accidents. Motor-cyc policemen and Hell's Angels alike believ it unlucky for their crash helmets to b touched by alien hands. Civil air pilo and even astronauts are reported to tak amulets with them on their flights, while th computer operator is coming to believ that his machine has a life of its own.

Superstitious fears are likely to arise i anyone — irrespective of social class o nationality — who feels himself threatene by forces lying beyond the range of h power. The form of a particular superstitic is determined by environmental and soci factors, but the function of superstitio itself seems to be unvarying.

Superstition may perhaps be defined a a form of personal magic which is used fo the purpose of coming to terms with th unknown. By false analogy a particula course of action which has proved successf in the past is associated with some obje worn or action carried out at the same tim which is then accorded a kind of talisman quality. The object or action is then use again or repeated, in the expectation o achieving a similar result at another tim Negative superstition, which may be define as the avoidance of certain acts with th object of preventing undesired contingencie arises from a similar false association o ideas. In all this activity, however, can b detected an awareness of some law of caus and effect, but it is the cause and effect o the savage, not that of the scientific ma the rule of assumption rather than though

ERIC MAPL

FURTHER READING: Paul Bauer, *Christia ity or Superstition* (Marshall, Morgan an Scott, London, 1966); Gustav Jahoda, *Th Psychology of Superstition* (Allen Lane, Th Penguin Press, 1969); Eric Maple, *Supe stition and the Superstitious* (W. H. Alle London, 1971).

Mansell Collection

…perish in flames with her dead husband as … act of purification was the duty of the high-…ste Hindu widow; a practice which survived …re and there, in defiance of the law, until as …cently as the 1940s

…UTTEE

…HE SELF-IMMOLATION of a Hindu widow … her husband's funeral pyre is described by … term *suttee*, more correctly spelt *sati*. …he literal meaning of sati is 'a virtuous …man', but early European writers applied … term erroneously to the ritual burning of …ch a woman with her dead husband. The …igin of the practice is not certain, but

parallels are found in many ancient cultures. The kings of Ur, for example, were buried with their wives, attendants and possessions, so that in the next world they should have all the comforts they were used to on this earth. Similar customs prevailed among the ancient Chinese, among early Indo-European peoples and also among the nomads of Central Asia.

There is no direct reference to the burning of widows in the most ancient Indian scriptures, known as the *Rig-Veda*. A funeral hymn describes how the widow lies down on the pyre beside her dead husband, but she is then called back to the land of the living. A reference in the later *Atharva-Veda* suggests, however, that subsequently the burning of widows became

A Hindu widow leaps into the flames of her husband's funeral pyre; men with poles pinned the sati down if her courage failed her. Some believed that this sacrificial act expunged the sins of both husband and wife: 18th century engraving

common. The Greek accounts from the time of Alexander the Great's invasion of India (327–325 BC) contain references to the self-immolation of widows, and among the high Hindu castes the practice continued intermittently until the 19th century when the British authorities declared it illegal.

The earliest memorial to a sati is an inscription on a pillar dated 510 AD, and similar monuments from later days are found in many parts of India. Some medieval writers declared that the sati by burning herself on her husband's pyre expunges both her own and her husband's sins, and that the two would enjoy millions of years of bliss in heaven. There was also the idea that the self-immolation of a widow would purify her own as well as her husband's family. If her husband had died far from home she was advised to take some article of his dress, tie it to her breast, and then ascend the funeral pyre. In theory the cremation of a sati was always voluntary, but social and family pressures to follow the custom may often have been irresistible, particularly in the case of high caste widows of warrior class.

Criticisms of the custom were not unknown even in ancient times, and in the Middle Ages writers of tantric sects (see TANTRISM) even declared that a woman burning herself with her husband would go straight to hell. Yet, the fate of widows in orthodox Hindu families was unenviable, and women without young children may often have preferred a self-imposed death to a life of privation, scorn and domestic servitude in the house of unsympathetic kinsmen of a deceased husband.

The circumstances and methods of conducting the cremation varied. In northern India it was the custom for the sati on her way to the pyre to mark the chief gateway of a temple with the impression of her hand steeped in vermilion, or to impress her stained hand on a stone, forming marks which would afterwards be made permanent by chiselling. Stones bearing such marks were considered sacred, and a woman who chose self-immolation was revered as a divine figure. A blessing given by a sati on the way to her death was highly valued and her curses were feared. The actual cremation was accompanied by elaborate rites. In some parts of India it was customary for the widow to sit beside her husband's corpse in a straw hut erected on a pyre, which she finally set alight with a torch. Elsewhere she lay beside the corpse surrounded with inflammable materials, and if her courage failed her she was pinned down in the flames by men wielding long poles. In southern India a fire was kindled in a pit into which the widow had to leap.

The practice of self-immolation of women was particularly common among Rajputs, people from the present-day state of Rajasthan in north-west India. Not only did many Rajput widows burn themselves with their husband's corpse, but on the capture of a fortress many of the noble women burned themselves in the rite known as *Johar* in order to escape dishonour.

In many places in northern India, and particularly on the banks of rivers or tanks, small masonry shrines dedicated to satis may be seen. Such a shrine is often decorated with a carving in stone representing the husband and his faithful wife. Women come to such shrines to pray for male offspring or for the health of their husband and children.

With Snakes to the Flames

The self-immolation of widows is paralleled by other instances of ritual suicide once practised in India. In the Punjab mothers were known to burn themselves with their dead children, and in the past it was not unusual for men to kill themselves in order to accompany a beloved lord and master to the next world. There are many historic references to ministers, courtiers and servants voluntarily ending their life after the death of a ruler, and those who sacrificed themselves in such a manner were held in high esteem. The cult of such heroes as well as that of women who chose the role of sati is closely linked with the whole idea of worshipping the sainted dead. Representations of snakes rising out of the masonry of sati memorials to receive the adoration of the living suggests such a connection with the cult of ancestral spirits. A legend tells how once upon a time in the Narbada River valley of central India, when the three widows of a man were burnt on his funeral pyre, two great snakes appeared and entered the flames to be burnt with them. The bystanders were convinced that these were two wives of the dead man in a previous birth, and when the memorial rite was performed it was done for six souls instead of four.

The prohibition of the burning of widows, though enacted during the period of British rule, was the result of a campaign by progressive Indians. A Hindu sect known as the Brahmo Samaj, which combined ethical doctrines derived from Christianity with traditional Indian beliefs, agitated for the abolition of the custom, and though vigorously opposed by orthodox Hindu opinion gained the support of the British authorities. In 1829 the custom then officially described as 'suttee' was prohibited in Bengal, and similar legislation soon followed in the provinces of Bombay and Madras. But in the independent princely states not affected by British legislation the practice continued unchecked, and there were cases of people from adjoining British territories going there to perform the rite. Gradually, several of the rulers of the larger states, such as Baroda and Indore, were persuaded to prohibit the immolation of widows, but resistance to the reforming movement was strong in Rajputana. The opposition to abolition was weakened, however, by a ruling from the chief Brahmin priest of Jaipur to the effect that the immolation of widows was less meritorious than the 'living suttee' of chastity and devotion. In 1846 several Rajput states prohibited the practice but as late as 1861 the cremation of widows openly took place in Udaipur (then a princely state). Secretly it continued very much longer, and in remote areas isolated cases of the immolation of widows occurred as late as the 1940s, though criminal proceedings were taken against those involved whenever a case came to the notice of the authorities.

C. VON FÜRER-HAIMENDORF

Detail from a 19th century engraving: a blessing given by a sati on her way to her death was highly valued and her curses were feared, for she was regarded as divine; the burning was accompanied by elaborate rites

WALLOW

HEN MAN BEGAN to erect solid buildings
e swallows found that the eaves provided
eltered niches for their nests. An ancient
gyptian papyrus refers to a lovesick girl
earing the swallows early in the morning
viting her into the countryside. Greek
riters often mentioned the bird which, in
mmon with other European peoples,
ey looked upon as a harbinger of spring.
nd it was a Greek writer, Aristotle, who
st wrote: 'One swallow does not make a
immer.' A black-figured Greek vase now in
e Vatican depicts an elderly man, a youth
nd a boy greeting the first swallow to
ppear in spring. The youth shouts 'Look,
ere's a swallow!,' the man cries 'By
eracles, so there is.' The boy exclaims
'here she goes,' and then, 'Spring has
me.' In the 2nd century AD boys went
om house to house on Rhodes singing:

The swallow is here and a new year he brings,
As he lengthens the days with the beats of his
    wings,
White and black
Are his belly and back.

Pay his tribute once more
With cheese in its basket,
And pork from your store,
And wine from its flasket,
And eggs from your casket, and bread
    when we ask it.

    springtime swallow song is still sung
in some areas of Greece. The Greeks had a
low opinion of the swallow's song which
they likened to a chattering in barbarous
tongues. In spite of its joyous spring associations, the swallow became associated with
wretchedness in the story of Philomela and
Procne (see NIGHTINGALE). In this myth,
Tereus cut out the tongue of his wife
Procne lest she should divulge that he had
violated her sister Philomela. Whereupon
the gods transformed all three into birds:
Tereus was turned into a hoopoe, Philomela
into a nightingale and Procne into a swallow.
Ever since, the swallow has only been able
to utter incoherent twitterings.

    Augurs claimed that they could interpret
the bird's call, and inferences were drawn
from its behaviour. The fluttering of a
swallow around the head of Alexander the
Great was regarded as a portent of tragedy,
but returning swallows were considered to
predict the safe return of Dionysus. Greek
and Latin writers mention that weather was
forecast from the swallow's flight; and
throughout Europe low-flying swallows are
still regarded, with some justification, as an
indication of bad weather.

    Observations of swallows flying low over
lakes and rivers may have inspired the
Chinese to throw swallows into water when
they prayed for rain. The associations
between swallows, rain and springtime
growth were responsible for offerings being
made to the genius of the house on the day
when the swallows returned. According to
one poem, heaven decreed that the swallow
should give birth to the Shang Dynasty.

**It was a common belief in many cultures that
the human soul might leave its body in the
form of a bird: Ani, a royal Egyptian scribe,
is represented after death as a swallow, in the
Theban Book of the Dead, c 1250 BC**

Its egg was said to have caused the pregnancy of the ancestress of the Shang line.

    The swallow has long been associated
with gifts of healing. The white or red
swallow-stones which were believed to be
secreted in the bellies of the nestlings had
medicinal value. During the Middle Ages,
this belief became elaborated into the
notion that the swallow fetches a pebble
from the sea-shore to restore the sight of
its fledglings. Confusion apparently arose
between the swallow-stone legend and the
ancient belief that the swallow brings to its
nest a herb which cures the young swallows
of their blindness. Parts of the bird were
widely believed to cure various diseases:
snake bite, epilepsy, rabies, and so on. Its
droppings cured diphtheria and turned hair
grey; and mud from its nest was a remedy
for erysipelas (a fever accompanied by
inflammation of the skin).

A Drop of Devil's Blood

In general the swallow has been viewed
as a helpful, propitious bird, but as is
often the case with other lucky birds, it
has in some localities been regarded with
suspicion. In regions of France and Hungary
it was said that if a swallow flew under a
cow's belly it would give bloody milk, and in
Scotland it was reputed to have a drop of

the Devil's blood in its veins. Yorkshire folk considered it a death omen when a swallow came down the chimney. If the first swallow seen by a girl in Czechoslovakia was alone she would be married within the year but if she caught sight of a pair she would remain unmarried.

It is widely believed that swallows should be kindly treated, and that ill luck befalls those who harm them. The Tyrolese say that if you destroy a swallow's nest your own house will be burnt down. In France it was believed that if a man robbed a swallow's nest his horse would go lame. The Chinese revere the bird, and although they use most organisms either as food or medicine, they do not molest the swallows nesting under the low eaves in city streets.

The helpful swallow plays a prominent part in Christian legends. The Swedes say that it hovered over the Cross crying 'Svala! Svala!', 'Cheer up! Cheer up!'. The Norwegian version is that it twittered 'Console him!'. In France it is said that the swallow picked off the Crown of Thorns ignoring the wounds made in her breast by the spines. Ever since, the swallow has borne stains of blood on her breast. Similar stories are told of the robin and crossbill, both of which have red breasts. According to another French legend magpies pricked Christ's feet and head with thorns while he was resting in a wood, but swallows came and extracted them. Because of this the magpie has been hated and forced to build its nest in tall trees, but

the swallow breeds in safety in man dwellings.

In English folk rhymes the swallow included among sacred birds:

> The robin and the wren,
> Are God Almighty's cock and hen;
> The martin and the swallow
> Are the two next birds that follow.

The disappearance of swallows in autum and their reappearance in spring caus speculation and gave rise to one of t oldest ornithological fallacies, that th had hibernated in crevices or even und water. Aristotle mentions this belief whi was substantiated by natural historia up to the 19th century.

E. A. ARMSTRON

Swami

Or svami, a Hindu holy man and teacher: in certain religious and ascetic orders, title of initiates who have reached the highest stage of spiritual progress and have renounced the world: a popular term in the West for almost any Hindu adept, teacher or occultist.

Camera Press

The belief that the swan sings while dying has a long history endorsed by poets down the ages: Shakespeare wrote in Othello, *'I will play the swan and die in music'*

SWAN

SEVERAL CHARACTERISTICS account for the swan's importance in mythology and folklore: they are among the largest birds of the Northern Hemisphere and, except for the Australian black swan, all swans have conspicuous white plumage. Moreover, except for the mute swan which makes a remarkable musical sound with its wings as it flies, the other species – the whooper, trumpeter and bewick – utter loud vocal calls.

Engravings and designs from the Old Stone Age onwards of long-necked birds resembling the goose or swan indicate that such species had a magico-religious significance in various ancient cultures. The Middle Bronze Age Urnfield folk of Central Europe and other later cultures incorporated such long-necked birds in designs which included a sun disc, showing that these birds were associated with solar beliefs. As swans and geese fly high and also frequent water they became linked as well with ideas about growth and fertility (see GOOSE). Swans appeared over northern tundra areas when the days were lengthening, the sun's path in the heavens was getting higher, and the snows

were melting and the flowers appearing. Thus swans are thought not only to accompany spring but to help usher it in. Even now, some of the inhabitants of the woodlands of northern Asia erect poles with wooden effigies of flying swans near sacrificial platforms; below they place carved wooden models of fish, symbolizing the powers of sky, earth and water.

Since myths in which people are transformed into swans are ancient and widespread, they evidently hark back to primitive modes of thought in which the distinctions between gods, men and animals were blurred. Aeschylus, the Greek playwright, mentions swan maidens; Aphrodite was represented in art riding on a swan or goose, and Ovid tells of Cycnus being turned into a swan by his father Apollo. Both Apollo and Venus rode in chariots drawn by swans. Zeus was said to have turned himself into a swan to couple with Leda. The sacred character of the swan is indicated by the belief held in areas as far apart as Siberia and Ireland that to kill a swan brings misfortune or death. In County Mayo the souls of virtuous maidens were said to dwell in swans.

For Love of a Swan Maiden

The most widespread swan transformation myth tells of a man who sees a flock of swans alight by the water, and watches them discard their feather garments, revealing themselves as beautiful maidens. He steals the robes of one of the swan maidens and lives happily with her until

one day she finds the garments, puts the on and disappears. In an Irish accou dating from the 8th century, Angus, t son of the Dagda, 'the good god', falls love with the swan maiden Caer who appea to him in a dream. On visiting Loch B Dracon at the time of the great Celt festival of *Samain* (1 November) he sees flock of 150 swans, each pair linked with silver chain, and among them his belove Caer wearing a golden chain and corone When he calls to her she leaves the flo and he, too, takes swan form. Togethe they circle the loch three times and, chantin magical music which puts to sleep all wh hear it for three days and nights, they f to the royal palace. Among the Buriats Siberia who regard the eagle as the paternal forbear and the swan as th mother of their race, a swan maiden tale told which has close affinities with Iris stories. There are also Indian version and in Malaya and Siam the theme form the basis of a dramatic performance. appears to have inspired the Japanes Noh play, *The Robe of Feathers*.

Christian elements introduced into swa transformation stories are obviously lat embellishments; this confirms that thes stories date from pre-Christian times. a Russian ballad, a swan maiden declar

The size of the swan and its flight high in th sky implies power, and its association wi water implies fertility: Zeus turned hims into a swan to father children on Leda; *Le and the Swan,* **school of Leonardo**

Myths in which gods or humans turn into swans are ancient and widespread, reflecting primitive concepts that blurred the distinction between gods, men and animals: Roman limestone relief of Leda and the swan, Crete

C. M. Dixon

that she will not marry the hero until he has been baptized, and a version of the beautiful Irish tale of the Children of Lir relates that after centuries had elapsed during which Fionnuala and her brothers, transformed into swans, swam the Irish sea, they were restored to human form in a very weak condition, and were baptized just before they died.

The belief that the swan sings while dying has a long history. Although Pliny contradicted this tradition it has been transmitted down the ages, and has been endorsed by poets almost up to our own times. This story may also have originated in the North. Although dying swans do not sing, a flock of bewick swans in full cry produces a resonant, mysterious, melodious tumult which seems to pervade the whole landscape. Chaucer refers in *The Parliament of Fowles* to 'swan-song'. Shakespeare wrote in *Othello* 'I will play the swan, and die in music', and in *The Merchant of Venice* 'He makes a swan-like end, fading in music'. Drayton in *Polyolbion* referred to 'swans who only sing in death' and Byron made the sad request:

> Place me on Sunium's marbled steep,
> Where nothing but the waves and I
> May hear our mutual murmurs sweep;
> There swan-like, let me sing and die.

Yet another poet to make use of this familiar theme was Alfred Lord Tennyson, in *The Dying Swan*.

The notion that swans are linked together or wear chains is also ancient. In *As You Like It* Celia says:

> And whereso'er we went, like Juno's swans,
> Still we went coupled and inseparable.

In Greek art, swans are depicted harnessed; a French medieval legend refers to six brothers and sisters whose transformation into swans depends on the possession of golden chains and in Grimm's tale of *The Six Swans* a golden chain is placed around the neck of the swan maiden. After Edward I had knighted his son at Westminster two swans with trappings of gold were brought into the palace. The stories of the Knight of the Swan both in France and in Germany also embody such traditions.

E. A. ARMSTRONG

WASTIKA

HE WORD SWASTIKA is derived from the anskrit, *svastika*, which means well-eing, good fortune, luck. Although the gure bearing this name has been extensively used as a decoration or mystical mbol in many parts of the world from rehistoric times onwards, the history of s origin and world-wide dispersion is bscure. Known as the *Hakenkreuz* (ooked cross) in German, its association ith Hitler's Germany is universally miliar and the symbol is therefore enerally equated with all the negative atures of the Third Reich: antisemitism ncluding genocide), aggression, persecuon and terror (see also CROSS).

Both before and after Hitler's rise to ower in 1933, German archeologists and ultural historians studied every conivable aspect of swastika symbolism, though without reaching definite conusions. The subject inevitably attracted the attention of 'lunatic fringe' researchers, ho went to irrational lengths to establish at it represented an ancient Germanic nd therefore acceptably Nordic symbol.

Guido von List (see LIST), for example, nfidently proclaimed that the runic quivalent of the letter G was a disguised vastika and quoted the *Edda* to prove that is rune had a secret and mystical signicance for ancient Scandinavian bards.

For many, including List, the swastika lso had a cosmic meaning, for example as 'sun wheel', symbolizing eternal rebirth nd eternal movement. One Germanic nthusiast asserted that it was an essentially hristian symbol until the Church adopted the crucifix in the 6th century. Friedrich öllinger proposed in his book *Baldur und ibel*: 'The hooked cross, also known as Sun wheel", can be found as a common oly symbol with all Germanic peoples, in the Near East as in Crete, alluding to the eligion of Odin (Wotan).' Ludwig Fahrenrog (see NEO-PAGAN GERMAN CULTS), the founder of one of the many Germanic eligious sects – non-Christian but not ways specifically pagan – that flourished Germany after the early 1900s, supposed at the form ᛋ suggested 'cessation' or way from God', while its counterpart ᛉ ieant 'genesis' or 'to God'. Here he followed ontemporary Theosophical concepts which ere based upon Buddhist traditions.

The date when the swastika first became ssociated with the ideology of the German *ölkisch* movement, emotionally inward-oking and intensely nationalist, is un-ertain. The few available clues point in the irection of the Austrian Pan-Germans, at is, followers of Schönerer, in the 1870s. uido von List, for instance, who was close Schönerer, was probably speculating bout the swastika as a Germanic symbol ng before it became identified with ölkisch groups in the Third Reich.

In Germany, Wilhelm Schwaner (b. 863), the publisher of one of the earliest ölkisch periodicals (*Der Volkserzieher*, 897) displayed a swastika on the title-age of his publication, which was intended

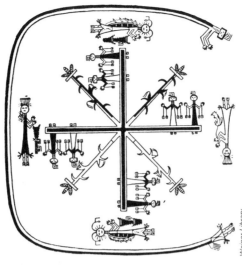

The swastika has been used as a decoration or mystical symbol in many parts of the world *Top* Swastika pattern of the Navaho Indians *Above* Adopted by the Nazis as their party badge, the swastika came to stand for Hitler's Germany in general, and for Nazi racial policies in particular, since it was chosen on the mistaken ground that it was a 'Nordic' emblem: 'few other symbols have become so widely associated with evil *Below* Swastika on a pot found at Argos in Greece, c 8th century BC

to inculcate truly Germanic (that is, völkisch) sentiments among its readers.

By 1912 half a dozen or more völkisch groups, some of them quite large, were using the emblem on the titlepages of their periodicals and on their stationery. It had also begun to appear on private letter-headings, either printed, rubber-stamped or drawn with a pen. This insistent exhibition of the swastika was intended to advertise an emotional and complete identification with truly völkisch sentiments, and these invariably included rigorously antisemitic attitudes. The swastika had by this time become a symbol of recognition for like-minded people. A number of firms, such as Ecklöh at Ludenscheid in Westphalia, began to manufacture swastika badges, tie pins, amulets and belts or buckles incorporating the device.

The famous pre-1914 youth movement, the *Wandervögel*, inevitably encountered the swastika by way of various völkisch writers and periodicals and the symbol was therefore completely familiar to the generation that fought in the First World War. Soon after Germany's defeat in 1918 it was adopted by various para-military Freikorps units, which included many ex-students and members of the *Wandervögel*. The famous Erhardt Brigade, which participated in the liberation of Munich from the Communists in April 1919, arrived at the Bavarian capital singing their marching song which began with the words: 'Hooked cross on steel helmets . . .' The swastika was soon no longer an exclusively romantic völkisch symbol but became associated with the 'national revolutionary' right-wing opposition to the Weimar Republic.

Hitler's National Socialist German Workers' Party had its roots in Anton Drexler's German Workers' Party, a minute völkisch group founded in Munich in January 1919. Hitler joined the latter in September 1919 and was largely responsible for re-naming it as the National Socialist German Workers' Party in February 1920. When Hitler and the Nazis adopted the swastika as their party emblem they therefore chose a symbol that already reflected all or most of the tenets of National Socialist ideology, and antisemitism in particular.

The form in which the Nazis used the swastika was designed by Dr Friedrich Krohn, a dentist who had belonged to various völkisch groups, including the Germanen Order (see GERMANEN ORDER), before 1914. He was aware of the Buddhist theory that the 'anti-clockwise' swastika signified 'fortune and well-being' and made his first design accordingly. It was shown to Hitler and others. The majority readily accepted Krohn's arguments but Hitler insisted that the clockwise alternative be adopted – some would say with disastrous consequences. The Party flag, badge and armband, all based upon Krohn's design, were in official use by the summer of 1920. Almost exactly 25 years later the swastika became a symbol of shame and defeat in Germany. It is probably true to suggest that few other symbols have become so widely associated with evil.

SWEDENBORG

A scientist turned visionary, Swedenborg claimed that the real meaning of the scriptures was revealed to him through his conversations with God and the angels

EMANUEL SWEDENBORG was born in Stockholm on 29 January 1688, the second son of the Lutheran Bishop of Skara, who had himself once been a professor at the University of Uppsala. Emanuel's father had changed his name from Swedberg when his family was ennobled in 1719. He was a remarkably learned and saintly man who was to have a longlasting influence on his son Emanuel.

From the first, Emanuel showed great promise in his scientific studies and, after graduating from Uppsala, travelled in Britain, Holland and Germany, pursuing his investigations. In England he met and was befriended by the astronomers Sir Edmund Halley and John Flamsteed, and on his return to Sweden had already established such a reputation that, in 1716, King Charles XII made him a special assessor to the Royal College of Mines. This work so absorbed him that he turned down the chance to follow in his father's footsteps as a professor at Uppsala, in order to continue with the practical work associated with the mines.

In 1718, he invented a means of transporting boats overland for 14 miles. While still a student, he had been concerned in 'a plan for a certain ship which, with its men, was to go under the surface of the sea and do great damage to the fleet of the enemy'. He had designed an air-gun with a magazine which could fire 60 or 70 shots without reloading and he had even busied himself with an attempt to design a flying machine.

Yet it was not as an inventor that he

gained his first international triumph. In 1734, Swedenborg produced a three-volume work *Opera Philosophica et Mineralia,* in which he developed his theory of 'nebular hypothesis' to account for the formation of planets, which predates the work of Kant and the French astronomer, the Marquis de Laplace, and is often erroneously attributed to them. Publication proceeded apace. In 1740 *Oeconomia Regni Animalis,* an anatomical work, was produced in Amsterdam; in 1743 *Miscellaneous Observations on Geology and Mineralogy* was published in Leipzig, and in 1744 he wrote, *On the infinite and final cause of Creation,* in which he attempted to discuss the relationship between the soul and the body. All these were major works of importance to the several branches of science to which they were addressed, yet all had the germs of his later religious preoccupation. Nevertheless, it was not until 1745, with the publication of *Worship and the Love of God,* that religion became his one and only concern.

No Flight of Fancy

His life became totally taken up with his religious work so that in 1747, at the age of 59, he resigned his assessorship and took a pension of half-pay so that he could devote himself to the new revelations. But he was in no sense a spiritist, for he believed that he had held conversations with these heavenly beings while still being very much aware of his surroundings and in much the same way that he might talk with another human being. His mysticism was not the mysticism of the trance or of the seance — it was a full-blooded avowal of his regular direct communication with beings from heaven. His religious writings are the record of these communications and he makes no concessions.

He was aware of the scepticism that such extraordinary claims would arouse, and in his first theological work he admitted: 'I am well aware that many persons will insist that it is impossible for anyone to converse with spirits and with angels during his lifetime in the body; many will say that such intercourse must be mere fancy; some, that I have invented such relations in order to gain credit; whilst others will make other objections. For all these, however, I care not, since I have seen, heard and felt.'

For statements of this kind to have any credence, it is important to remember that Swedenborg was neither a dreamer, nor an ascetic with little experience of the world, but a practical applied scientist who had preferred the real business of mining to becoming the Professor of Astronomy in the University of Uppsala.

Swedenborg's theological works are not easily read and they are certainly not the products of a slapdash mystical enthusiast. Just as in his earlier days he had learned about watch-making by apprenticing himself to a watch-maker, so he set about studying theology, becoming well-skilled in Greek and Hebrew and in the standard commentaries. Although his work was all based upon his own direct mystical experience of God, he did not neglect scholarship, and

the large volumes, written in Latin, we intended for the serious student and we in no sense considered as the means popularizing a new religion.

Despite the enormous claims made his writings, Swedenborg remained throug out his life a modest and simple perso working enormously hard, never marryin and without any intention of founding a ne sect, believing that his followers could be any denomination.

'God is a Man'

What then were the special doctrines whic he taught, and how did he make his infl ence felt? The key to it all is in his beli that he was a divinely-appointed instr ment of God's revelation to man. He put special gloss on Christianity, except inc dentally, for it was his view that his writin fulfilled the New Testament story, just the gospels had fulfilled that of the O Testament. He thus approached the gospe as one with superior knowledge. Swedenbo believed that his scholarship was informe by his own direct contact with God. H spiritual world was not seen through an i spired individual approach to scripture whic Mary Baker Eddy, the founder of Christia Science, claimed as her contribution; nor wa it seen as the result of the miraculous dis covery of a new book of revelations, like th Book of Mormon; but it was revealed to hir personally by God himself, who had led hir along the paths of heaven, enabling hir to talk directly to the angels. Indeed Swedenborg spoke as if heaven and i inhabitants were his 'second home'. H knows them as he knows human beings an his knowledge enables him to maintain tha man's real self is in form exactly as is h physical body, and if it had not been f the Fall, the body would have been slough off like a snake-skin. Instead, men nee to die before they move on to a higher plac So important is this concept of humannes that Swedenborg continually emphasize that it is only through man's own eyes tha he can see God, that God exists only in th terms that man can see him, and that thos terms are human terms.

This position undoubtedly comes fro Swedenborg's reliance on his visions, and i these, God certainly does appear as a mar Of course, he would admit that God in hi essence is unknowable, but insists that it i part of the essential God to be known i human form. It would be misleading, say Swedenborg, for us to think about God i human symbols if those symbols were n more than mere forms, but instead the must be an essential part of the reality God himself. This explains the otherwis baffling comment: 'God is a man'. It cann to taken totally literally and yet it is n merely symbolic. There is a real sense i which God shares the human form.

Swedenborg retained the doctrine of th Trinity, but twisted it slightly to fit in wit the experience of his vision. The Father absolute — God in his essence, unconditior ally, worthy to be called Jehovah. Whe Jehovah determined to save mankind, b assumed the humanity of the Son. Tha humanity was complete, with all its defec

…d all its blemishes. Thus God took on the …norance of the child, was tempted with …al temptations, which played upon …al human desires and weaknesses. Like …l humanity, the humanity of the Son …uld reach towards perfection – he was not, … in orthodox Christianity, perfect God …nd perfect Man.

The redemption of the world was the …ystical redemption of this humanity …ecoming perfect and thus reaching to the …ivine Father and reuniting the now …erfect humanity with him who is perfect …ivinity. This example makes it possible for …l men to come to the Father.

…taircase to Heaven and Hell

…ll this is based upon a very special …octrine of creation which acknowledges …an as the highest form of life on earth, but …oes not see him as created. Man is a form …hich is capable of receiving the life which …onstantly flows into him from God. Life is, … fact, Love-Wisdom, and this was received …ladly before the Fall, when man accepted …ne harmony with God. Once he began to …nore the fact that his life came from God, …nen he had to stand alone. God did not …ave him without a help to perfection, but …nstead provided him with the old dispen-…ation, which led him towards a stage at …hich he was able to receive the revela-…on of God's human form. God did not …ecome man, but merely clothed his divinity … man's form. This revelation is to be found … the New Testament, and it in turn has …een elucidated by the direct communi-…ation of God with Emanuel Swedenborg.

Once again, returning to this direct revela-…on, Swedenborg *saw* heaven and hell. He …lso saw the intermediate place to which we …o at death and from which we move, as our …pirit leads us towards perfection or destruc-…on. For those on the upward 'escalator', …ne approach towards God is inevitable. …or those on the downward, the Devil is …eached by easy stages. Swedenborg …escribes the spiritual world, with its …piritual patterns of all that there is in the …aterial world, and he calls this vision the …econd Coming of Christ. For him, the …dvent is not a physical return, but the …piritual vision of Christ in his true surround-…ngs. This vision comes to us all as we near …erfection and pass to that state of spiritual …ision which Swedenborg reached and upon …hich all his religious writings are based.

The revelation which God makes to man …s, in fact, a kind of distillation of the Word …hich is found in God himself. There is a …reat danger in revealing to unready minds …he full force of this truth and therefore the …ible contains a 'sifted-down' version of the …Vord which has descended until it has …eached the level at which man can under-…tand it. Of course on other planets, says …wedenborg, there are beings far brighter …han man, for whom revelation has been

presented in more direct a form. Yet in the sifted state in which the scriptures reach us, they make a direct appeal to the spirit of man, who has the capacity to understand and search out the real meanings contained within them.

This enables us to see that there is among the books in the Bible, a true canon of books which are really the Word, and which can be read for their spiritual meaning, and some others which are merely devotional aids. This view allowed Swedenborg to concentrate his work on the Pentateuch (the first five books of the Old Testament); Joshua, Judges, I and II Samuel; I and II Kings; the Psalms, and most of the prophets. He also accepted the four gospels and the Apocalypse as of this specially divine nature. Their real meaning was revealed to him in his understanding which came from contact with the other world, and from his direct conversations with spirits and with God.

From this understanding, Swedenborg was able to see that the Atonement did not reconcile God with man, but made it possible for man to relearn the way to union with God – a way he had lost through choosing to love other than God at the Fall. When Christ had shown this way, he put off all the weaknesses of humanity and put on the divine humanity, given him by Jehovah. This was the glorification which is so much a part of Swedenborgian philosophy.

A Challenge to the Intellect

Now a knowledge of the truth is to be found in the Church. It is this knowledge that shows the way back to God. The Church is the true Church in so far as it has the truth. Therefore the founding of the Swedenborgian Church – or the New Church, as its adherents prefer – does not imply that other Churches are wrong; it is merely to help to point the way and to complete the revelation which may already be seen by people in other Churches. Nor is it the final

revelation, for no doubt God may wish to show more of himself when the time is ripe. Swedenborgians claim, therefore, to be one of God's instruments, guided by the direct revelations made to Emanuel Swedenborg by God and his angels. These revelations they believe to be true, but in no way unique or exhaustive. They are not easy to assimi-late, for the truths are theologically compli-cated and unarresting to the ordinary person, yet they have seized upon the minds of some great intellects. Much of William Blake's work, for instance, is imbued with the Swedenborgianism he embraced and then left behind. Despite his satire on Sweden-borg's *Heaven and Hell* – which Blake called *The Marriage of Heaven and Hell* – he continued to be inspired by the directness of the revelations of a real other world which is the hallmark of Swedenborg's message (see BLAKE).

In our own day, Helen Keller, who was born blind and deaf, wrote of her love for the writings of Emanuel Swedenborg, 'If people would only begin to read Swedenborg's books with at first a little patience, they would soon be reading them with pure joy.' Miss Keller recognized that her hero was at first not easy to understand, and it is certainly true that for most people he does not get any easier even upon closer acquaintance, yet for some, he does appear to 'bring men by a won-drous way to God's city of light'.

His appeal is not universal. The New Church has never been very large, and its adherents have been few. Swedenborg presupposes a dedication to heavy reading. It would be surprising if the God who appeals to all men should have chosen so esoteric a character to continue his revelations made manifest in the carpenter's son. Neverthe-less, here is obviously a mighty mind at work – a mind which was convinced of its personal and direct contact with God and which set out to describe that contact for the enlighten-ment of an inevitably dedicated readership.

JOHN SELWYN GUMMER

…he founding of the **Swedenborgian Church, or** …Jew Church, **'does not imply that other** …Churches are wrong: it is merely to help to** …oint the way and to complete the revelation** …vhich may already be seen by people in other** …Churches'; etching of the New Church, Bath**

SWEDISH WITCHCRAFT

BY CONTRAST with Germany, France, England and Scotland, the Scandinavian countries were comparatively free of organized witch hunts. But that fear of witches existed and could arouse hysteria and panic is shown by the case of the witches of Mora in Sweden, who were accused of taking children to a mysterious place called the Blocula and there enrolling them in the service of the Devil.

In July 1668 the Lutheran pastor of Elfdale in central Sweden, an area with a suitably evocative name in view of what was to happen, reported to his bishop that a girl named Gertrude Svensen had learned

the art of magical incantation from a servant, Marit Jonsdotter, and had stolen several children of the district for 'the evil genius', the Devil. Her activities had been detected by a boy of 15, Eric Ericson, who also accused several others of stealing children for the Devil. One of them, a woman of 70, admitted that the accusation was true, but the others denied it. Officials of the royal government had investigated and discovered that the accused had stolen consecrated wine from the church, the implication being that they could only have a diabolical use for it.

The accusations caused great uproar locally. Rumours spread that hundreds of children had been delivered into the Devil's hand and that the evil genius himself had

been seen going about the countryside. I May 1669 the royal government (Kir Charles XI was then aged 13) instructe the bishop to appoint worthy ministers join members of the royal council in commission to restore peace and orde without the use of imprisonment or tortur In June the bishop was told to order publ prayers throughout his diocese to ward o the Devil's wrath, and this may perhap have made the panic worse, for when th commission met, on 13 August, 300 people came flocking to hear its deliberation

After an investigation lasting t 25 August, the commission found that 30 children had been involved, and identifie 70 witches. Far from being treated mildl 23 who freely admitted their guilt we promptly beheaded and their bodies the burned to ashes. The other 47 were sel to the town of Falun, where they wei later executed in the same way. In additio 15 of the children were executed, 36 age between nine and 15 were made to run th gauntlet and condemned to be public beaten on the hands with rods eve Sunday for a year, and 20 more, aged und nine, were to be beaten on the hands three successive Sundays.

Man in Gray

The atmosphere of dream or fantasy s often found in the confessions of accuse witches hangs thickly round the Mora cas According to the evidence given to th commission, the children were dressed red or blue clothes and carried by th witches to the Blocula, riding on goats sticks or cooking spits or on the bodies men who were fast asleep. The Blocula itse sounds like a place from a dream. It wa 'situated in a delicate large meado whereof you can see no end'. There was gate, painted in various colours, an behind it a smaller meadow and a hous The beasts the witches rode were left the smaller meadow and the bodies of th sleeping men were propped up against th wall of the house. Inside, in one huge roo there was a very long table at which th witches sat down to feast, and near it wa another room, 'in which there were ve lovely and delicate beds'.

Every witch had to take a child wi her, such was the Devil's dubious fond ness for young souls, and he bullied the and whipped them if they did not. Some them took as many as 15 or 16 childre with them. The children were made to der God. They were baptized anew by th Devil's priests and their names we written in blood in the Devil's book.

The Devil appeared as a man. He ha a red beard and he usually dressed in gray coat, a high-crowned hat with line of various colours wrapped round it, an stockings of red and blue with long garter When they sat down to eat, those who stoc highest in the Devil's favour were place nearest him. The children stood by th door and the Devil himself gave the their food and drink.

Afterwards the witches danced, caree ing round and round astraddle on halbere (weapons which were a combination of

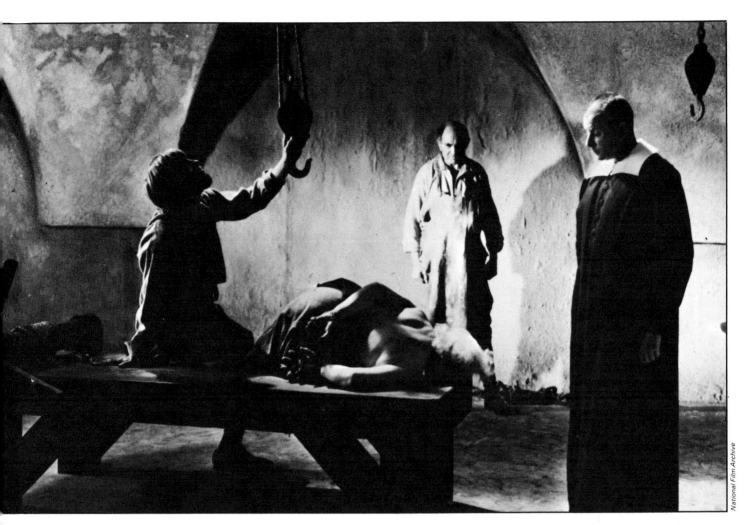

National Film Archive

The Scandinavian countries were relatively free of organized witch-hunting, but fear of witches existed and could arouse panic and hysteria *Left* **Detail from a contemporary illustration of witches in Sweden in 1669: they were accused of stealing children for the Devil** *Above* **A suspect about to be tortured, a still from the Danish film** *Day of Wrath*

spear and a battle axe), while the Devil roared with laughter and played the harp with fingers which were like claws. The dancing culminated in a mixture of fighting and copulation. The Devil had children as a result of sexual intercourse with the witches, but they bore toads and snakes through their intercourse with each other.

The witches also said that they used to meet at a gravel pit which was near a crossroads, and there they would cover their heads with garments and dance. On the beasts or instruments which the Devil provided they would be carried over churches and high walls. He gave them ointment which they smeared on themselves, and a saddle to ride on. He would give a witch a purse in which were shavings filed off a clock. It had a stone tied to it, and the witch would drop it into water, saying, 'As these shavings of the clock do never return to the clock from which they are taken, so may my soul never return to heaven.'

The panic spread beyond Elfdale. In 1670 commissions of investigation were appointed in the Uppsala area and in Helsinki, in the Swedish province of Finland. In 1674 and 1675 a royal commission

inquired into allegations of witchcraft in the parishes of Thorsaker, Ytterlannas and Dahl, and there was another holocaust.

In 1676 there were investigations in Stockholm and six women were executed. Many more were imprisoned, and many of them insisted that they were guilty. A Finnish woman named Magdalen Mattsdotter was accused by several children and servant girls, and her own two daughters said they had seen the Devil standing beside her. She denied the accusations and was burned alive, her younger daughter walking all the way to the stake with her trying to persuade her to confess. Later it became clear that the servants had accused her out of envy and malice, and they were condemned to death in their turn. The case contributed to a revulsion of feeling, Charles XI banned all further accusations, and the hysteria died away.

Christian Thomasius, a German lawyer and author of *De Crimine Magiae* (1701), who was head of Halle University (which his opponents nicknamed Hell University), said that he met one of the Swedish officials appointed to investigate accusations. The official told him that he and the other lay judges easily saw through the evidence, which was based on the lies and fantasies of children. But the Lutheran ministers, who dominated the proceedings, were convinced that the Holy Spirit spoke through the children and would never allow them to tell lies in such a case, citing the text 'out of the mouths of babes and sucklings' (Psalm 8, Matthew 21.16). After

many innocent people had been put to death, one boy accused a man everyone respected. One of the commissioners offered the boy money to admit that he had made a mistake and had really meant to accuse somebody else. This the boy readily did, and the ministers on the commission decided that the Holy Spirit did not speak through the children after all. They gave the boy a beating and abandoned the inquiry.

Fighting in Germany during the Thirty Years War, Swedish generals had put a stop to witch trials in areas under their control, on the orders of Queen Christina, who believed that persecuting supposed witches simply entangled increasing numbers of people in 'an inextricable labyrinth', a conclusion which all the European evidence bears out. H. R. Trevor-Roper has commented (in *The European Witch-Craze in the 16th and 17th Centuries*) that the subsequent persecutions in Sweden itself followed on the new intolerance of the Swedish Lutheran Church in the 1660s. 'Like the established Calvinist Church in Scotland, it had shaken itself free from other, more liberal Protestant parties, and its Puritan leaders prepared to advertise their purity by a great witch-hunt.'

FURTHER READING: H. C. Lea, *Materials Towards a History of Witchcraft* (Yoseloff, 1957 reprint, 3 vols); M. A. Murray, *The Witch-Cult in Western Europe* (Peter Smith, 1967 reprint); R. H. Robbins, *Encyclopaedia of Witchcraft and Demonology* (Crown, 1959).

SWORD

Regarded with mystical reverence in the Dark Ages, the sword was credited with a personality and power of its own; in dances of immensely ancient lineage it replaced the sticks and clubs of victory celebrations and seasonal fertility rites

UNLIKE SPEARS AND AXES, which can be traced back to the Stone Age, the sword never existed in primitive times, for it presupposes a certain skill in metallurgy, and a certain sophistication in war; also, a social class willing to support the craftsman and learn the best use of his handiwork. For these reasons, the sword has a mystique which cruder weapons lack.

According to an Arabian tradition, swords were invented by the Hebrews, and first made on a hill near Damascus where Cain slew his brother Abel. Archeology, however, favours a European origin. The oldest known specimens are Bronze Age products dating from the second millennium BC, and found in Crete and north-western Europe. The sword appears to have developed originally as an enlargement of the knife or dagger, and repeated sharpening produced tapering blades that came to a point. When these were found to be deadly, smiths hit on the idea of a greatly elongated dagger with a sharp end.

The earliest swords of all were primarily for thrusting rather than slashing. Engraved gems from Mycenae portray warriors running their opponents through; an Irish sword from Lissane resembles a rapier. And although slashing with the sharp edge must

have developed early, it was not until the 18th century that any swordsmen explicitly fenced with the point alone. However, the amount of practice required for this modern art suggests that the early thrusting swords must have demanded considerable skill. They imply a warrior elite with the time and inclination to undergo training.

It is not surprising, therefore, that legends of superhuman armourers lay stress on their sword-making. A letter written in 520 AD by Cassiodorus, secretary to the Gothic king Theodoric, thanks another monarch for a gift of swords 'so beautiful that one is tempted to attribute them to Vulcan': for this late classical writer, Vulcan's fame for such weapons is a literary cliché. The Teutonic peoples had their counterpart for Vulcan in Volund or Wieland, who made Siegfried's sword, Balmung. In England, Wieland became Wayland the Smith (see SMITH) and had a forge in a cave near Lambourn, Berkshire. Testing Balmung on a rival, Amilias, he cleft him down to the thighs so adroitly that Amilias only realized he had been struck when he tried to walk and fell apart.

The sword with which Beowulf, the Anglo-Saxon epic hero (see BEOWULF), kills the mother of the monster Grendel, whom he had mortally wounded, is the work of giants, not men. According to Geoffrey of Monmouth, King Arthur's sword Caliburn (an early form of the better-known name Excalibur; see ARTHUR) was forged in the enchanted island of Avalon. Several other fabulous swords are the gifts of fairy folk.

While classical legend acknowledges a divine armourer, its interest in swords is not nearly as pronounced as that shown later by the barbarian and Christian worlds. However, the two most famous classical stories do reflect the weapon's association with royal status and power.

It is said that when Alexander invaded Asia Minor, he visited a temple of Zeus where a cart was tied up with a complicated knot of bark, known as the 'Gordian Knot'. Gordius, the father of Midas and king of Phrygia, had gained the throne in obedience to an oracle when he arrived riding in the cart, which he dedicated to Zeus. A prophecy declared that whoever could undo the knot would become ruler of Asia. Alexander wasted no time; drawing his sword, he cut the Knot, and became ruler of Asia.

The second legend, preserved by Cicero, has given rise to another proverbial phrase. Damocles, a sycophant of the Sicilian tyrant Dionysius, wishing to flatter him, remarked how happy a man in such a position must be. Dionysius invited him to a banquet and offered him the royal chair. Damocles sat down on it, and suddenly realized that a sword was suspended above his head by a single horsehair. From this he could draw a moral about the insecurity of greatness.

On the whole, the Greeks and Romans did not regard their weapons with mystical reverence. The precursors of the romanticized swords of medieval chivalry are Teutonic and Celtic, not classical. Iron swords of the *La Tène* Celtic culture, in the last centuries BC, have almost parallel edges

In pagan legends of northern Europe a great hero frequently has a magic sword, possessed of wonderful powers and a life of its own, and the swords of Viking chieftains bore such names as Odin's Flame, Battle Snake or Sea-King's Fire. In the Middle Ages the mystique of the sword was adapted to a new symbolism, including the concept of Church and State as the 'Two Swords' *Left* The English Great Sword of State, symbolizing royal power and authority *Right* The Sword of Justice, in a British propaganda poster of the First World War

and rounded points, foreshadowing the massive two-handed swords of the knights. According to Livy and other sources, the swords of 'barbarian' Europe were always associated with social rank; common men seldom possessed them. Their special aura is pagan long before it is Christian. Tacitus, writing of a German tribe, notes a reverence for weapons: 'no business, public or private, is transacted except in arms'.

A Life of Its Own

Numerous swords have been found in the peat bogs of Denmark, which were originally meres. They were laid under the water with care, sometimes deliberately bent, in fenced-off areas. This northern practice belongs to the early centuries of the Christian era. It may have been partly sacrificial, but it may also have been akin to the custom of burying swords with the noblemen who owned them. The idea was not simply that the dead man might need his weapon in the hereafter; the sword symbolized his power, and was linked with him personally. It shared his life and had a life of its own. Hence, anyone else would be rash to take it. It might injure him or fail him in battle, or the owner's ghost might return to claim it. So even when the corpse of the owner lay elsewhere, it might be advisable to put his sword out of others' reach at the bottom of a mere, for instance, under magical protection. The implied personality of the sword itself is a frequent motif in northern mythology. Those recovered from chieftains' graves of the period 400–700 AD show a fineness of workmanship, a richness of

Sword

Although many sword dances are now show-pieces, it is thought that they originated as rituals honouring and promoting virility, victory and fertility. The swords may be used more as props than as weapons, but dances in which a combat is danced out are believed to be descended from mock battles between individual groups representing summer and winter, fertility and sterility *Below* Sword dancing at the Braemar Games *Bottom* The North Skelton Long Sword Dance, from the English Midlands *Right* Turkish dancers in mimic combat *Far Right* A Javanese fighting dancer

Spectrum Colour Library

Picturepoint, London

ornament, which accord with many literary indications that a sword was more than a utilitarian object. It was a living being with a name and a character. If not buried with its lord, it might be handed on in his family.

When Beowulf prepares for his combat with Grendel's mother, the royal herald Unferth lends him a weapon:

> Not the least or the worst of his war equipment
> Was the sword the herald of Hrothgar loaned
> In his hour of need, Hrunting its name,
> An ancient heirloom, trusty and tried;
> Its blade was of iron, with etched design
> Tempered in blood of many a battle.
> Never in fight had it failed the hand
> That drew it, daring the perils of war.

Many of the swords in other folklore and legend have outright supernatural properties. They shine, and discharge lightning-bolts. They grow and shrink at need, they make the owner invisible, they give him the power to travel fast over long distances, and they run with blood when he dies. Heroes pierce rocks with them, splinter arrows in flight, and create hills and springs by striking the earth.

Numerous tales of magic further reveal the personality of the weapon, and its independent wisdom and virtue. There are swords that can cause death whenever drawn, or throw enemies into an enchanted sleep. Some, on the other hand, can release the spellbound, keep the dying alive, and even resuscitate the dead. Swords act by themselves, striking out of the air in forests,

or falling on an enemy. They speak to save their masters from danger, and understand when spoken to themselves.

Reserved for a Special Task

A number of stories tell of a sword's gift of discrimination. Some are unwilling to deal a wrongful blow. When the owner of one tries to attack a friend, it becomes too heavy for him to lift. Others turn to wood when somebody raises them against an innocent victim.

The use of these marvellous weapons is governed by many rules and hazards. Some can only be moved at all by the right person. Some are reserved for a single appointed task (as when a son must take up his father's sword to kill his father's murderer).

Sonia Halliday

Picturepoint, London

Some must be handled in a special manner, for example, they must be drawn, and sheathed, and drawn again a fixed number of times before the battle.

A hero's vulnerability may be bound up with the magical qualities of his weapon. He may wear an impenetrable garment which his own sword alone can pierce, and eventually does. His sword may be bewitched so that it will break in one particular peril, or fail in one crucial crisis. However potent the sword's virtue, a hostile magic can be stronger. It can be dulled or otherwise neutralized, perhaps by an incantation, or by scratching a counter-charm on the blade. A magic wand may break it, or an evil spirit get into it. Grendel's mother is a case in point. She is a troll woman living in a cave under a

Picturepoint, London

lake. Beowulf assails her with the sword Hrunting, but finds it useless against the demon:

> He swung his war sword with all his strength,
> Withheld not the blow, and the savage blade
> Rang on her head its hymn of hate.
> But the bold one found that the battle-flasher
> Would bite no longer, nor harm her life. . . .
> That time was the first for the treasured blade
> That its glory failed in the press of the fray.

On the wall, however, Beowulf spies an ancient sword made by giants. He manages to seize it, kills the troll woman, and cuts off the head of Grendel, whose corpse is still lying in the cave. The monster's blood melts the iron, so Beowulf can take only the hilt back with him. When he returns the ineffectual Hrunting to Unferth, despite its almost disastrous failure, 'the great-hearted hero spoke no word in blame of the blade'. Hrunting deserves a human courtesy for doing its best.

The swords of the Vikings have many descriptive phrases and nicknames applied to them: Odin's Flame, Battle-Snake, Battle-Fire, Sea-King's Fire, Tongue of the Scabbard, Ice of Battle, Dog of the Helmet, Mail-Coat's Terror. Several sagas refer to Skofnung, 'the best of all swords which have been carried in northern lands'. Made for Hrolf Kraki, a 6th century king, it uttered a cry when it saw wounds. Skofnung was buried with its master, but 200 years later a warrior named Skeggi opened the grave and appropriated the sword.

Such an action was fraught with danger, though Skeggi himself knew the weapon's secrets and could handle it. Skofnung must never be drawn in the presence of a woman, or casually, with no immediate intention of fighting. Nor must the sun shine full on its pommel, which was protected by a cover. It had a 'life stone' as an accessory and wounds inflicted by the sword could be healed only by rubbing with the stone (archeology supplies evidence for these magical stones, which were large beads attached to the hilt by a thong). Skeggi reluctantly lent Skofnung to a young friend, Kormak, who had challenged a rival to a duel. Handing it over, Skeggi gave him all the necessary warnings and added that when the time came to fight, Kormak should breathe on the blade and a little snake would creep out under the guard.

Scornful of all this cryptic advice, Kormak made every possible blunder. When he got home he tried to draw the sword to show to his mother (a double error) and it stuck in the scabbard, making a weird noise when he pulled harder. On reaching the duelling ground, he removed the cover so that the sun shone on the pommel. The snake appeared, but 'it was not handled as it should have been, and the luck of the sword was changed'. Again archeology sheds light: the snake would have been a faintly etched design, a charm of some sort, which showed up when the blade was breathed on.

In the medieval romances of Charlemagne and his peers, a similarly respectful spirit is evident. The Emperor's sword is Joyeuse, and that of his champion Roland is called Durandal. Joyeuse, 'the unconquered' was made by the smith Gallas and took him three years to finish. The gold-hilted coronation sword of the kings of France, now in the Louvre, is traditionally described as the sword of Charlemagne. Apart from a new grip fitted by Napoleon, it does appear to be 9th century work, though its identity as Joyeuse cannot be proved. A second sword in Vienna, said to have been given to Charlemagne by Haroun al-Raschid, the Caliph of Baghdad whose adventures are recounted in the *Arabian Nights*, is probably Hungarian.

The kinship of the Charlemagne cycle to the masculine world of Skeggi and Beowulf is reflected in an allusion to the sword Durandal, in the *Song of Roland*. When Roland is dying and recalls the things dearest to him, he is sad that Durandal will be masterless, but he does not think of Aude, his betrothed. In the more cultured romances of King Arthur (later as literature, though referring to an earlier period historically), women can, and usually do, put swords in the shade. Yet it is Arthur's sword, rather than Charlemagne's or Roland's, which has become immortal: doubtless because the advance in sophistication was also an advance in magical fantasy.

Arthur becomes king after passing the test of pulling a sword out of a stone, which no other claimant had succeeded in doing. In some versions, but not in all, this is said to have been the famous Excalibur which he wields later. Arthur's sword in the *Mabinogion* is called Caledvwlch, a

The warrior's sword is a common motif in heraldry and on military medals *Above (left)* Nazi war insignia awarded for 75 military engagements, *(centre)* the arms of the Howard family, *(right)* badge of the Order of Merit military division *Right* Richard, Earl of Warwick is dubbed Knight of the Garter: the method of conferring knighthood by striking the candidate on the shoulder with a sword is still used

Celtic name of uncertain derivation. In Geoffrey of Monmouth it becomes Caliburn. The form 'Excalibur' is supposed to be based on the Latin phrase *ex calce liberare* 'to liberate from the stone'.

In Sir Thomas Malory's *Morte D'Arthur* Excalibur is distinguished from the sword in the stone, and a different story is told of how Arthur came by it. Here Merlin brings Arthur to a lake, and he sees 'an arm clothed in white samite' rising above the surface with a sword in its hand, richly jewelled, in a fine scabbard. The Lady of the Lake approaches. In return for Arthur's promise of a boon to be specified later she agrees to let him have the sword. He rows out and takes it, and the hand vanishes under the water. Merlin tells him to prize the scabbard also, for while he wears it, no wound can ever cause him to lose blood. Many years afterwards, Excalibur has to be thrown back into the water. The hand rises to catch it.

One suggestion to account for this story is that there may have been a tradition of sinking the weapons of dead chiefs in meres, as practised in Denmark. The Lady of the Lake was perhaps a priestess in charge of the sacred place, who allowed a particular sword to be recovered in order to endow a new chief with an old one's authority.

Twin-Edged Blade

Medieval legends name many other wonderful swords belonging to British, French, Scandinavian, German and Spanish heroes. The mystique did not die with the triumph of the Church, but it was Christianized. During the 12th century the sword was adapted to a new symbolism; it looked like a cross, it was wielded by crusaders against the infidel, and the twin edges of its blade could stand for truth and loyalty. Medieval political theory symbolized the spiritual and secular powers as the 'Two Swords', and the

Receive this sword in the name of the Father, and the Son, and the Holy Spirit, and use it in thine own defence and that of the Church of God ...'

more ambitious popes claimed the right to carry both. The figure of Justice on the Old Bailey bears the secular sword.

In Germany, there are accounts of swords being introduced into marriage ceremonies. Sometimes the bridegroom held out the ring lying on the blade. One ritual required the bride to place her thumb on the pommel. A poem tells how an unwilling girl clenched her fist so tightly that the marriage could not proceed. The weapon's function in pledges and oaths of other types was by this time already ancient. When Hamlet says 'Swear by my sword', he is following a custom traceable a long way back to pagan Teutons.

Swords played an important part in the rituals of knighthood. Here too there were pagan antecedents. In *Beowulf* the king of the Geats honours the hero by giving him a rich sword. A Norwegian law manual describes the ceremony when a new member of the royal bodyguard, the Hearthmen, took the oath of allegiance. The king rested his own coronation sword, sheathed, on his right knee, with the hilt pointing forward with his hand covering it. The new Hearthman knelt before him, placed his own right hand under the hilt, and kissed the hand of the king.

In Christendom, when a knight went to church to be admitted into an order of chivalry, he handed his sword to the priest, who laid it on the altar, blessed it, and gave it back, saying: 'Receive this sword in the name of the Father, and the Son, and the Holy Spirit, and use it in thine own defence and that of the Church of God, and for the confusion of enemies of the cross of Christ and the Christian faith.' The knight brandished it three times, sheathed it, and passed it to his sponsor. In the East too, the Samurai of Japan made the sword an object of reverence and ritual.

The lore of symbolism and magic gives the sword a variety of roles according to context. Viewed structurally, as a union of blade and guard, it stands for conjunction; functionally, as an instrument with the power to wound, it stands for liberty and strength; sexually, it is ambiguous. The straight Western type of sword is male, the curved oriental type is female. Despite the relationship with the scabbard, it is often

emblematic of chastity, because of its brightness and also its power to separate. Many characters in legend, for example, Siegfried, sleep beside a woman who must not be touched, with a sword between them.

For alchemists the sword is a symbol of purifying fire. In the magician's hands, it is a protection against malevolent ghosts and hostile enchantments. Its polished surface can be used like a crystal ball for 'scrying'. It figures in Arthurian legend as one of the four Hallows or sacred objects seen by Grail seekers: the sword, the cup, the dish and the lance. Occultists assert a connection between these Hallows and the four suits of the Tarot pack, in which swords correspond to the spades in the ordinary pack.

GEOFFREY ASHE

Sword Dances

In sword dancing the swords are used as props and not necessarily as weapons; dancers wield swords to build up elaborate group figures or for use in dance tricks. There are many variations and types of sword dances, but they share some characteristics: for instance, they are exclusively performed by men, they are highly stylized even when they portray combat, and they derive from cultic and perhaps mythological sources.

Although many sword dances are now showpieces, they probably all originated in pre-Christian rituals in honour of virility, victory and fertility. For instance, the *Moriscas* ('Moorish dances', in which a ritualistic form of battle is mimed) and the various types of sword-or-stick dances have intrigued scholars over a long period. These dances have now been traced, not to Moorish origin, but to very ancient spring-time seasonal rites for the return of the sun and of vegetation, culminating in a human or animal sacrifice. The combat signified the battle between summer and winter, night and day; and the leaps and high kicks promoted growth. In the Iron Age, the sticks and clubs were replaced by metal swords, especially in mining areas, and the symbolic developments became increasingly complex.

Whatever the aboriginal motivation, the overt meaning of the Morisca type of sword dance changed during the Crusades and the Moorish invasion of Spain. In the

The Sword of Arthur

And there I saw mage Merlin, whose vast wit
And hundred winters are but as the hands
Of loyal vassals toiling for their liege.

And near him stood the Lady of the Lake,
Who knows a subtler magic than his own —
Clothed in white samite, mystic, wonderful.
She gave the king his huge cross-hilted sword,
Whereby to drive the heathen out: a mist
Of incense curl'd about her, and her face
Wellnigh was hidden in the minster gloom;

But there was heard among the holy hymns
A voice as of the waters, for she dwells
Down in a deep; calm, whatsoever storms
May shake the world, and when the surface rolls,
Hath power to walk the waters like our Lord.

There likewise I beheld Excalibur
Before him at his crowning borne, the sword
That rose from out the bosom of the lake,
And Arthur row'd across and took it — rich
With jewels, elfin Urim, on the hilt,

Bewildering heart and eye – the blade so bright
That men are blinded by it – on one side,
Graven in the oldest tongue of all this world,
'Take me,' but turn the blade and ye shall see,
And written in the speech ye speak yourself,
'Cast me away!' And sad was Arthur's face
Taking it, but old Merlin counsell'd him,
'Take thou and strike! The time to cast away
Is yet far off.' So this great brand the king
Took, and by this will beat his foemen down.

Tennyson *Idylls of the King*

ew of the anthropologist George Foster, he trail of Iberian Moriscas spread from orth to south along with the gradual xpulsion of the Moors, from Lérida in 150 to Andalusia in the 14th century. further two centuries later, the Moriscas ere taken by the Spanish to the New World.

Meanwhile, in the Middle Ages the sword ances of central Europe became attached guilds as well as to male fraternities, nd in Austria this is still the case. In Austria nd in Spain and Portugal, the sword dances e traditional, while in England they were vived after 1900, thanks to the efforts of ecil Sharp, the famous collector of folk ng and dance; today they are losing their remonial meanings, even in the villages. In merica they are kept alive by the enthusiasm f folk dance societies.

Despite the widespread diffusion of vord dances within the Old World and to le New, the celebrations have retained me of the original costuming and music, nd a great deal of the aboriginal and edieval seasonal timing. They are held uring the season of new life, from Epiphany Corpus Christi. Moriscas abound during arnival time at Corpus Christi, sword ances on Plough Monday (first Monday fter Twelfth Night) and during Whitsuntide r at May Day. Some dances are performed t unusual times, such as the September uild observance of the Hallein dancers om Austria, who also observe Whit Sunday.

rossed and Wielded Weapons

cholars have divided sword dances into arious groupings. Solo dances which ature the brandishing of a sword or abre predominate in the Near East. The rab *Aissoua* is performed in a semi-ance culminating in self-mutilation. The krainian *Zaporotchez* and the *Lezginka* the Lezgis, Georgians, and Tartars the Caucasus Mountains appear as a isplay of virtuosity, but probably origi-ated in an old fertility rite, or at least a ourtship rite for the display of masculine rowess. Before his female partner, the gorous male leaps and whirls while he ourishes a sabre.

Stepping between two crossed swords a sword and scabbard, or perhaps two ossed sticks, or pipes, originated as a ctory dance. The best-known examples, l from Europe, are the Scottish *Gillie*

Left The Greek hero Theseus raises a stone to take his father's sword: Roman terracotta relief, 2nd century AD. In the Arthurian legends, Arthur becomes king by drawing a magic sword from a stone, which in some versions is identified with his great sword Excalibur *Below* In alchemy the sword was a symbol of purifying fire; and when God drove Adam from the garden of Eden he placed an angel at the gate with 'a flaming sword which turned every way, to guard the way to the tree of life': detail from the Bedford Book of Hours

British Museum

Callum, the English *Bacca Pipes*, the Finnish *Skin Kompasse*, the Catalan *L'Hereu Riera*, and the Hungarian *Kanász Tánc*. Gillie Callum is now as popular among Scots in America as it is in Scotland, and women and children have been admitted as performers. The soloist follows a set routine to the traditional bagpipe music. With an elegant, erect carriage, and with extended arms and hands held to form a semi-circle, he lightly steps among the four spaces between the crossed sword and scabbard, executing a series of *jétes, pas de basques,* and other steps familiar to ballet dancers.

Combat mime by a pair of opponents or two opposing factions involves the use of metal or wooden weapons. Among primitive tribes the weapon is usually a spear, a long staff or a war club, as in the Bontoc and Igorot war dances of the Philippines. More advanced civilizations have used metal in the construction of swords. In China and Japan swords feature in stylized, theatrical presentations of warrior dances. In Europe (except for Scandinavia), Latin America and the Caribbean, swords of metal or wood serve as weapons in the Moriscas. Closely connected to these are the Dalmatian *Moreshka*, a battle mime between two factions involving elaborate formations, and the Portuguese *Mouriscada* featuring the combat between beautifully-dressed men and demonic masked dancers. In Spain and Mexico *Los Moros y Cristianos,* the Moors and the Christians, is a drama of combat, ending with the victory of the Christians. The obvious reference to the Crusades has been reinterpreted by scholars such as Cecil Sharp and Curt Sachs as a medieval version of an ancient, pagan vegetation rite, a battle between the seasons, with the inevitable victory of the good, warm season. The drama usually includes dialogue, always elaborate costuming and masking, sometimes even realistic additions such as horses. If the Christian group has a leader called Santiago (St James, patron saint of Christendom), it is termed *Santiagos.* The English Morris Dance, despite the similarity of its name, differs from the south European Moriscas in the extreme stylization, the absence of actual conflict or the clash between sticks in set patterns, and the presence of side actors portraying a death and resurrection theme (see MORRIS DANCES).

When Spanish missionaries taught

Moriscas to their converts in Latin America, they apparently received a warm welcome. And they were able to substitute these vegetation combat dramas for the indigenous Indian dramas. Today, in Mexico, most religious fiestas include Los Moros y Cristianos under various names. The male dance-actors have substituted medieval costumes and masks for their aboriginal outfits; they clash with swords, usually of wood, instead of the aboriginal war clubs; the words spoken in Spanish or their native tongue are about the victory of Christianity. But they dance in a way that is earthly, relaxed, and retentive of ancient native styles.

Such importations have taken root in other areas colonized by the Spanish: the Philippines, Trinidad, Peru, Bolivia. In Brazil they have mingled with Negroid styles, as in the Mocambique of Sao Paolo, for the agrarian saint, San Benito. Here, the swords have become sticks and the battle features complex, syncopated rhythms and African steps. In the course of the fray, the swords are not only weapons, they are also used as percussion instruments. In time with the musical accompaniment usually of flute and drum, metal swords clang rhythmically and wooden swords clash with a duller sound. In some areas, such as Papantla in eastern Mexico, excitement is intensified by the dancers' high-pitched, monotone yells, and by the stamping of feet. These martial sounds synchronize with the visual effects of encounter, retreat, and advance.

Geometric Patterns

Sword dances of western Europe lack the element of combat; they create excitement by the steady evolutions of geometric patterns and metric beat of drum and stepping. In this dance, swords are not weapons. They connect the male dancers, usually six, sometimes ten or more. In her book *Sword Dance and Drama* (1962) Violet Alford describes the link:

> It begins by each man grasping his hilt in his right hand and in his left taking the point of his neighbour's sword. A closed chain or ring is thus formed, a sword between each man and the next, and except for the weaving of broadswords at fixed moments into a pentagon, hexagon, or octagon according to the number of swords and dancers, it never comes undone until each figure is finished.

In this book Miss Alford points to the frequency of sword dances in mining regions, perhaps as magical cults of sword forgers. She supports this discovery by giving lists of mining sites, in which she includes, however, some sites that are salt mines, such as the one near Hallein, Austria. Some scholars, like the folklorist Douglas Kennedy, regard sword dances as vestiges of seasonal rites. Kennedy supports this theory by describing two aspects of death and resurrection, the symbolic killing of a captain or the Fool in an associated acting group, and the revival by a doctor (see FOLKPLAYS).

In Kennedy's book *England's Dances* he also suggests a further theory, of influenc from invading Norsemen. British swor dances are indeed concentrated in norther England, with long-sword dances in Danis Mercia (covering the present-day Midlands and Rapper Sword Dances in Northumbri (much of northern England). They ar further north than the Morris dances, and i distinct areas.

Elsewhere in Europe, hilt-and-poin sword dances abound in the mountainou regions of northern Spain and the Basqu provinces, and in the mountainous area of Austria. Everywhere the dances shar basic formations and types of costume an music, although regional differences ar often evident.

The dances usually progress in a sun wise circle or weave within a circle, bu the Flamborough Sword Dance straighten out into longways formations. The characte of the figures depends on the length of th swords. A ring-and-step usually start the dance, that is, a circling with a stead run, shifting the sword from shoulder t shoulder; this section concludes with foo tapping, 'stepping' in place, and sometime with a clash, that is, a meeting of the sword in a central pyramid. Afterwards follo evolutions such as the 'single-under' an 'double-under', in which the dancers i succession twist under the upraised swords the 'single-over' and 'double-over', in whic they successively step over the lowere swords; the 'roll' or 'waves', in which th parallel swords are successively raised an lowered and the dancers pass under an he basis of the sword's mystique is its fficiency as a killer combined with its use by a warrior elite in advanced societies, skilled in metallurgy and comparatively sophisticated echniques of war *Left* Effigy of a crusader: the word looked like a cross, it was wielded by hristian knights against the infidel, and its two dges could stand for truth and loyalty *Right* he triumphant Ottoman leader Mehmed II at he death of Uzun Hasan, ruler of northern Mesopotamia

ver; the 'reel' or circular hey with raised words; and 'threedling' with double over-ead arches. In the final, triumphant 'lock' he swords are linked into a star shape. Then the leader displays the star during epping, or the group wraps the lock around he neck of an attendant character and ircles clockwise in the 'rose'. This leads to he decapitation and to the resurrection hat follows.

Among the many variations, the dance gures at Dürrnberg near Hallein are parti-ularly ingenious. In addition to the basic ormations, they include symbolic presenta-ions of mining activities, along with hymed speeches by the sergeant. In the bridge' sequence the dancers stand in two parallel lines, with lowered swords. The ergeants step across and the files follow. or the shaft the dancers form a vault with heir raised swords; they conclude with a apid winding movement for the joyous eturn homeward.

Richard Wolfram, who has published many books and articles in German on the opic, considers these semi-realistic forma-ions recent inventions, superimposed on lder, basic patterns of sun-circling and nterweaving. He agrees with Kennedy that he probable origin was an ancient vegeta-ion cult, long preceding the first historical eference of 1398. He associates the custom ith pre-Christian brotherhood initiations, ince he has observed that these dances are lways performed by members from within a losed fraternity group.

In every setting, from village green to ymnasium, the well-performed versions f these dances continue to enchant the erformers and to captivate the audiences, ot only due to the skill and beauty of the xecution, but also thanks to a primordial nagic of intent and geometry.
See also DANCE; FOOL).

GERTRUDE KURATH

URTHER READING: For sword: H. R. Ellis Davidson, *The Sword in Anglo-Saxon England* (Oxford Univ. Press, 1962); R. E. Oakeshott, *The Archaeology of Weapons* Praeger, 1963). For sword dances: Violet Alford, *Sword Dance and Drama* (Dufour, 963); Violet Alford and Rodney Gallop, *The Traditional Dance* (Methuen, London, 935); Douglas Kennedy, *England's Dances* (Clarke, Irwin, 1949).

Sonia Halliday

is the role of religious symbols,' said [C.] G. Jung, 'to give a meaning to the life of [ma]n': it is increasingly suggested in the West [tha]t the lack of adequate symbols is part of [the] Western malaise

SYMBOLISM

'[T]HE GREAT function of symbols,' wrote [th]e distinguished German Protestant [th]eologian Paul Tillich, 'is to point beyond [th]emselves, in the power of that to which [th]ey point, to open up levels of reality which [ot]herwise are closed, and to open up levels [of] the human mind of which we otherwise [ar]e not aware.' There is no doubt that [m]an's tendency to see in everything around [hi]m intimations of a veiled reality, and to [pe]rform actions which are themselves [sy]mbolic, has played an immensely impor[ta]nt role in the history of religion and [m]agic, but the elucidation of symbols is a [hi]ghly precarious business. This is because [a] symbol is essentially an attempt to express [wh]at is otherwise inexpressible, which [m]eans that it cannot be expounded satis[fa]ctorily in words. The more powerful the [sy]mbol, the more this is so. Having caught [it] in your butterfly net, you can only display [it] with its wings spread out and a neat [cl]assificatory label underneath if you pop [it] in the killing bottle first. It is now un[fo]rtunately dead – it has lost the elusive [qu]ality which made you want to capture it [in] the first place.

Major religious symbols have about them [a] tantalizing vagueness or, put the other [w]ay round, a haunting richness, with an [ai]r of holding the key to a secret beyond [th]e grasp of rational intelligence. It is [b]ecause they are felt 'to open up levels of [re]ality which otherwise are closed' that [so]me Christian writers have suggested that [if] God has chosen to disclose himself to [m]an, symbols would be the natural vehicles [of] his revelation. Whether this is accepted [o]r not, it is at least impressive evidence [of] one of the cardinal facts about symbols (as [di]stinct from minor conventional signs, [li]ke trademarks or traffic lights), that the [im]pact they make on the mind is one of [re]cognition, not of invention. They are [fe]lt to be discovered, not devised.

What is discovered, however, may vary [co]nsiderably from one mind to another. [E]ven within the same broad tradition, a [sy]mbol will have different connotations for [di]fferent people (and even for the same person [a]t different times). A telling example is [pr]ovided by Mary Douglas in her book

Natural Symbols, in connection with the Roman Catholic rule of abstaining from meat on Fridays. This was originally a symbol of 'personal mortification, a small weekly celebration of the annual celebration of Good Friday. Thus it pointed directly to Calvary and Redemption.' Among sophisticated Catholics the rule is increasingly ignored and its symbolism regarded as empty. But the rule is strictly maintained by many Irish immigrants to England, in a country where they have no roots and often no relatives or friends. To them, abstaining from meat on Fridays is a vital symbol of 'allegiance to a humble home in Ireland and to a glorious tradition in Rome.'

Another factor which makes the interpretation of symbols difficult is the confusing variety of ways in which the symbolic is related to the real. A symbol, by definition, is not what it represents. It stands for, suggests, reveals to the mind a reality other than itself. But in practice the symbol is frequently treated as if it *is* what it represents. When someone insults the American flag in the United States, for example, the violence of the reaction provoked among some patriots suggests that what has been maltreated is not merely a piece of cloth but America itself. Both the culprit and the patriot know perfectly well that the flag is not the same as America, but represents it, but they also feel that in a more profound sense it is America that has been damaged, not just the piece of cloth.

This principle applies to much religious

Left Greek figure of the god Dionysus as a [yo]uth, holding a cock and an egg, symbols of [cr]eator and created, youth and age, death and [re]birth *Right* At the simplest level, the cross [m]erely represents the instrument of Christ's [de]ath, but it has a great wealth of symbolic [re]ferences, leading the mind on to the idea of [sa]crifice and suffering, resurrection, a burden [to] be borne, trust in God's will, reconciliation [be]tween God and man, reconciliation of [op]posites, the essential unity of all things: *[C]rucifixion*, by Antonello da Messina

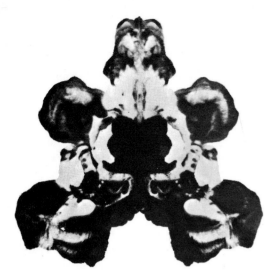

Practically everything of which human beings have become aware has been used as a symbol, but the same symbol will have different connotations for different people: the Rorschach test, devised by a Swiss psychiatrist, follows the principle of the child's inkblot game and takes the shapes, scenes and characters which you see in the blots as clues to your personality

and magical symbolism. When a sorcerer inflicts injuries on a puppet which represents his victim, he believes that he is inflicting the same injuries on the real body of the victim, and all imitative magic depends on the belief that the symbol of a thing *is* the thing (see IMITATIVE MAGIC).

Christ and the Host

The host, or communion wafer, is a symbol of Christ but when it has been properly consecrated in the Mass, it also *is* Christ. The Pope's Encyclical letter *Mysterium Fidei*, issued in 1965, observes that it is wrong 'to be so preoccupied with considering the nature of the sacramental sign that the impression is created that the symbolism – and no one denies its existence in the most holy Eucharist – expresses and exhausts the whole meaning of Christ's presence in this sacrament. Nor is it right to treat of the mystery of transubstantiation without mentioning the marvellous change of the whole of the bread's substance into Christ's body . . . Nor, finally, is it right to put forward and to give expression in practice to the view which maintains that Christ the Lord is no longer present in the consecrated hosts which are left over when the sacrifice of the Mass is over.'

On the other hand, there are many contexts in which the symbol is sharply distinguished from the reality, which it merely stands for. And between the two extremes is a large 'in between' area, in which the symbol is felt to be intimately connected with the reality without fully being it. Magical systems of correspondences, for instance, create links of this sort between symbols and realities (see CORRESPONDENCES). The Hungarian students who, in the uprising of 1956, hanged a bust of the Stalinist politician Matyas Rakosi from a lamp post, probably felt that they were doing something more effective than making a mere gesture of

defiance. Going back to the Eucharist for a moment, there is a whole range of responses from Christians of different denominations to the nature of Christ's presence in the sacrament, as being 'real' or 'spiritual' or 'merely symbolic' (see MASS; SACRAMENTS).

Practically everything of which human beings have become aware has been recognized somewhere by somebody as a symbol of something. Unusual events are treated as omens, signs of an underlying maladjustment of the order of Nature which will bring death or disaster. The rustling of trees, the fall of lots, the speech of a person in trance, the lines on a hand or the stars in the sky, are interpreted as symbols of the will of the gods or the pattern of fate (see DIVINATION; OMENS; ORACLES). Animals, plants, features of landscape, thunder and lightning, parts of the body, clothes, numbers, buildings and innumerable other objects are felt to have greater significance than appears on the surface. A rolling wheel may be a symbol of the sun or the course of the year, and the sun and the year themselves may be symbols of the divine. An early Christian writer, Hippolytus of Rome, said of Christ: 'He the Sun, once he had risen from the womb of the earth, showed the 12 Apostles to be as it were 12 hours . . . Once they were gathered together, the 12 Apostles like 12 months proclaimed the perfect year, Christ.'

In Green Pastures

People and their occupations may be symbols. Among the symbols associated with the pharaohs in Egypt were the herdsman and the shepherd. 'The functions of the state,' said Henri Frankfort (in *Before Philosophy*), 'were to own, control, drive, discipline, and defend; they were also to cherish, nurture, shelter, and enlarge the population. The god-sent controller of the Egyptian people was the herdsman who kept them in green pastures, fought to secure fresh pastures for them, drove off the voracious beasts who attacked them, belaboured the cattle who strayed out of line, and helped the weaklings.' He went on to point out that, 'The concept of the herdsman has its negative pole in the implication that men are simply cattle, property on a lower stage of existence.'

Similarly, the king could be thought of as a shepherd. The sun god had appointed him, 'to be shepherd of this land, to keep alive the people', watching by night and by day. One of the earliest emblems of Egyptian kings was the shepherd's crook. The imagery of the shepherd has also played an inspiring role in Judaism and Christianity. In the Old Testament God is a shepherd ('The Lord is my shepherd, I shall not want' – Psalm 23) and, in the New, Jesus says: 'I am the good shepherd . . . and I lay down my life for the sheep' (John, chapter 10). Christ or the Church or the priest cares for the 'flock' of humanity, including its 'black sheep', and the crosier, or pastoral staff, of a bishop, may be descended from a shepherd's crook and is an emblem of firmness and mercy, and of the authority that combines both these qualities (see also GOOD SHEPHERD; SHEEP).

Evocative and long-lived myths a[re] powerful symbols, stories which are f[e] to reveal otherwise inexpressible truth[s] Religious and magical rites and action[s] are symbols, ranging from an initiatio[n] ceremony in which the candidate symboli[c]ally dies and is reborn (see INITIATIO[N] to such simple gestures as the kiss [of] peace, the finger held to the lips as a sig[n] of silence, kneeling as a mark of humilit[y] standing as a mark of respect, sitting as [a] mark of authority, in the case of a king or [a] judge (see also GESTURE). But even [an] apparently simple gesture may have u[n] suspected depths. In Islam, prostration is a[n] expression of humility before God, but to t[he] Sufi mystics it is something much mor[e] meaning 'no less than extinction, a ritu[al] affirmation that there is no room in t[he] Divine Presence for more than the On[e] (see SUFIS).

The Key and the Net

Some symbols have a basic meani[ng] which is obvious enough and depends o[n] some evident resemblance or analog[y] though many will see deeper significan[ce] below the surface. Inverted symbols, f[or] example, things which are upside dow[n] backwards, the wrong way round, are gene[r]ally connected with evil, black magic an[d] witchcraft because they reverse accepte[d] standards of what is good. To turn a cruci[fix] upside down, with deliberate intent, is [to] state allegiance to God's adversary, t[he] Devil. A key opens a lock and so it stand[s] for access to some spiritual truth or co[n]dition. In Christian art St Peter is show[n] with the keys of heaven as a sign of t[he] authority and function which Jesus conferre[d] on him (Matthew 16.19). More broadl[y] a key may be a symbol of the longing for G[od] which opens the door of Christian hop[e] More broadly still, it may be a key of wisdo[m] or eternal life, of initiation, of entrance in[to] mysteries (see HOUSE). A net is an obviou[s] image of entanglement, of difficulties an[d] snares. It appears in the book of Ezeki[el] as a weapon in the hand of God, who w[ill] throw a net over an offender and entrap hi[m] But also in Ezekiel, and in the New Testa[ment], the net is connected with fishin[g] and in Christian symbolism it is linked wi[th] the apostles and their successors as fishe[rs] of men, the Pope is called the Fisherman.

Other symbols are not approached s[o] simply (or deceptively simply). Receptacle[s] are, in general, symbols of woman, f[or] obvious reasons, but they are readi[ly] spiritualized: one of the emblems of t[he] Virgin Mary, for instance, is a golden vas[e] filled with white lilies (for purity). The cu[p] is a female sex symbol but it also carrie[s] connotations of nourishment and abu[n]dance. When it becomes the cup of t[he] Eucharist, and still more when it become[s]

A dream-like painting by Chagall, *Time is [a] River without Banks*: both the Freudian an[d] Jungian schools of psychoanalysis treat t[he] scenes and images which appear in dreams [as] symbols which reveal unconscious mental pr[o]cesses, and Jungian methods of interpretatio[n] relate them to symbols in alchemy, myth[s] legends and folktales

the Grail, it has clearly far transcended its simple anatomical reference (see GRAIL).

One of the functions of a symbol is to act as what has been called 'a rallying point for meaning'. Through it the mind connects together several meanings which are not outwardly or immediately connected. Mircea Eliade cites as an example the symbolism of the moon, which links together the moon's changing cycle in the sky, the rhythms and cycles of life on earth, woman, the waters, death and rebirth, and human destiny (see MOON). 'The symbol is capable of revealing a perspective in which diverse realities can be fitted together or even integrated into a system.' This is why symbols are used in meditation, in many traditions, to lead the mind on to the

realization of unsuspected truths or aspects of truth.

The Christian cross, at the simplest level, merely represents the cross on which Jesus died, but it has a great wealth and variety of symbolic references. The mind which dwells on it may be led on to ideas, among others, of death, suffering, sacrifice, resurrection, of a crisis to be endured or a burden to be borne, of God's love, of trust in God's will, of the reconciliation of God and man, the reconciliation of opposites, the unity of all things (see CROSS).

The cross can lead on towards the symbolism of the centre. The directions of east, west, north and south have their own symbolism, as do left and right (see DIRECTIONS), and up and down are naturally connected with

ideas of progress and decline, superiori and inferiority, good and evil, heaven i the sky and hell underground (see SK STEPS). The cross on which Christ die can be thought of as an emblem whic connects the directions and the centre, an in Christian tradition it was erected at th centre of the world. The cross was als thought of as a tree, and in various myth a great tree is the *axis mundi*, 'axis of th world', its trunk connecting the underworl the earth and the sky, and affording a mear of communication between the differer levels. The tree reconciles the opposites sky and earth, 'above' and 'below', Christ's death on the glory tree made possible for men below to be reconciled wit God above. (Or the tree may be an *imag mundi,* a diagram of the world, as it is i the Cabala — see CABALA; TREES.)

A sacred mountain is sometimes though to stand at the centre of the world, i 'roots', so to speak, beneath the surfac and its summit in the sky. The Hind heavens are located in a 'divine enclosure said to lie somewhere north of the Himalaya at the centre of which, marking the cent of the universe, is Mt Meru, a towering pea of pure gold, round which the heaven bodies revolve. Alternatively, a shrine city may be said to stand at the navel centre of the earth, and sites where th divine is believed to have revealed itse become sacred 'centres', places whe communication is possible between differer levels of existence, between men and th gods, or the living and the dead (se MOUNTAIN; NAVEL; PILGRIMAGE).

In myths, legends and folktales a templ a palace, a castle, may be a centre in whic is concealed a secret goal of overwhelmir importance, a holy of holies, the Grail, th enchanted princess, the treasure hoard. maze contains a hidden centre, the way which is hard to find, but in reaching th heart of the labyrinth a man penetrate perhaps to the Heavenly Jerusalem, pe haps to the underworld, perhaps to th innermost recesses of his own being (se MAZE). It is interesting that a map Christian's journey in *Pilgrim's Progres* reproduced earlier (page 2147), show his path as a spiral, circling in from th periphery to the Celestial City at the centr suggesting a journey inwards.

The Hero Within

That symbols illuminate the world withi us, whether or not they reveal the wor without, is one of the answers to the vie which regards a symbol as at best unimpor tant and at worst undesirable, because stands in place of a reality instead of bein the reality itself. In practice, as suggeste above, important symbols are not treate as reality substitutes but as things close connected with a reality which could not approached without them. In many societie outside the West symbols and symbol actions are essential ingredients of huma understanding of, and relationships wit reality, including relationships with th human as well as the sacred (see, f instance, MENSTRUATION; RITES C PASSAGE; RITUAL). In the West, it

increasingly suggested that a lack of adequate symbols is part of the modern malaise.

For example, in his last book, *Man and His Symbols,* C. G. Jung said: 'It is the role of religious symbols to give a meaning to the life of man. The Pueblo Indians believe that they are the sons of Father Sun, and this belief endows their life with a perspective (and a goal) that goes far beyond their limited existence. It gives them ample space for the unfolding of personality and permits them a full life as complete persons. Their plight is infinitely more satisfactory than that of a man in our own civilization who knows that he is (and will remain) nothing more than an underdog with no inner meaning to his life . . .

'Today, for instance, we talk of "matter". We describe its physical properties. We conduct laboratory experiments to demonstrate some of its aspects. But the word "matter" remains a dry, inhuman, and purely intellectual concept, without any psychic significance for us. How different was the former image of matter – the Great Mother – that could encompass and express the profound emotional meaning of Mother Earth. In the same way, what was the spirit is now identified with intellect and thus ceases to be the Father of All. It has degenerated to the limited ego-thoughts of man; the immense emotional energy expressed in the image of "our Father" vanishes into the sand of an intellectual desert.'

Both the Freudian and Jungian schools of psychoanalysis maintain that the scenes and images which the mind throws up into consciousness, especially in dreams, may begin to make sense if treated, not at their face value, but as symbols which reveal unconscious mental processes. Jungian methods of interpretation relate these scenes and images to symbols in alchemy and in myths, legend and folktales from all over the world. Common features in numerous hero legends, for instance, suggest that the myth of the hero is really about the process of psychologically growing up. 'In the developing consciousness of the individual the hero figure is the symbol by which the emerging ego overcomes the inertia of the unconscious mind, and liberates the mature man from a regressive longing to return to the blissful state of infancy in a world dominated by his mother' (this and following quotes are from Joseph L. Henderson's essay in *Man and His Symbols*).

The 'tutelary' figure often found presiding over the upbringing and education of the hero (the centaur Chiron who taught

Louvre/Hamlyn Group Library

Left Jung believed that alchemical symbolism expressed ageless realities of the human mind and that the alchemists were exploring their own innermost depths: symbols of alchemy and science mingled on the title page of Athanasius Kircher's *Ars Magna Lucis et Umbrae,* 1671 *Above right* Rembrandt's *Philosopher with an Open Book* suggests the light of illumination penetrating the darkness of ignorance, and the spiral stairs recall the alchemical motif of a return to the womb as a penetration of the recesses of the self

Achilles, for example, or Merlin in the case of Arthur) becomes on this view a symbolic representation of the 'whole psyche, the larger and more comprehensive identity that supplies the strength that the personal ego lacks', and his role in the story suggests that 'the essential function of the heroic myth is the development of the individual's ego-consciousness – in a manner that will equip him for the arduous tasks with which life confronts him.'

When the hero does battle with dragons, monsters and evil beings, he is really in combat with his own 'regressive' trends, with the dark and negative side of his personality, with the shadow in himself. When he rescues a beautiful girl from danger – the damsel in distress theme – he is really liberating his own 'anima', the female component in his being (a woman's male component is the 'animus'). The hero eventually falls, betrayed or sacrificed, because 'the human ego can be exalted to experience godlike attributes, but only at the cost of over-reaching itself and falling to disaster' (a theme which many who are not Jungians have seen in the story of Adam and Eve, or in the Faust legend, and which flourishes in science fiction).

The hero myth, on this interpretation, is concerned with individuation, the process of becoming a 'whole person', which has parallels in the processes of alchemy and magic, where the attempt is made to find the true inner self and expand it, as it were, into the whole man, who is the divine man (see ALCHEMY; MAGIC).

The Jungian approach has been criticised on various grounds, among them that it involves talking about 'the' hero myth, when in fact there are many hero myths, which have to be stretched or lopped on a bed of Procrustes to fit them into the desired pattern, and similarly with other types of myth; and that it equally blurs the different meanings which people recognize in the same myth or symbol. The archetypes, or symbolic figures and patterns which the Jungians identify, do not appear as regularly as Jungians maintain; and when they do, they may be more easily explained as images drawn from the ordinary conscious experience of humanity than as images from the unconscious.

The Collective Unconscious

Jung explained the appearance of the same themes over and over again by locating them in the 'collective unconscious', but it was difficult to explain how this reservoir of images, if it exists, is transmitted from one generation to the next. In *Man and His Symbols* Jung suggested that the human mind has a tendency to form symbolic representations of a motif, 'representations that can vary a great deal in detail without losing their basic pattern', and that this tendency is 'an instinctive *trend,* as marked as the impulse of birds to build nests . . .'

Common themes and symbols in different societies can no doubt often be explained as the result of common human tendencies and common human experience, but

Symbolism

The dignity of work, strength in unity, rejection of war and desire for peace – these concepts are symbolized in a Victorian trade union membership certificate

symbols can also be seen migrating from one culture and religion to another. Obvious examples are Old Testament symbols which were adopted and adapted by the early Christians. In the Old Testament God is the Father, as he remained in Christianity, and he is king, judge and shepherd, which all became symbolic roles of Christ. He is also the cultivator of vines, which are his people ('My beloved had a vineyard on a very fertile hill' – Isaiah, chapter 5). Ignatius of Antioch, expanding on the theme in the 2nd century, said: 'Christ the tree of life . . . has the Apostles for branches, the redeemed for fruit, words for leaves; baptism is the root, and the Father, the gardener.' In St John's gospel again, Jesus is 'the bread of life' (chapter 6), referring back to the manna on which the Israelites fed in the wilderness, and this symbolism became linked with the host in the Mass.

The Christians saw figures and events in the Old Testament as 'types', or symbolic foreshadowings, of Christian figures and events. Jonah emerging from the belly of the whale, for example, was a type of Christ's resurrection from the dead (see JONAH). And, in one of the supreme examples, Christ was identified with the 'suffering servant' of Isaiah (chapter 53): 'He was despised and rejected by men; a man of sorrows, and acquainted with grief . . . upon him was the chastisement that made us whole and with his stripes we are healed.'

(See also numerous other articles, including ALPHABET; BODY; BURIAL; CIRCLE; COLOURS; DREAMS; ICONOGRAPHY; LANDSCAPE SYMBOLISM; MANDALA; PHALLIC SYMBOLISM).

RICHARD CAVENDISH

FURTHER READING: J. E. Cirlot, *A Dictionary of Symbols* (Philosophical Library, 1962); Mary Douglas, *Natural Symbols* (Pantheon Books, 1970); Mircea Eliade, *Patterns in Comparative Religion* (World Publishing, 1958); G. Ferguson, *Signs and Symbols in Christian Art* (Oxford Univ. Press, 1966 reprint); C. G. Jung ed, *Man and His Symbols* (Dell, 1968).

Sympathetic Magic

Term coined by Sir James Frazer, in *The Golden Bough* for the principle that 'things act on each other at a distance through a secret sympathy'; combining two basic assumptions of magical thinking, the principle of mimicry, 'that like produces like, or that an effect resembles its cause', and the law of contact, 'that things which have once been in contact with each other contrive to act on each other at a distance after the physical contact has been severed.'

See IMITATIVE MAGIC.

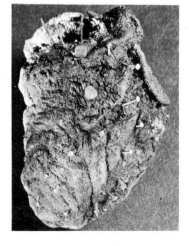

Syncretism

The mingling in one religious system of elements drawn from different systems: for example, the blending of cults in the Roman Empire as Eastern religions spread to the West and gods of different regions were identified with each other; or the blending of Egyptian, Greek, Christian and other elements in Gnosticism; or the mingling of eastern and western ideas in some modern occult systems.

The great bull god El and the dying and rising god Baal, with his consort Anat, were worshipped in rites which were ceaselessly denounced by the Old Testament prophets; yet nevertheless, their pagan temples withstood Syria's official adoption of Christianity

SYRIA AND PALESTINE

THE FULLEST contemporary record of religion in Syria is the texts in alphabetic cuneiform from ancient Ugarit, Ras Shamra, about 12 miles north of Latakkia and two miles from the coast. Theophoric names (personal name including in its form a divine name) as in the Egyptian Execration texts, lists of offerings to various gods, ritual texts, incidental references in legends and above all myths of the fertility cult illustrate the religion of Syria in the 14th century BC. The many gods, both Semitic and non-Semitic, reflect the mixed population of this city in north Syria, but only the cult of the fertility god Baal (see BAAL) and the goddess Anat and their associates is documented sufficiently to permit a reconstruction of the cult.

From these texts we learn that the senior god was El ('god'), the King Paramount, Father of the Exalted Ones and Father of Men and Creator, depicted as enthroned at the remote 'source of the streams'. His strength and procreative influence is expressed in his title 'the Bull', but he was the principal god in social relationships, and this aspect of his character is expressed by his title, 'the Kindly, the Compassionate'.

El's executive king is Baal, whose proper name was Hadad ('the Thunderer') or Baal Ramman ('the Thunderer'), which Jewish scribes parodied as Rimmon ('pomegranate'). He establishes his kingly power and order in Nature in a primeval conflict with Sea-and-Ocean Currents and associated monsters like Letan (Leviathan of the Old Testament) and Tannin, also

Goats figure frequently in the religious art of western Asia: he-goat in a thicket, in gold and lapis lazuli, from Ur in Mesopotamia, the city which Abraham, the Jewish patriarch, left to settle in Canaan

known in this connection in the Old Testament, and has his 'house' built as a visible token that he is the reigning king. He is obliged, however, to reassert his kingship in a seasonal conflict against Sterility, or Death (Mot) in a myth which is believed to be related to the chief seasonal crisis in Syria, at the autumn equinox.

The Fertility Cult

In this myth Baal is the god of thunder, lightning and winter rains, 'He who Mounts the Clouds', and is, like the Mesopotamian Tammuz, a dying and rising god, whose fortunes fluctuate with the vegetation he promotes (see DYING GOD). In his eclipse in the summer season his sister and consort Anat (the north Syrian counterpart of Astarte; see ASTARTE) is particularly active. Baal, as the vegetation he promotes, succumbs to Mot. His dead body is sought over hill and dale by Anat, called in the Ras Shamra texts 'the Virgin Anat', a rite which had its counterpart in the fertility cult throughout the Near East (see APHRODITE; DEMETER; OSIRIS; TAMMUZ). There is definite reflection of the mourning of Anat on the recovery and burial of the body of Baal in the Old Testament (Zechariah 12.11) in 'the mourning for Hadad-Rimmon in the plain of Megiddo'. Anat proceeds to avenge Baal. She cuts down Mot, winnows him, parches him with fire, grinds him with a millstone and scatters his remains in the fields for the birds to eat. This obviously relates to the desacralization of the new crop, setting it free for common use, as in the offering of the first sheaf of 'new grain from fresh ears, parched with fire,' in Leviticus 2.14.

In myth related to ritual strict logical consistency is not expected, and Baal revives. His revival is anticipated in a dream by El, who is the final authority in these texts and intervenes at significant junctures to confirm a decision or to foreshadow the future. El's vision is of the skies raining olive oil and the wadis running with honey, which recurs in the liturgies of Israel reflected in Amos 9.13 and Joel 3.18. With similar lack of consistency Mot is introduced in a final 'showdown' with Baal, out of which Baal emerges victor and again vindicates his kingship. This conflict is set 'in the seventh year' and may be related to the seven-year cycle marked in Israel by an artificial famine, when the land lay fallow on the principle that drought must be given full play in order that its force might be exhausted. Thus in the seasonal tension after the long dry summer, pending the coming of the 'early rains', the Syrian peasant relieved his anxiety and predisposed providence by homoeopathic magic, which was the genesis of drama in Greece in the cult of the wine god Dionysus at Athens. In Syria no such dramas are attested, but all the elements of drama are in the Baal myth.

The Canaanite mother goddess Athirat or Ashera, was probably a form of the Mesopotamian goddess Ishtar, shown with a palm tree on this Assyrian seal: the fertility rites of Canaan were fiercely denounced by the Old Testament prophets

It will be seen that Israel inherited the liturgic theme of the great autumn festival which she developed in the light of her own historical tradition of the great deliverance from Egypt and the Covenant, but the essential features of the seasonal festival survive conflict with the forces of destruction and disorder, the demonstration of the effective kingship of God and the establishment of his government, often by judgement. This is expressed notably in the Enthronement psalms in the Old Testament, in passages in the Prophets which reflect this liturgic theme and in passages on the Day of the Lord in Jewish and Christian apocalyptic, for example, Revelation. There the sea and certain sea monsters are arch-enemies of God's ordered government, as in the Baal myth of Ras Shamra in the New Year festival in Canaan.

The role of the king in his sacral function as executive of Baal as the Divine King in his 'passion' and triumph in the great autumn festival cannot be established on the evidence of the Ras Shamra texts, but on the analogy of the corresponding occasion in Mesopotamian religion it is likely. With the necessary changes, it may certainly be demonstrated that in Jerusalem the Davidic king was the temporal guarantee of the effective Kingship of God, which was expressed in the liturgy of the great autumn festival. For Canaan Ezekiel's denunciation of the King of Tyre (chapter 28) expresses the conception of the king as the representative of God, the channel of divine blessings, and, as representative of the community, the royal man in the garden of God. The Legend of King Krt at Ras Shamra speaks of the king as 'the son of El', and the crown prince is 'suckled by the fertility goddesses Anat and Athirat'. The conception of the king as the upholder of the social justice which is the concern of God is expressed in the royal texts from Ras Shamra and, as in Psalm 72 and Isaiah 11.1–9, he is the medium of blessings in Nature. It is not difficult to see here an ideology from which the conception of the Messiah in Israel developed.

The protagonists of this cult are well known through texts, sculpture and figurines. Baal is the active young warrior god, El is an elderly god on his throne and footstool, both being associated with the bull in virtue of procreative interests. Anat, like Astarte in the Old Testament, is the goddess of love and appears naked in moulded reliefs and pendants, either devoted to shrines or given in return for the payment of a vow and used as amulets to promote childbirth. Sexual rites of imitative magic associated with the Canaanite fertility cult survived in Israel and are constantly denounced by the Prophets. Anat was also the goddess of war like Ishtar in Mesopotamia, and is involved in what is evidently a bloody massacre in her temple in an episode in the Baal myth at Ras Shamra, which may really describe a blood-letting rite, like the self-laceration of the devotees of Baal at Carmel (1 Kings 18.28), or perhaps circumcision. The mother goddess Athirat (Ashera of the Old Testament) appears as the consort of El and is probably the goddess represented as the nourisher of life who offers ears of corn to

Michael Holford

Bronze figures of Canaanite gods, thought to be El (*left*) and Baal (*right*): El was the paramount deity, father of gods and men, the kindly and compassionate; Baal, god of storm and the winter rains, was a dying and rising god, linked with the seasonal death and rebirth of vegetation; both El and Baal were associated with the bull

two rampant caprids (goats) on an ivory relief from the seaward quarter of Ugarit. The motif is a development of the rampant caprids reaching up to the fruit of the Tree of Life, which is familiar throughout the Near East. In the references in the Old Testament to the *ashera* as a feature of sanctuaries this is a tree, either natural or stylized, representing the mother goddess Ashera as the receptive element in Nature and as the universal nourisher. The Tree of Life is closely associated in the ancient Near East with the king in his sacral function as mediator of the divine blessing, as in Assyrian sculpture and on the royal couch from the palace of Ras Shamra.

The Will of the Gods

Significant as the fertility cult of Canaan undoubtedly was, it is possible that the dramatic nature of the Baal myth gives an incomplete picture of the actual situation. In royal legends for instance, in dynastic succession and other historical and social situations the predominant deity is not Baal but El, to whom chiefly sacrifice is made in a fast-liturgy on the occasion of a national emergency. This and a certain text from Ras Shamra containing oaths by certain attributes of El indicate a more spiritual conception of El, which is nearer to the Hebrew conception of God.

Among many other deities in Canaanite religion Dagan, the god of corn (*dagon*), is known at Ras Shamra from offering lists, from Baal's stock epithet 'the Son of Dagan', and from dedication inscriptions on stelae

from a temple adjoining that of Baal at Ras Shamra, which dates from c 2000 BC. Reshef was the god who slew men by war and plague. He is known from Egyptian sculpture and may be recognized in bronze figurines of a striding warrior with offensive weapon and shield, well known from archeological sites in Syria and Palestine. In one of the Ras Shamra texts he is called Reshef of the Arrow, and in the Graeco-Roman period he was assimilated to Apollo with his pestilential arrows. From later inscriptions from Sidon, Eshmun is known as the god of healing, assimilated to Asclepius in the Graeco-Roman period, as Baal was to Hercules, by whose labours also order was sustained against the constant menace of chaos. The sun, regarded as a goddess, is a minor figure in the Baal myth of Ras Shamra, and the moon god and his consort Nikkal were also worshipped, particularly at Harran in north-west Mesopotamia, and in north Syria (see HARRANIAN RELIGION). Ritual texts from Ras Shamra indicate that special rites and sacrifices, in which the king was involved, were observed at certain days of the month, probably at lunar phases.

The will of the various gods was consulted and communicated in various ways. In the 2nd century AD, Lucian of Samosata mentions oracles according to the movement of statues of the gods, doubtless at the manipulation of priests in response to specific questions, conveying a simple 'Yes' or 'No', like the sacred lots Urim and Thummim in early Israel. Divination by the entrails of sacrificed animals was also practised, the liver being especially significant, as is indicated by clay models from archeological sites, charted and annotated for consultation or instruction. The medieval Arab writer Ibn an-Nadim mentions divination at Harran by the direction of the gaze or the expression in the eyes of the dying victim. Texts from the Amorite city of Mari on the mid-Euphrates mention diviners who consulted the auspices in this way and communicated their findings to the king in matters of ritual or state. There were also communications by ecstatic devotees, who suggest 'the sons of the prophets' in the Old Testament and dervishes of later Islam.

At Byblos c1100 BC there is an instance of the will of the god communicated to the king in an affair of state by an ecstatic of his household and considered authentic by the king. The account of the distress of King Saul before his last battle (1 Samuel 28) mentions prophets and dreams as the media of the communication of the will of God in a crisis, and the patriarchal narratives in the Old Testament and the passage in the Baal myth where El sees the revival of Baal in a dream indicate the significance attached to dreams as communications of the will of God in future events or on the

significance of the present situation. People would often resort to shrines in ritual incubation when dreams were taken as sure communications of the purpose of the god.

The temple in Syria varied in form, but the general conception was a large area within the sacred precinct in which the temple proper was the focal feature. This conception is best illustrated in the sanctuary of Bel, or Baal, in the early Roman period at Palmyra in the Syrian desert and the Moslem sacred precinct at Jerusalem. At Ras Shamra and Hazor in the 14th–13th centuries BC, the tripartite temple is known, comprising an outer court with a great altar, shallow vestibule, main nave and inmost shrine, or 'Holy of Holies'. This is the plan of Solomon's Temple at Jerusalem, which was constructed by Phoenician craftsmen. Administrative texts from Ras Shamra attest hereditary office in a large number of professions among temple personnel, priests, votaries both male and female, temple prostitutes, singers, makers of sacred vestments, sculptors, potters, launderers, slaughterers, augurers, or possibly Temple herdsmen, and merchants who traded on account of the Temple. The king of course was the supreme priest, though except on special occasions he would delegate his duties.

Sacrifice of the Infants

The myths and legends of Ras Shamra in their fuller context amplify the simple listing of various types of sacrifice in the offering lists. Thus from the description

Left Statue of Baal Hammon, the principal god of Carthage, the Phoenician colony in North Africa: the name Hammon may derive from Ammon, god of the Siwa oasis in Libya; 1st century AD, from Tunisia *Below right* Ruins of a temple of Baal in Tunisia *Above right* Roman ruins at Palmyra in Syria, where the moon god was venerated by the caravan merchants

Tyrian colony of Carthage (see PHOENI-CIANS), in Punic inscriptions and in the writings of the African Church father Tertullian (3rd century AD). Those may have been first-born children dedicated thus as firstlings, but in King Mesha's sacrifice of his eldest son (2 Kings 3), like those in Judah in the latter period of the kingdom, they may have been sacrifices in extremity, to which Philo of Byblos (64–161 AD) alludes. Other cases, such as that which Diodorus Siculus attributes to the Carthaginians in Sicily after a victory over the Greeks in 307 BC, may be a case of 'death-devotion' (*herem*), a great act of renunciation of the spoils of war, to which King Mesha also refers in his inscription recording his war of liberation from Israel (c 835 BC). The sacrifices would thus correspond to Samuel's 'hewing Agag in pieces before the Lord' (1 Samuel 15.33).

The Dead and the Afterlife

Besides the commemoration of the dead as recipients of the divine favour ritual texts from Ras Shamra refer to the family god ('*il 'ib*), certain of these alluding to 'offerings at the aperture of the divine ancestor'. This is amplified by the discovery of grave-installations of such apertures as pipes or bottomless jars to communicate offerings, especially libations, to the defunct, probably to promote fertility of the earth, over which the dead were believed to have some influence. Such offerings to the dead may be the substance of the ban on offerings of a portion of the harvest to the dead in Deuteronomy 26.14. The dead were termed *repa'im* by the Phoenicians as in Israel, the name for the 'weak' shades in the Old Testament, and were possibly referred to in funerary inscriptions of King Tabnith of Sidon (5th century BC) as 'divine', or at least supernatural, as in the passage on King Saul and the Witch of Endor (1 Samuel 28.13), where the shade of Samuel is described as 'a god'. In this case the king sought revelation of the future.

As recipients of offerings, givers of fertility and revealers of the future, the departed in ancient Syria were regarded as not quite defunct. The Aramaean king Panammu in his inscription (c 750 BC) expects his descendants to invoke him when they make an offering to Baal, so that 'his soul may eat and drink with Baal'. The existence of the shade in the gloomy underworld is familiar in the Old Testament, particularly in Job chapter 3. Though quite undesirable this was apparently still an existence, however insubstantial, and this attenuated life was sustained by offerings, particularly libations, though one of the more recently discovered texts from Ras Shamra refers to animal sacrifice 'for the life of the family god', or the divine ancestor. The belief in

Sonia Halliday

of the duties of the son and heir of the king in the royal legend of Prince Aqhat at Ras Shamra it is known that communion meals were eaten in the sanctuary. The blood and vitals were offered to the god, and the rest was cooked and eaten by the community, thus effecting solidarity of the participants with the god and with one another. The shrine might also house memorials of the ancestors of the community, represented by standing stones, as in the Canaanite sanctuary of Hazor, and probably also at Gezer. By offerings at this tangible token of a favoured ancestor the community hoped to continue to share in the blessing which had been his.

Besides communion sacrifices there were those that were offered wholly to the

gods either as food or as an act of total renunciation on the part of the worshipper, being wholly burnt on the altar; and other such offerings were made for purification, as doves were sacrificed in Israel after childbirth, and as firstlings of crop and flock and of game in hunting. In Israel and among the Carthaginians in North Africa animals were sacrificed in redemption of first-born sons, and this was almost certainly done also in Syria.

Archeological evidence has been claimed from Gezer and Tell al-Fara by Nablus for foundation sacrifice of children, but this is disputed. Multiple infant sacrifice, however, is attested by jars full of calcined bones of infants and young animals from the sanctuary of the fertility goddess Tanit at the

Alan Irvine

Sonia Halliday

this insubstantial life of the dead who require to be revived by libation survives among Arab peasants in Syria and Palestine, who believe that the dead come at dusk to wells, springs and rivers to drink; however, this was but a tenuous existence. In the Legend of Prince Aqhat in the Ras Shamra texts occurs the passage:

As for mortal man, what does he get as his
    latter end?
What does mortal man get as his inheritance?
Glaze will be poured out on my head,
Even plaster on my pate,
And the death of all men will I die,
Yea I shall surely die.

These lines express the typical view of the afterlife in ancient Canaan.

Incantations and Amulets

Apart from the regular cults, men in Syria, as elsewhere and at all times, sought to enlist the powers of the supernatural or to ward off their evil influences by charms and amulets. Prophylactic charms in Aramaic are known, and at least one excerpt from the Baal myth of Ras Shamra was probably used as an aphrodisiac charm. The figurines of the nude fertility goddess were probably also used to promote procreation and childbirth. Besides, a great number of amulets have been found in excavations. Those are chiefly Egyptian, the cat and the intelligent ape, the hippopotamus, which was both a sinister force to be placated as the representative of chaos or, in the form of an upright female, a beneficent patroness of mothers.

The grotesque dwarf Bes, the protector of children and pregnant women was also popular. From the Egyptian cult of the fertility god Osiris, the goddess Isis and their son Horus, who survived a hazardous infancy to avenge Osiris' death (see HORUS), small images of the infant Horus were favourite amulets, and also the 'Eye of Horus' with its fertilizing tear-drops. Small gold flies and other insects resembling lice, which were found by Sir Flinders Petrie at a site at the mouth of the Wadi Ghazzeh in Palestine, may have had a prophylactic purpose to ward off disease, like the gold mice referred to in 1 Samuel 6.4, which were sent back with the ark by the Philistines.

In describing the religion of Syria the documents of Ras Shamra have been taken as the basis of this account, firstly because they are a contemporary statement, the fullest and most reliable that is available, and secondly because they document the fertility cult, which was the most conspicuous aspect of local religion that impressed Israel as she settled in Palestine. Ugarit, however, was but one city state in Syria, and in the history of the land it is notable that, despite a general community

In the Graeco-Roman period the Canaanite gods were identified with classical deities: coins of the 2nd century AD show Baal (*top left*) who was assimilated to Hercules; Eshmun (*top right*) the god of healing, with twin serpents, assimilated to Asclepius; the sea (*bottom left*) assimilated to Poseidon, the city god of Beirut; the sanctuary of Byblos (*bottom right*)

of religion in any given period, there were local variations and different emphases. So too over the long period of paganism until Christianity was established as the faith of the majority (c 500 AD), different variations of the old religion developed through time and in different localities.

The Blood of Adonis

In the settled land the old gods were assimilated to the gods of Greece and Rome, as Baal to Zeus the sky god with his thunderbolt, the fertility goddesses Astarte, Anat, and Ashera to Aphrodite and Juno. Baal in his role as a dying and rising vegetation god was assimilated to Adonis, the lover of Aphrodite, or Venus, but retained his Syrian title Adonis ('lord'); their cult was practised at the source of the River Adonis just south of Beirut. When it ran red, as it did at a certain time in summer, it was considered to be discoloured by the blood of Adonis, who was lamented at that time by the Syrian women. Baal, the divine king who must always struggle to vindicate his kinship and order against the forces of chaos, was assimilated to the labouring Hercules, particularly at Tyre and her colonies in the coastal plain of Palestine south of Jaffa. The god Reshef, with his power of life and death, was assimilated to Apollo with his bow and arrows as plague-shafts, and Anat the goddess of love and war was assimilated to Athene and Minerva. The sea was assimilated to Poseidon, who appears as the city god of Beirut on coins from the Graeco-Roman period, and the healing god Eshmun to Asclepius with his serpents. The latter was particularly venerated at Sidon, judging from the name Eshmunazzar, which was borne by two kings of Sidon.

In the caravan city of Palmyra, between Damascus and the Euphrates, the needs of the caravan merchants in the first three centuries of the Christian era are indicated by the cult of the moon, which was also venerated at Harran, another great caravan city in north Mesopotamia. The moon had evidently a peculiar significance for those merchants and their distant and protracted enterprises. The Venus star Athtar, the brightest star in those latitudes, the first to rise at evening and the last to disappear in the morning, was also greatly venerated at Palmyra, where as two gods Arsu and Azizu ('the Gracious and the Fierce') they are represented as mounted respectively on a camel and a horse.

Christianity did not easily oust the Nature religion of Syria, even after it became the official religion of the Roman Empire. Indeed when Porphyry the Bishop Elect of Gaza went to his see at the end of the 4th century AD the lusty heathen impeded his journey; and according to his deacon and biographer, there were eight pagan temples and many private shrines in Gaza and only 280 Christians out of between 50,000 and 60,000 inhabitants, and that after an Imperial edict against paganism.

JOHN GRAY

FURTHER READING: John Gray, *The Canaanites* (Praeger, 1964); *Near Eastern Mythology* (Paul Hamlyn, London, 1970).

British Museum

Table Turning
Or table tilting, a popular method of communicating with 'spirits'; the table tilts up and raps on the floor with its foot in response to questions, without being consciously pushed by the experimenters, who rest their fingers on it.
See OUIJA BOARDS.

Rules of behaviour which govern the human uses of things and people, taboos are not isolated restrictions; they are always part of a whole system and cannot be understood outside their social context

TABOO

TABOO (sometimes spelt tabu) is a ban or prohibition; the word comes from the Polynesian languages where it means a religious restriction, to break which would entail some automatic punishment. As it is used in English, taboo has little to do with religion. In essence it generally implies a rule which has no meaning, or one which cannot be explained. Captain Cook noted in his log-book that in Tahiti the women were never allowed to eat with the men, and as the men nevertheless enjoyed female company he asked the reason for this taboo. They always replied that they observed it because it was right. To the outsider the taboo is irrational, to the believer its rightness needs no explaining. Though supernatural punishments may not be expected to follow, the rules of any religion rate as taboos to outsiders. For example, the strict Jewish observance forbids the faithful to make and refuel the fire, or light lamps or put them out during the Sabbath, and it also forbids them to ask a Gentile to perform any of these acts. In his book *A Soho Address*, Chaim Lewis, the son of poor Russian Jewish immigrants in London's Soho at the beginning of this century, describes his father's quandary every winter Sabbath: he did not want to let the fire go out and he could not ask any favour outright. Somehow he had to call in a passerby and drop oblique hints until the stranger understood what service was required. Taboos always tend to land their observers in just such a ridiculous situation, whether it is a Catholic peasant of the Landes who abstains from meat on Friday but eats teal (a bird whose fishy diet entitles it in their custom to be counted as fish), or a Maori hairdresser who after he had cut the chief's hair was not allowed to use his own hands even for feeding himself and had to be fed for a time like a baby.

In the last century, when the word gained currency in European languages, taboo was understood to arise from an inferior mentality. It was argued that primitive tribes observed countless taboos as part of their general ignorance about the physical world. These rules, which seemed so peculiar to Europeans, were the result of false science, leading to mistaken hygiene, and faulty medicine. Essentially the taboo is a ban on touching or eating or speaking or seeing. Its breach will unleash dangers, while keeping the rules would amount to avoiding dangers and sickness. Since the native theory of taboo was concerned to keep certain classes of people and things apart lest misfortune befall, it was a theory about contagion. Our scholars of the last century contrasted this false, primitive fear of contagion with our modern knowledge of disease. Our hygiene protects from a real danger of contagion, their taboos from imaginary danger. This was a comfortably complacent distinction to draw, but hygiene does not correspond to all the rules which are called taboo. Some are as obviously part of primitive religion in the same sense as Friday abstinence and Sabbath rest. European scholars therefore took care to distinguish on the one hand between primitive taboo with a mainly secular reference, and on the other hand rules of magic which infused the practice of primitive religion. They made it even more difficult to understand the meaning of foreign taboos by importing a classification between true religion and primitive magic, and modern medicine and primitive hygiene; and a very complicated web of definitions was based on this misconception.

In the Eye of the Beholder
The difficulty in understanding primitive taboo arose from the difficulty of understanding our own taboos of hygiene and religion. The first mistake was to suppose that our idea of dirt connotes an objectively real class from which real dangers to health may issue, and whose control depends on valid rules of hygiene. It is better to start by realizing that dirt, like beauty, resides in the eye of the beholder. We must be prepared to put our own behaviour under the same microscope we apply to primitive tribes. If we find that they are busy hedging off this area from that, stopping 'X' from touching 'Y', preventing women from eating with men, and creating elaborate scales

Methods of purification in Arnhem Land, Australia: water is poured over a girl *(below)* and a man is purified by sweat from another's armpits *(above)*. Many of the rules of primitive societies, breach of which might cause a pollution that needed to be cleansed away, used to be termed taboos, with the implication that they stemmed from inadequate knowledge and inferior mentality: in fact, all societies have rules which may appear irrational in isolation but are part of a larger and necessary system of classification

Uniphoto (London)

of edibility and inedibility among the vegetable and animal worlds, we should realize that we too are given to this ordering and classifying activity. No taboo can ever make sense by itself. A taboo is always part of a whole system of rules. It makes sense as part of a classification whose meaning is so basic to those who live by it that no piecemeal explanation can be given. A native cannot explain the meaning of a taboo because it forms part of his own machinery of learning. The separate compartments which a taboo system constructs are the framework or instrument of understanding. To turn round and inspect that instrument may seem to be an advanced philosophic exercise, but it is necessary if we are to understand the subject.

Above left A seller of dye for caste-marks, in India: the Hindu caste system involves elaborate rules regulating behaviour between the castes *Above right* Street scene in Morocco: for centuries it has been taboo in Arab countries for women to appear unveiled out of doors *Below* A ban on wearing shoes on holy ground is a common religious rule: special slippers provided for worshippers at a mosque

The 19th century scholars could not understand taboo because they worked within the separate compartments of their own taboo system. For them religion, magic, hygiene and medicine were as distinct as civilized and primitive; the problem of taboo for them was only a problem about native thought. But put in that form it was

insoluble. We approach it nowadays as a problem in human learning.

First, discard the idea that we have anything like a true, complete view of the world. Between what the scientists know and what we make of their knowledge there is a synthesis which is our own rough and ready approximation of rules about how we need to behave in the physical world. Second, discard the idea that there can ever be a final and correct world view. A gain in knowledge in one direction does not guarantee there will be no loss or distortion in another; the fullness of reality will always evade our comprehension. The reasons for this will become clear. Learning is a filtering and organizing process. Faced with the same events, two people will not

necessarily register two identical patterns, and faced with a similar environment, two cultures will construe two different sets of natural constraints and regular sequences. Understanding is largely a classifying job in which the classifying human mind is much freer than it supposes itself to be. The events to be understood are unconsciously trimmed and filtered to fit the classifications being used. In this sense every culture constructs its own universe. It attributes to its own world a set of powers to be harnessed and dangers to be avoided. Each primitive culture, because of its isolation, has a unique world view. Modern industrial nations, because and insofar as they share a common experience, share the same rules about the powers and dangers aroused. This is a valid difference between 'Us' and 'Them', their primitive taboos and ours.

For all humans, primitive or not, the universe is a system of imputed rules. Using our own distinctions, we can distinguish firstly, physical Nature, inorganic (including rocks, stars, rivers) and organic (vegetable and animal bodies, with rules governing their growth, lifespan and death); secondly, human behaviour; thirdly, the interaction between these two groups; fourthly, other intelligent beings whether incorporeal like gods, devils and ghosts or mixtures of human and divine or human and animal; and lastly, the interaction between this fourth group and the rest.

The use of the word supernatural has been avoided. Even a small amount of reading in anthropology shows how very local and peculiar to our own civilization is the distinction between natural and supernatural. The same applies even to such a classification as the one just given. The fact that it is our own local classification is not important for this argument as the present object is to make clear how taboos should be understood. Taboos are rules about our behaviour which restrict the human uses of things and people. Some of the taboos are said to avoid punishment or vengeance from gods, ghosts and other spirits. Some of them are supposed to produce automatically their dreaded effects. Crop failures, sickness, hunting accidents, famine, drought, epidemic (events in the physical realm), they may all result from breach of taboos.

The Seat of Mana

Taboos can have the effect of expressing political ideas. For example, the idea of the state as a hierarchy of which the chief is the undisputed head and his officials higher than the ordinary populace easily lends itself to taboo behaviour. Gradings of power in the political body tend to be expressed as gradings of freedom to approach the physical body of the person at the top of the system. As Franz Steiner says, in *Taboo* (1956): '. . . in Polynesian belief the parts of the body formed a fixed hierarchy which had some analogy with the rank system of society . . . now the backbone was the most important part of the body, and the limbs that could be regarded as continuations of the backbone derived importance from it. Above the body was, of course, the head, and it was the seat of mana. When we say

this, we must realize that by "mana" are meant both the soul aspect, the life force, and a man's ritual status. This grading of the limbs concerned people of all ranks and both sexes. It could, for example, be so important to avoid stepping over people's heads that the very architecture was involved: the arrangements of the sleeping rooms show such an adaptation in the Marquesas. The commoner's back or head is thus not without its importance in certain contexts. But the real significance of this grading seems to have been in the possibilities it provided for cumulative effects in association with the rank system. The head of a chief was the most concentrated mana object of Polynesian society, and was hedged around with the most terrifying taboos which operated when things were to enter the head or when the head was being diminished; in other words when the chief ate or had his hair cut . . . the hands of some great chiefs were so dangerous that they could not be put close to the head.' Since the Polynesian political system was very competitive and chiefs had their ups and downs, great triumphs or total failures, the system of taboo was a kind of public vote of confidence and register of current distributions of power. This is important to correct our tendency to think of taboo as a rigidly fixed system of respect.

We will never understand a taboo system unless we understand the kind of interaction between the different spheres of existence which is assumed in it. Any child growing up learns the different spheres and interactions between them simultaneously. When the anthropologist arrives on the scene, he finds the system of knowledge a going concern. It is difficult for him to observe the changes being made, so he gets the wrong impression that a given set of taboos is something hard-and-fast handed down the generations.

In fact, the classifying process is always active and changing. New classifications are being pushed by some and rejected by others. No political innovation takes place without some basic reclassification. To take a currently live issue, in a stratified society, if it is taboo for lower classes or Negroes to sit down at table or to join sporting events with upper classes or whites, those who assert the rule can make it stronger if they find a basis in Nature to support the behaviour they regard as right. If women in Tahiti are forbidden to eat with men, or in Europe to enter certain male occupations, some ultimate justification for the rule needs to be found. Usually it is traced back to their physical nature. Women are said to be constitutionally feeble, nervous or flighty; Negroes to smell, lower classes to be hereditarily less intelligent.

Rules of the Game

Perhaps the easiest approach is to try to imagine what social life would be like without any classification. It would be like playing a game without any rules; no one would know which way to run, who is on his side or against him. There would be no game. It is no exaggeration to describe social life as the process of building classification

systems. Everyone is trying to make sense of what is happening. He is trying to make sense of his own behaviour, past and present, so as to capture and hold some sense of identity. He is trying to hold other people to their promises and ensure some kind of regular future. He is explaining continually, to himself and to everyone else. In the process of explaining, classifications are developed and more and more meanings successfully added to them, as other people are persuaded to interpret events in the same way. Gradually even the points of the compass get loaded with social meanings. For example, the west room in an Irish farmer's house used to be the room where the old couple retired to, when the eldest son married and brought his wife to the farm. West meant retirement as well as sundown. In the Buddhist religion, east is the high status point; Buddha's statue is on a shelf on the east wall of the east room; the husband always sleeps to the east of his wife. So east means male and social superior. Up and down, right and left, sun and moon, hot and cold, all the physical antitheses are able to carry meanings from social life, and in a rich and steady culture there is a steady core of such agreed classifications. Anyone who is prepared to support the social system finds himself impelled to uphold the classification system which gets meaning from it. Anyone who wants to challenge the social system finds himself up against a set of manifold classifications which will have to be rethought. This is why breach of taboo arouses such strong feeling. It is not because the minor classification is threatened, but because the whole social system (in which a great investment has been made) looks like tottering, if someone can get away with challenging a taboo.

Classification involves definition; definition involves reducing ambiguity; ambiguity arises in several ways and it is wrong to think that it can ever be excluded. To take the classification of animal species, they can be classified according to their obvious features, and according to the habitat they live in, and according to how they behave. This gives three ways of classifying animals which could each place the same beasts in different classes. Classed by behaviour, using walking, swimming or flying as basic types, penguins would be nearer to fish; classed by bone structure and egg laying, penguins would count more clearly as birds than would flying fish, which would be birds in the other classification. Animal life is much more untidy and difficult to fit into a regular system of classification than at first appears. Human social life is even more untidy. Girls behave like boys, there are adults who refuse to grow up, every year a few are born whose physical make-up is not clearly male or female. The rules of marriage and inheritance require clear-cut categories but always there will be some cases which do not fit the regularities of the system. For human classifications are always too crude for reality. A system of taboos covers up this weakness of the classification system. It points in advance to defects and insists that no one shall give recognition to the inconvenient facts or behave in such a way as to undermine the acceptability and clarity of the system as a whole. It stops awkward questions and prevents awkward developments.

Sometimes the taboo ban appears in ways that seem a long way from their point of origin. For example, among the Lele tribe, in the Kasai district of the Congo, it was taboo to bring fishing equipment direct into the village from the streams or lakes where it had been in use. All round the village fishing traps and baskets would be hung in trees overnight. Ask the Lele why they did this and they replied that coughs and disease would enter the village if the fishing things were not left out one night. No other answer could be got from them except elaboration of the danger and how sorcerers could enter the village if this barrier were not kept up. But another kind of answer lay in the mass of other rules and regulations which separated the village and its human social life from the forest and streams and animal life. This was the basic classification at stake; one which never needed to be explained because it was too fundamental to mention.

Injecting Order into Life

The novelist William Burroughs describes the final experiences of disgust and depression of some forms of drug addiction. What he calls the 'Naked Lunch' is the point where all illusions are stripped away and everything is seen as it really is. When everyone can see what is on everyone's fork, nothing is classed as edible. Meat can be animal or human flesh, caterpillars, worms or bugs;

Keystone

In the West women and 'dirt' have long been the subjects of powerful taboos *Above* Suffragettes campaigning for votes for women *Below* The London Stock Exchange is still barred to women *Right* Marcel Duchamp's *The Fountain* (1917): sent to a New York art exhibition, this urinal was greeted with a mixture of outrage and delighted shock

soup is equally urine, lentils, scotch broth or excreta; other people are neither friends nor enemies, nor is oneself different from other people since neither has any very clear definition. Identities and classifications are merged into a seething, shapeless experience. This is the potential disorder of the mind which taboo breaks up into classes and rules, and so judges some activities as right and proper and others as horrifying.

This kind of rationality is the justification for the taboos which we ourselves observe when we separate the lavatory from the living room and the bed from the kitchen, injecting order into the house. But the order is not arbitrary; it derives from social categories. When a set of social distinctions weakens, the taboos that expressed it weaken too. For this reason sex taboos used to be sacred in England but are no longer so strong. It seems ridiculous that women should not be allowed in some clubs or professions, whereas not so long ago it seemed obviously right. The same for the sense of privacy, the same for hierarchy. The less we ourselves are forced to adopt unthinking taboo attitudes to breaches of these boundaries, the easier it becomes to look dispassionately at the taboos of other societies and find plenty of meaning in them.

In some tribal societies it is thought that the shedding of blood will cause droughts and other environmental disasters. Elsewhere any contact with death is dangerously polluting, and burials are followed by elaborate washing and fumigation. In other places they fear neither homicide nor death

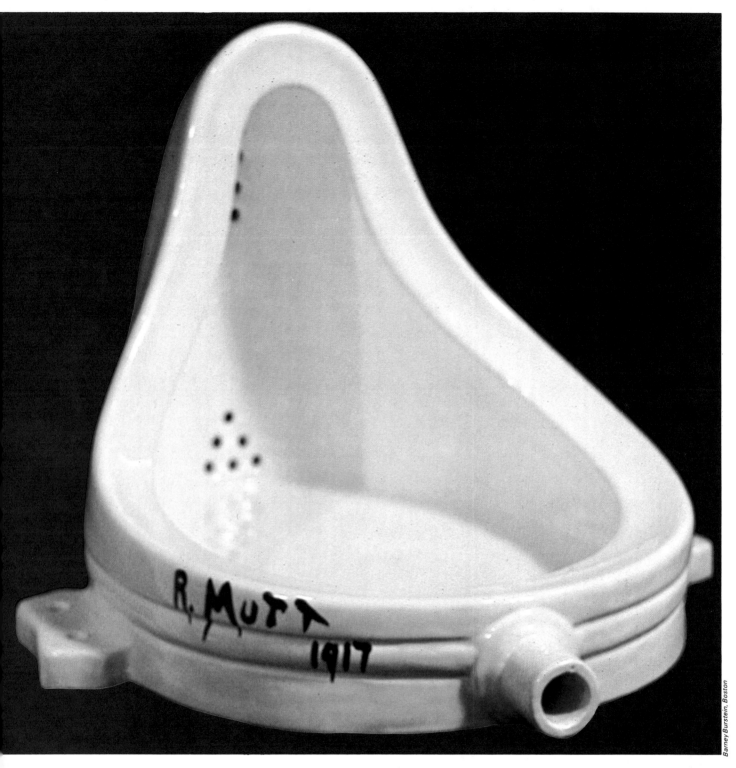

pollution but menstrual blood is thought to be very dangerous to touch (see MENSTRUA-TION). And in other places again, adultery is liable to cause illness. Some people are thickly beset with taboos so that everything they do is charged with social symbolism. Others observe only one or two rules. Those who are most taboo-minded have the most complex set of social boundaries to preserve. Hence their investment of so much energy into the control of behaviour.

A taboo system upholds a cultural system and a culture is a pattern of values and norms; social life is impossible without such a pattern. This is the dilemma of individual freedom. Ideally we would like to feel free to make every choice from scratch and judge each case on its merits. Such a freedom

would slow us down, for every choice would have to be consciously deliberated. On the one hand, education tries to equip a person with means for exercising private judgement, and on the other hand, the techniques of education provide a kind of mechanical decision-making, along well-oiled grooves. They teach strong reactions of anxiety about anything which threatens to go off the track. As education transmits culture, taboos and all, it is a kind of brain-washing. It only allows a certain way of seeing reality and so limits the scope for private judgement. Without the taboos, which turn basic classi-fications into automatic psychological reflexes, no thinking could be effective, because if every system of classification was up for revision at every moment, there

would be no stability of thought. Hence there would be no scope for experience to accumu-late into knowledge. Taboos bar the way for the mind to visualize reality differently. But the barriers they set up are not arbitrary, for taboos flow from social boundaries and support the social structure. This accounts for their seeming irrational to the outsider and beyond challenge to the person living in the society.

(See also FOOD AND DRINK; MANA; MAORI; POLYNESIA.)

MARY DOUGLAS

FURTHER READING: Mary Douglas, *Purity and Danger* (Praeger, 1966); Franz Steiner, *Taboo* (Penguin, 1967 reprint).

Likened to a sword and a shield, a talisman may be defined as an object which has been magically endowed with the power of attracting good fortune, while an amulet is something which naturally possesses protective properties

TALISMANS

THE WORD TALISMAN is defined in the *Oxford English Dictionary* as an 'object engraven with figures or characters to which are attributed the occult powers of the planetary influences and celestial configurations under which it was made; usually worn as an amulet to avert evil or bring fortune to the wearer'. The word is traced to the

Greek *telesma*, meaning in this case a consecrated object, one over which a rite has been completed. An amulet, according to the same authority, is 'anything worn about the person as a charm or preventive against evil, mischief, disease, witchcraft, etc.': its derivation is traced through the Latin, *amuletum.*

It will be seen that in these definitions no clear distinction is made between amulets and talismans. According to Sir E. A. Wallis Budge, the Egyptologist, expert opinion is divided on the subject; he himself considered that the essential difference between an amulet and a talisman is that while an amulet exercises its protective powers continuously and in general over its owner, a talisman is called upon to perform some

isolated task of protection. In this artic it is proposed to treat the two as differing nature. A talisman is an object ceremonial endowed with the power of attractin favourable influences: it reinforces, and ma be thought of as a sword. An amulet is a object naturally possessing the power turning away evil or undesired influence it *protects,* and may be likened to a shield.

The idea that special influence, luck, protection is somehow inherent in objects universal. Anthropologists have collecte great stores of information on the subjec of *mana* (see MANA), belief in whic directs innumerable customs in many cu tures throughout the world. Mana is perhap especially potent in the substances and fluid of the body, and so might be equated wit the idea of 'personal magnetism'. Henc possession of items endowed with mana possession of the soul-code of the perso a tiny tuning-fork as it were, to which h must automatically respond. So hair, teet saliva or blood, are powerful levers in magi black or white, the psychic equivalent of telephone number.

From Diamonds to Skulls
Ancient Egypt was pre-eminently the lan of amulets. They were worn by the livin and placed in great abundance within th inner coffin of the mummy. The head of th mummy rested on a circular piece of line inscribed with magical figures. Chief amon the mummy amulets were the Uzat or Eye Horus, left and right eyes representing th sun and moon (see HORUS); the Tw Fingers, in obsidian or haematite; and th Five Steps. Probably best known is th scarab beetle, symbol of the sun god Khepr whose revolutions were pictured in the rollin movement of the beetle (see SCARAB). Th list is long: the Buckle of Isis, the Hear Papyrus Sceptre, the Tet (backbone tree-trunk), Vulture, Frog, Serpent's Hea Menat, Nefer (a musical instrument), Ank or life-symbol, and the Sam, symbol union, and so on. Modern Freemasons woul recognize the Angle or Square, symbol protection, and the Plumb-line. Most of th amulets were fashioned either in certai materials or in certain colours, althoug they could be in a precious metal such as gol

All races have traditional amulets. Th jungle Negro hangs from his neck hi personal charm or *gris-gris*; the Chines carry an object engraved with a characte from the ancient text, the *Shu-Ching*; th Mohammedan a verse from the Koran; th Christian a scapulary or relic; and the Je fastens at his door a little roll of parchmer inscribed with SHADAI, the ninth of the te divine names of the Cabala. The followers Zoroaster have an amuletic garment, sacred shirt and cord which is woven with peculiar holy thread made of fine wool wove by the wives of Parsee priests, with speci invocatory charms. The sacred book, th *Khordah-Avesta* describes how, standing sitting, and wherever he may be, the garme

Talismans are objects believed to attra favourable influences, like these toker hung up in a church to obtain cures or heaven protection

ill protect him from injury from slings, rrows, knives or clubs.

Pieces of the wood of the True Cross were eld in especial reverence for their power by he Christian nations in the Middle Ages. lthough orthodox teaching stated it to e all of oak, some ancient writers maintained that four kinds of wood were used. he stem was of cypress, the cross-piece f cedar, the superscription of board pine, nd the block to support the feet, of boxwood.

A wide variety of natural objects from ewels and semi-precious stones (see EWELS) to berries and animals' hairs have een used as amulets. Coral, especially the ed or pink variety, has always been believed o have amuletic properties; and one of the nain reasons for its being used with bells n babies' rattles was that it was reputed to afeguard against the Evil Eye (see EYE). erdinand I of Spain wore a small branch of oral suspended about his neck, which he vould point at anyone whom he suspected f having a malignant influence. In the Middle Ages it was held to be a protection rom lightning, storm and witches.

Garnets were popular as amulets in Egypt, where they were known as 'happy tones'; the Romans called them 'loyal tones'. Jet was also highly prized. In 1841 n Cologne a stone coffin of about the 5th entury was found which contained, in addiion to human remains, beautifully made jet rnaments such as armlets, rings, buckles, necklets and hairpins. Jet was considered aluable not only as a remedy for toothache nd tumours, but as a revealer of unfaithulness. Sardonyx was supposed to ensure narital happiness, and in classical times it lso had a reputation as an aid to the elouence of lawyers. Pliny relates that a lawyer amed Paulus hired a sardonyx ring to wear vhen he defended a wealthy widow; he won is case and the widow as well.

Jade was believed to keep off kidney omplaints; and even in this century it has een reported to be effective in curing eadaches, when pressed to the forehead. he star sapphire is undoubtedly in the mulet class. It is greatly sought after for this urpose in Thailand, where a tourist was old recently, 'Should the world come to an nd, it will protect you from all harm!' Rock rystal is said to stimulate clairvoyance, and vas made into polished spheres for crystalazing in quite ancient times. A ball of

Above Talisman of the moon, intended to harness the moon's influence to protect the wearer against evil *Below, left to right* Lucky charms, from a set of Wills's cigarette cards of the 1920s: jade hei-tiki, used by the Maori in New Zealand; the ankh, the ancient Egyptian symbol of life; hand, making the gesture of blessing; tau cross, protecting against disease and snakebite

this stone surmounts the sceptre of the Scottish regalia. Some of the crystal balls preserved as healing stones were no doubt originally intended for divination. A diamond is said to have been the Schamir stone in Solomon's magic ring, which was reputed to have the power to preserve his throne.

Amulets in Reverse

Vegetable and animal products also have a place in the lists of amulets or charms. In India the *rudraksha* berry and beads from the *tulsi* or Indian balsam plant are believed to have properties making them suitable for necklaces of the rosary type. In Africa, the stout hairs from the elephant are plaited into lucky rings, and elsewhere the rabbit's paw has been used as an amulet.

There are several cases of human skulls being associated with a particular family and house, the removal of which is said to affect the owners' fortunes unfavourably. In this sense the skull must be regarded as an amulet (see HAUNTED HOUSES; SKULLS).

Certain objects, usually gems, have a documented history of bringing evil and disaster upon their possessors, rather than

good fortune. The Hope Diamond is perhaps the best known. In 1965 it was disclosed that it had been on loan for study at the De Beers' laboratories in Johannesburg, and it was found that after exposure to ultraviolet light it glowed for several minutes like a red-hot coal, a phenomenon which had not occurred with other diamonds.

It seems as if an atmosphere or aura of violence lingers about these articles, and acts as a kind of detonator when it again enters a field of intense emotions. But this would hardly apply in the case of Mephisto's Ring. This was a ring set with a large and beautiful emerald which came into the possession of the Spanish royal family in the reign of Philip II, who sent the ill-fated Armada. Centuries later the ring was presented to a church at the time of the Spanish-American War of 1898. Soon after, the church burned down, but the ring was rescued and placed in a museum. The museum was severely damaged by lightning and the ring was sent back to the royal family. That same week they received news of the defeat of their navy at Manila. Mephisto's Ring was then sealed up in a strong box and buried in the ground.

The Healing Talisman

A common use of talismans down the ages has been for the purpose of healing. In the New Testament, simple cloths became effective talismans when charged with the power of Paul the Apostle (Acts 19.11–12): 'And God did extraordinary miracles by the hands of Paul, so that handkerchiefs and aprons were carried away from his body to the sick, and diseases left them and the evil spirits came out of them.'

The case of a woman who seemed to be afflicted with an incurable eye inflammation is cited by Eliphas Levi, the 19th century occultist. She was suddenly and mysteriously cured, and confessed to her priest that she had had recourse to magic. For a long time she had pestered a scholar – whom she supposed to be a magician – to give her a written charm to carry, and finally the scholar had given her a little roll of parchment with the advice to wash three times a day in cold water. The priest made her bring the parchment, and when he opened it he found it inscribed in Latin with these words: 'May the devil dig out your eyes and fill the empty spaces with dung!' He

THE HEI-TIKI.

THE ANKH.

THE HAND.

THE TAU CROSS.

translated the words to the woman, who was thunderstruck, but nevertheless cured.

This anecdote illustrates one aspect of the use and effect of talismans. The wearer's thoughts are constantly turning towards the talismanic object and picturing its purpose or quality. If it has been impregnated by the act of a powerful will, when one who has faith concentrates his thought upon the talisman, he draws from it a strong suggestion which his own will-power reinforces. Even where there is no 'magnetic charge', as apparently in the case of the roll of parchment, the wearer's belief quickly builds up a charge which is effective at subconscious levels.

A talisman kept by a Scottish family, the Lee Penny of the Lockharts which is said to have originated with the Moors in Spain in the 14th century, has a long record of healings by water in which it was dipped. Sir Simon Locard of Lee obtained the talisman as part of the ransom of an emir whom he took prisoner in Spain. The emir's mother explained the powers and method of using the penny, which was a silver groat with a dark red triangular stone set in the middle. It could stop bleeding, cure fever, and especially cure animal diseases by means of the water in which it was dipped three times and then swirled round. The last record of its successful use was before the First World War when one of Sir Simon Lockhart's guests accidentally sustained a deep cut in his hand which bled obstinately. Sir Simon 'magnetized' a basin of water with the penny, and the guest soaked his bandaged hand in it. The bleeding stopped, and the cut healed rapidly.

As J. G. Lockhart, who has written a full record of this famous healing stone, says: 'It might be observed that the Lee Penny appears to have been at least as successful in dealing with the complaints of its time as in a later day the Ministry of Agriculture has been in dealing with Foot and Mouth Disease. The Penny was at any rate reputed to cure where the Ministry can only kill.' It was the Lee Penny, incidentally, which inspired one title of Sir Walter Scott's novel, *The Talisman*.

How to Make a Talisman

An old work, Sepharial's *Book of Charms and Talismans* is still widely read for its delightful blend of Hebrew-inscribed medieval cabalistic diagrams and Victorian descriptions of their usefulness. Consider, for example, what the 'Talisman for Travelling on Land or Sea,' engraved on a Monday in silver, can do: 'Train drivers and guards should certainly wear it, and signalmen too. All those who hold any position on board ship from Commodores and Captains down to waiters and stokers should wear it as it will assist from the safety standpoint, will help to prevent seasickness and will cause the ordinary work to seem less arduous.'

Ancient Egyptian amulet, c 1250 BC, showing the head of the popular god Bes, a squat, dwarfish, cheerfully grinning deity, who presided over fun and music, and helped women in childbirth: numerous amulets depicting him have been found

In making a talisman, your will, and to a secondary degree your personal emanation, can impregnate a suitable chosen piece of material with lasting power. You can set up in it a 'field' or charge of a particular type of force. But the material to receive this should be new or virgin, although used material can be cleaned and purified.

The type of material will affect the permanency of the result. Parchment is more enduring than paper and has other advantages; the nobler metals such as platinum, gold, silver, and even nickel, are less absorptive of gross vibrations; while gem stones, containing the most highly developed mineral life, can sing the same vibrational song over thousands of years. Sensitives will tell that this is so in the case of many of the Egyptian symbolic jewels and the inscribed gnostic gems used in initiation ceremonies in the past. The serpent-entwined rod of the caduceus was charged with power and when laid along the spine of the candidate in the Mysteries, produced a stirring of power and intuition in him.

On the other hand, for a temporary purpose, you can make an effective talisman for a friend from a short length of new cord. Holding it, you make a loose knot, and then concentrate with all the intensity you possess on the quality you are to give. When you feel supremely charged, picture that charge pouring down your arms and concentrating in the knot as you pull it tight with a fierce jerk. Make seven knots like this and you have your talisman.

Supposing you wish to give a ring or jewel for a talismanic purpose, the technique is to visualize a sheet of tense etheric matter between the curved forefinger and thumb of your left hand and, holding the object in your right hand, pass it through the web several times with the intent that all past 'magnetism' be combed out. The object can then be made potent by a process of tension and discharge into it, somewhat similar to the knotting procedure just described. All authorities agree that many types of talisman are better enclosed in silk, and not exposed to the gaze of the inquisitive.

Although the human will is the most powerful element in its creation, it is usual to take into account the best possible astrological conditions in deciding the time. It is unwise, say the astrologers, to wear the birthstone traditional for your sign if in your nativity map the sun has serious adverse aspects; so you require to know your personal horoscope. Very few occultists nowadays would care, however, to go through the elaborate ceremonial with dress, colours, and invocations at exactly appropriate times, feeling that they mainly serve as psychological props and aids to concentration.

C. NELSON STEWART

FURTHER READING: E. Clodd, *Magic in Names* (Singing Tree Press, 1967 reprint); W. B. Crow, *Precious Stones* (Weiser, 1968); J. G. Lockhart, *Curses, Lucks and Talismans* (Midway, 1938); A. E. Powell, *The Etheric Double* (Theosophical Publishing House, 1925); W. G. O. Sepharial, *Book of Charms and Talismans* (Wehman, 1965).

TAMMUZ

THE HEBREW PROPHET Ezekiel tells how, in the year 592 BC, in a mystic vision he saw the iniquity of the Jewish inhabitants of Jerusalem. In particular, he relates how he was brought to 'the north gate of the house of the Lord; and behold, there sat women weeping for Tammuz' (8.14). The prophet thus, unintentionally, witnesses to the widespread influence of the cult of the Mesopotamian god Tammuz and to a notable feature of that cult. The Jewish women were performing a ritual lamentation for the death of Tammuz, which was annually mourned at the summer solstice when the year begins to wane and vegetation has withered under the sun's heat. The mourners chanted in their lament:

> How long will the springing up of verdure be
>   withheld?
> How long will vegetation be withheld?

The Hebrew name 'Tammuz' derived from the Sumerian 'Dumuzi', which was both the name of an ancient Sumerian deity and of the month in which he was specially commemorated. In the Jewish calendar there is also a month 'Tammuz', as there is with the Arabs under the name 'Tamuz'. The god was known, too, by the title *Adoni*, 'my Lord', which passed into Greek and Latin as Adonis (see APHRODITE). Although this ancient deity was so widely known and abundant reference is made to him in Mesopotamian texts, our modern knowledge of him is pieced together from a variety of material, most of it fragmentary.

The Sumerians, who originally conceived of this deity, called him 'Dumu-zi-abzu', meaning 'True son of Apsu'. The Apsu was the personification of the sweet waters, as opposed to Tiamat, the personification of the salt waters or sea (see CREATION MYTHS). Since it was the sweet waters (as rivers or rain) which fertilized the earth, Dumuzi's filial relationship to the Apsu doubtless indicates some original connection with fertility. There is indeed evidence of this aspect of his nature; however, in Sumerian mythology the god appears in various guises. Thus, in one myth concerned to exalt agriculture over a pastoral economy, Dumuzi is a shepherd god, who competes unsuccessfully with Enkimdu, the farmer god, for Inanna, the fertility goddess.

Dumuzi's connection with Inanna ('Ishtar' in Akkadian; see ISHTAR; MESOPOTAMIA) constitutes the most celebrated feature of his mythology, but the evidence about it is curiously ambivalent. Although represented in the previous myth as the rejected suitor of the goddess, in another myth he appears as her husband; but the relation had direful consequences for him. For Inanna became desirous of ruling in the underworld as she did in the world above. Consequently she descended to the realm of Ereshkigal, the Sumerian goddess of the dead, to challenge her sovereignty. But Ereshkigal was too strong for her, and Inanna was held prisoner in the 'Land of No Return'. Eventually the god Enki secured her release and return to the upper world, but on condition that she found a substitute to take her place. To save herself, Inanna delivered Dumuzi to the demons who accompanied her, as the required substitute, and Dumuzi was carried off to the grim domain of Ereshkigal.

Sacred Prostitutes

In the famous *Epic of Gilgamesh* (see GILGAMESH), curious reference is made to Ishtar's responsibility for the fate of Dumuzi. In repelling the amorous advances of the goddess, the hero Gilgamesh includes Dumuzi among the list of her victims; but he adds 'To the god Dumuzi, the lover of thy youth, thou hast ordained lamentation year by year'. This cryptic statement doubtless refers to some aspect of the myth which found expression in an annual ritual lamentation for Dumuzi, in which Ishtar was involved. Further information, though still of a cryptic nature, is provided in the later Akkadian version of the myth of Ishtar's descent into the underworld. In this version there is no mention of Dumuzi's being a substitute for Ishtar. However, at the end of the narrative, after the account of Ishtar's return from the 'Land of No Return', reference is suddenly made to Tammuz (Dumuzi): 'Tammuz, her young husband, wash with pure water; anoint him with goodly oil; clothe him with a resplendent robe; let him play on the flute of lapis lazuli; let the courtesans appease his wrath! . . . On the day when Tammuz comes up to me, and the lapis lazuli flute with him, and the carnelian ring, come up to me. When those who lament, men and women, come up with him to me. May the dead arise and smell the incense.'

These invocations or injunctions clearly relate to an elaborate ritual drama in which the death and resurrection of Tammuz were portrayed. The 'courtesans' were undoubtedly the sacred prostitutes who served in the temples of Ishtar. However, it is difficult, in turn, to relate the myth of Ishtar's descent into the underworld to these rubrics concerning Tammuz. The obvious explanation that Ishtar descended there to rescue the dead Tammuz is not actually supported by the Akkadian text; and it is certainly contradicted by the Sumerian version. However, the Akkadian text does imply a ritual connection of some kind.

The general bearing of the extant evidence indicates that, whatever may have been his original Sumerian form, in Mesopotamia later, and in other adjacent lands, Tammuz was the central figure of a death and resurrection ritual which was related to the annual cycle of vegetation, and in which the fertility goddess Ishtar was intimately implicated (see VEGETATION SPIRITS; DYING GOD).

As a 'dying-rising god', Tammuz naturally suggests comparison with similar types of deity, and above all with Osiris of Egypt (see OSIRIS). Such phenomenological similarity makes it reasonable to ask whether Tammuz also played the role of the saviour god in Mesopotamian religion which Osiris so notably did in the religion of Egypt. The answer is that Tammuz did so, but in a different way, and the reason for the difference is interesting and important.

The religion of the ancient Mesopotamian peoples was based upon an evaluation of human nature that precluded any hope of a happy afterlife. Death irreparably shattered the constitution of the individual person, and what survived (the *etimmu*) descended to the grim Land of No Return. Hence, Tammuz could never assume that role in a mortuary ritual which Osiris had in Egypt, whereby the dead participated in the resurrection of the divine hero. However, ritual texts do exist in which salvation was sought through Tammuz; but the salvation was from sickness, not from death.

An attempt has been made to show that there existed in Sumer a myth and ritual pattern in which a divine king represented Tammuz. This pattern involved the sacred marriage of the king and the chief priestess of Inanna, and the death and resurrection of the king. The purpose of the rites was to ensure the fertility of men, flocks and land. The theory has not, however, found general acceptance among scholars.

S. G. F. BRANDON

FURTHER READING: S. N. Kramer, *Sumerian Mythology* (Harper and Row, 1961); H. W. F. Saggs, *The Greatness That Was Babylon* (Praeger, 1969).

Sumerian seal showing the mother goddess, a worshipper and Dumuzi, or Tammuz: in the 6th century BC the prophet Ezekiel described how the women of Jerusalem lamented the god's death

TANTRISM

Sven Gahlin

In tantric philosophy the interplay of two basic forces, Shiva and Shakti, male and female, underlies the entire universe: the female principle is the dominant one and the male the subordinate, for 'Shiva without Shakti is a corpse'
Previous page Copies of statues from the temple of Konarak, c 1000 AD, showing the male and female principles embraced
Left and *right* 18th century pictures of Kali, a personification of the elements of terror and dread in Shakti, dancing on and dominating her male partner, Shiva

that are the fountainhead of all Hindu orthodoxy; and the Buddhist frowns upon most of its teachings and practices, which to the puritan border on the scandalous.

Tantrics, the followers of Tantrism, claim that theirs is perhaps the oldest religion in India. Yoga (see YOGA), now regarded as one of the six orthodox systems of Aryan Hindu philosophy, is in their view basically tantric. A figure in a typical squatting posture, and a priest gazing at the tip of his nose, which both suggest yogic breathing and meditative techniques, have been found impressed in seals of the Indus Valley civilization (c 2000 BC), which preceded the arrival of the Aryans in India by more than 1000 years.

This priority can, of course, be disputed, but the tantrics' claim to uniqueness admits of little doubt. Theirs is a special cult; its teachings confer personal and social emancipation; it liberates the follower from the bondage of all moral restraints. The tantrics regard themselves as the elect, and all those outside the sect as *pashu*, or the animal herd.

Most tantric writings are traceable to a period after the 10th century AD. Many of the earlier manuscripts were destroyed by Hindu zealots, and the bulk of the remainder by a succession of invaders who conquered India, and to whom the doctrines appeared unworthy of perpetuation or remembrance. The monasteries where they were taught were razed to the ground, the libraries burned, and the monks slain. The nucleus of the teaching was thereafter preserved with great secrecy.

According to tantric philosophy the whole universe is built up of and pervaded by two basic forces which are in intimate and intricate union. These forces, named Shiva and Shakti, are personified as male and female deities. Of this divine pair, Shiva is the subordinate one, for it is the Female Principle that ultimately underlies all manifestation, and everything, including Shiva himself, is contained within the Female Principle. There is a tantric saying, 'Shiva without Shakti is a corpse.'

So important is the Shakti concept in this philosophy that Tantrism is often known by the alternative title of Shaktism, the Tantras spoken of as the Shakta writings, and tantric cults often called the Shakta cults. Among the various reasons advanced by tantrics as the basis for their claim to

Believing that the generative organs are instruments of a supreme magical operation, the tantrics seek salvation through sex, but in their highly disciplined rites sensual pleasure is incidental

UNTIL THE END of the last century comparatively little was known in Europe about Tantrism, although it is one of the most extraordinary cults of the East. Today in one form or another it plays an essential role in certain occult societies, both in Europe and America. It is in a sexual context that this philosophy is usually considered because its treatment of sex is so remarkable, but Tantrism touches on a great deal more than sexual matters.

The name comes from *Tantra*, a general

term used for the texts in which this system is expounded, as a rule in the course of a dialogue between the Hindu god Shiva and his consort Shakti (see SHIVA). Tantrism is practised with local variations in India, Nepal, Bhutan and Sikkim, and before the Chinese occupation it formed part of certain lamaist sects of Tibet. Its philosophy is as complex as any that can be found in the orthodox religions of these countries, and some of it reaches heights of subtlety and finesse to match anything in the more traditional theologies. But there are critics who maintain that it bears the same relationship to orthodox Hinduism and Buddhism that the Black Mass bears to Christianity. Though an outgrowth of Hinduism it is opposed to the *Vedas*, the sacred writings

Women are treated on terms of complete equality with men, and in many of the rites are assigned superior status

superiority over orthodox Hinduism is the high place assigned to women. The latter are treated on terms of complete equality with men, and in many of their rites are assigned an even superior status, as living embodiments of Shakti, the mother goddess.

The main subjects dealt with in the Tantras include the creation of the world, and its final dissolution; the various gods and goddesses and the worship appropriate to their status and powers; physical culture; mental and spiritual discipline; and the rites by which magical powers can be acquired to enable one to control oneself, control others, the forces of Nature, and, on the highest plane, even the gods themselves. This emphasis on magic has brought Tantrism into further disrepute, and the term 'tantric' retains its overtones of black magic in India to this day.

Indeed, there is hardly an occult procedure that is not dealt with in Tantrism. Some of its rituals are reminiscent of the forms of ceremonial magic described in the Western grimoires. Candles, incense, bells, magical wands, spells, magic circles, bodily postures, occult gestures, symbolical designs, words of power, are as much part of the tantric's paraphernalia as of the Western magician's. Much of the ritualism has in fact been embodied into their own traditions by Western magicians who have been largely influenced, especially in rites of sex mysticism and sex magic, by what they have found in tantric manuals or learned from tantric teachers.

Long periods of preparation and training in techniques of highly specialized physical culture are a pre-requisite to tantric progress. In particular, great emphasis is laid on *pranayama* or respiratory exercises (see BREATH); on heliotherapy or invigorating the body by adoration of the sun and exposure of the body to the sun; on the control of certain autonomic functions, that is, of those physiological processes not under the direction of the conscious mind, such as body temperature, pulse rates, and the reflexes that trigger ejaculation; on methods of superconcentration that bring all bodily functions under the control of the will; and on very subtle processes of internal alchemy. Certain exercises are motionless stances with the limbs fixed in prescribed symbolic attitudes during which the internal exercises are carried out. Running parallel with these

Sven Gahlin

'Acts that cause the moral degradation of the ordinary man, by those very acts does the wise one obtain salvation'

practices is the intonation of holy *mantras* or spells of a special abbreviated kind. Like the physical exercises, the voicing of such mantras is first minimized, and then carried on interiorly (see MANTRA).

Rousing the Sleeping Snake

The alchemy expounded in the tantric texts, like its counterpart in the writings of the Western alchemists, is replete with esoteric passages and little can be made of their jargon. The secret door will not open to the uninitiated without a key. In tantric writings a curious symbolism underlies the outward meaning, much of it couched in metaphorical language or expressed as though an actual laboratory experiment were being described.

Though ostensibly concerned with the transmutation of baser metals into gold, and with the vessels, implements and apparatus of commerce and the ritual movements of the alchemist in his workroom, this alchemy actually takes place within the body itself. It is a hermetic distillation, as it were, from the bodily fluids, with the aid of instruments and utensils provided by the body itself, of the gross substance within oneself, into the subtle quintessence that can reinvigorate the physical frame, make the body glow, activate one's supernatural faculties and put one in communication with any entity in the universe. All the processes as described are carefully concealed parallels of physiological processes by which the internal ingredients manufactured within the body are heated to an even heat by the bodily fires, and rising upwards through various stages are distilled in the brain to produce the alchemical liquor of transcendence – the celestial dew of the hermetic philosophers of the Western tradition (see ALCHEMY).

This naturally presupposes a complex system of subtle anatomy and physiology, by which the invisible transmutation is effected, and such indeed is the case. It is based on the *chakras* or plexuses of the etheric body, situated along an axis that passes from tail-bone to skull (see KUNDALINI). They are seven in number, like lotuses of variegated colour, located roughly at the base of the spine (the basal chakra), the sex organs, the solar plexus, the heart, the throat, between the eyebrows, and at the crown of the head (the *sahasrara*). There is a

connection between the base and crown chakras, between the abode of Shakti and Shiva. In some texts the head is compared to an inverted bowl and the pelvis to a basin, the two being joined by a hollow tube. All power is promised to him who can siphon the lower energy towards the upper, but in the ordinary man this is an almost impossible task for the tube is blocked at the stages marked by the chakras, each of which has a formidable gate that will never open to anyone without the password.

The basal chakra is inhabited by the mysterious *kundalini*, which is likened to a tiny snake, normally lying curled and asleep near the tail-bone. Its arousal is the goal of an elaborate technique taking many years to master and requiring the personal guidance of a guru. When aroused, the serpent begins its upward ascent, piercing the gates of the chakras one by one until it reaches the summit.

Sometimes the chakras are compared to focuses of occult fire, lying dormant. There is an ember flickering in the kundalini which is the incendiary point, but normally quiescent. A sympathetic resonance exists between the chakras. By tantric method the kundalini can be made to blaze up and when the blaze reaches the chakra next above it, ignites it and in this manner the stream of flame going from chakra to chakra reaches the crown, the sahasrara.

The dangers of this discipline can be very real for unless one has been trained to deal with this fire-force it can leave madness or even death in its trail. But words fail in attempting to describe the climax of the operation if it is successful. For then Shakti and Shiva are united and their ecstasy is known with a hundred variations under countless names. It is the Great Awakening, the Immortal Draught, the Supreme Bliss.

Transcending Good and Evil

Besides personal disciplines there are a number of rites which are regarded as essential to the tantric's progress. They include nudism, sexual freedom, group sexuality, adultery, incest and, in the higher planes, intercourse with elemental creatures, female demons and goddesses. Tantrism has therefore been condemned as representing the worst side of religion and a travesty of Hinduism and Buddhism. But its advocates

Early 19th century figure of Parvati, the consort of Shiva and another aspect of Shakti, the female principle of Tantrism: the tantric scriptures contain dialogues between Shiva and Parvati in which the doctrines of Tantrism are expounded

defend it as a noble and inspiring philosophy, condemned and vilified only by misrepresentation and prejudice.

Since the law and the social code are opposed to the doctrines, tantrics feel that attempts cannot be made early enough to wean the initiate from traditional standards of morality and set forth the virtues of the tantric code. Sex may be impure if treated solely as an animal function, on an equal footing with the other animal functions performed by man. But even on grounds of its naturalness alone it should be free from any unpleasant overtones, and no more subject to moral stricture than drawing breath. Part of the discipline therefore consists in a gradual psychological indoctrination that inures the disciple to the new outlook and conditions him by precept and practice to the tantric view. The mind must be jolted into a new way of thinking, and this is achieved by deliberate antinomianism or working against the law and acting against the dictates of morality and conscience. Just as two lovers, ravished by their passion, care not whether their love is moral or permissible but only that they should continue in their loving, and in this manner override society and its laws and the conventional standards of right and wrong, even so must the mind of the tantric, absorbed in the sublimity of the tantric doctrine, transcend the ideas of good and evil, and move to a higher level of morality to a condition beyond the jurisdiction of family, society and state.

Human existence in the so-called civilized environment is cluttered with convention, artificiality and superfluity. Lessening the load is therefore a pre-requisite to success along the tantric path. But no half-hearted or apologetic contravention of the dictates of society is worth the effort: what is needed is a complete and total denial of their validity. The Tantras repeatedly preach the need for going against the established order of things so that the will might be strengthened, the new way of life properly understood, and accepted in its true sense.

William MacQuitty

'Acts that cause the moral degradation of the ordinary man, by those very acts does the wise one obtain salvation', runs a typical tantric text. Another says, 'Just as a thorn in the foot can be removed by another thorn, and poison neutralized by poison, so can sin purge sin.' 'Actions that cause a man to burn in hell, are those by which the yogi attains beatitude.' And to sum up: 'Perfection is gained by satisfying all one's desires'. This is the idealization of Self, for within the self dwells Shakti. What you desire, that do, for this gratifies the goddess.

Organized society, religion, law, are all inimical to the doctrine of spontaneity. What is natural is right. The mind must be emptied of all its familiar preconceptions and prejudices or the tantric doctrine will be resisted. What is natural must be freely enjoyed. There can be no sin in spontaneity, for Nature cannot be transgressed. Eating and drinking, breathing, sleeping, sexual intercourse, there is no 'moral' difference between them.

Salvation through Sex

In the higher reaches of this line of thought the idea of good and evil is altogether abandoned as a purely artificial distinction. And down the line the whole set of conflicting opposites is similarly thrown overboard. There is no difference between rich and poor, between prince and pauper. In fact social stratification is non-existent among tantrics, and the only hierarchy is one of cultic eminence. Still more carefully must one try to grasp the idea that there is also no difference between wisdom and folly, industry and idleness, food and offal. And among some tantrics offal is actually eaten, as part of a ritual to symbolize the rejection of all traditional values imposed by habit and convention and acquired taste.

One rite commonly celebrated in many tantric sects is known as the *chakra-puja* or circle worship, where the participants sit in a circle, which implies complete mutual equality among those present. Male and female participants sit next to each other on the floor, and in the middle of the circle sit another couple, who represent Shakti and Shiva. Sometimes a nude girl occupies the central place as Shakti, or else a drawing of the yoni (female genitals) may be made

The terrifying aspects of Shiva and Shak■ are the subject of tantric meditation graveyards during rites of contact wi■ corpses

Left Lamaist temple banner from Tibe■ 18th century, showing the goddess of terr■ surrounded by deities and demons

Right Mandala of Shiva in his awe-inspir■ aspect as Bhairava (from *bhairav*, 'terror■ Bhairava was said to have been born from■ drop of Shiva's blood and became the perso■ fication of his rage and hatred

on the floor, this symbol being taken ■ signify the presence of the goddess. Then a■ the members partake of a ceremonial me■ consisting of wine, flesh, fish, and brea■ followed by a rite of sexual intercourse■ These five items have been the subject ■ much philosophical speculation; they ar■ said to represent certain fundament■ categories and are equated either with th■ elements or with the interior faculties of th■ body. The wine symbolizes fire and th■ subtle draught of immortality that th■ tantric must learn to distil and drink; th■ flesh symbolizes air and the bodily functio■ that must be brought under control; fis■ stands for water and the techniques ■ sexual occultism; the bread is the earth, ■ the natural environment which must b■ understood and controlled. *Maithuna* ■ sexual intercourse symbolizes ether, th■ quintessence of all the elements, and is th■ final goal of all tantric endeavour, for throug■ it one apprehends the ultimate reality. I■ this context the esoteric meaning of ma■ thuna must be clearly understood. The se■ act in its normal, gross form may occasional■ bring a fleeting revelation of eternal trut■ but that would be rare, for the smoke ■ passion clouds the mind. Sex as a sacre■ ritual, unclouded by passion can, on th■ other hand, help one to apprehend th■ ultimate Unity. The genuine rite can revea■ Being, expand consciousness, confer bliss■ The way through *bhukti* (pleasure) can lea■ one to *mukti* (redemption). Sex, in othe■ words, can be a way of salvation. And thi■ profoundly mystical belief is the tantri■ secret.

The gods have ordained that the evolutio■ and purification of man's soul can only b■ achieved by living in an earthly incarna■ tion and experiencing life on the physic■ plane. So it is the destiny of the initiate t■ utilize the sex organs for the purpose ■ discovering the ultimate principles of th■ universe. Union of male and female bring■ about the union of man and God. In th■ religious art of many Indian sects the pro■ creative organs are stylized in the form of th■ lingam (phallus) and yoni. The lingam bein■ the symbol of transcendent life is regarde■ as worthy of adoration, and anointed, ga■ landed and given homage. The yoni, sym■ bolizing regeneration, is drawn on th■ ground in the form of mandalas (se■ MANDALA), often in composite designs ■

three or nine yonis; sometimes little vessels representing the lingam and yoni in union are used as lamps to keep the symbol of the divine encounter ever before the eyes of the worshipper.

Woman, the Opposite

The human organs that perform the divine rite of maithuna receive veneration for special reasons. In tantric theory the seat of pleasure during the sex act resides not in the active members but in the heart, so the members do not need to be venerated for the pleasure they are erroneously thought to give. The apparent purpose of food is the satisfaction of one's appetite, whereas only after the food has passed from plate to palate and the taste buds have been satisfied, does the actual process of nourishment take place. Only the pashu, or animal, thinks of sex in terms of pleasure or procreation. The gross product of the sex apparatus results in children, but such procreation is not a human prerogative. All animals procreate; in tantric belief they derive greater pleasure from the act than men; they produce more abundantly, and procreation is therefore rightly for the pashu. The human sex organs are instruments of a supreme magical operation of which no animal can possibly be aware. They help the participant of the sex rite to transcend the physical, to transcend the mental, and rise to a psychic and spiritual state. Sex, like every other blessing can be debased and become a mere lustful interlude in which the worst elements of human animality are given full play, and the erotic components of smell, sight, touch, taste and hearing are directed towards a purely sensual gratification. But to the tantric pleasure plays only an incidental part in the process.

Woman provides an element that nothing else can give a man, for she represents the Opposite, the contrasting and vitalizing component that brings the vision of the goddess. Again, only the pashu thinks of the female in terms of intercourse with her. There is no room in Tantrism for the man who seeks out women for their beauty, youth, status, wealth, pleasure or progeny. The unique quality about a woman is her sex, and it is imperative that one's motivation should be moved from all considerations of personal desire to the pure fact of experiencing sexual union.

The further a woman is removed from all deceptive allures the better, for then the power of the female can be brought into operation in a pure unadulterated state, transcending all considerations at the physiological or social level. To the adept it makes no difference whether his sexual partner is a Draupadi (a voluptuous heroine of the *Mahabharata*) or a dombi (a low-caste untouchable woman). Beauty is a snare and an impediment, and in order to avoid its attraction it is necessary to overcome the obstacles of conventional revulsion. To avoid all possibility of desire entering into the rite, the true adept often insists that his partner be an old or ugly woman.

In the tantric circle worship it therefore becomes important that no claim should be made on any partner, and that no personal preferences should be allowed to decide the selection. Various means are used to ensure that the partners should pair not by choice but by chance. One method is for each woman on entering the sanctuary to deposit her bodice in a box, and at the end of the preparatory ceremonies for each man to pick one and take as his partner for the occasion the woman to whom it belongs, be that woman his wife, another's wife, his daughter, sister or even mother. This last requirement is explained away by some tantrics as symbolizing certain other mysteries.

Each stage of the tantric exercise demands some form of personal discipline. The asceticism of the unenlightened person involves resisting, conquering and killing physical desire. This latter does not dam the turbulent stream of sex, but only muddies it. The tantric practises *tapas*, which means both 'heat' and 'asceticism', and in tapas sexual desire is not obliterated but vitalized and used. It is a means whereby sexual energy is brought to a controlled intensity and then re-absorbed into the system. In one curious rite the tantric undertakes to serve the female like a domestic, for three months. He sleeps in the same room with her, but on the floor, while she sleeps on the bed. Later he sleeps in the same bed, but at her feet; then beside her, but clothed; then they lie together nude in each other's arms. But at no time during this cycle of 'closed intercourse' does he have sex with her. He builds up an inner tension, deliberately controlled by long self-discipline and complex yogic techniques so that his system becomes a reservoir of power and he is ready for the very difficult sex procedures that follow. One tantric text says, 'The man who knows the fiery form of Shiva procreates himself anew at every intercourse. His body glows, his mind is crystal clear, his spirit in harmony with heaven'.

(See also BUDDHISM; SEX.)

BENJAMIN WALKER

FURTHER READING: Agehananda Bharati, *The Tantric Tradition* (Hillary House, 1965); S. B. Dasgupta, *An Introduction to Tantrik Buddhism* (Calcutta Univ. Press, 1950); Benjamin Walker, *Hindu World*, 2 vols. (Praeger, 1968) and *Sex and the Supernatural* (Macdonald, London, 1970).

Typical of the many paradoxes contained in this ancient philosophy is the fact that 'Tao' means the 'Way', yet it does not prescribe a particular path; Tao is simply 'the uncomplicated essence of what is right'

TAOISM

ONE OF THE THREE great religions of China, Taoism, like the other two, Confucianism and Buddhism, has a traditional founder. He is Lao Tze, born in 604 BC in a hamlet in Honan province. During his long life he held a number of public offices and was for a time the curator of the royal library in Loyang. Confucius, more than half a century his junior, visited him and was overawed by his presence and his phenomenal learning. After the interview Confucius told his disciples, 'I understand how birds move through the skies, how fish swim in water, how animals run over the hills. Things that fly can be snared; things that swim can be caught in nets; things that run can be trapped. But what can one do with a dragon that soars into the heavens, trampling on the clouds and riding the storms!'

At an advanced age Lao Tze retired from government service and travelled westward on buffalo-back to the borders of the barbarian lands somewhere in the region of the Gobi Desert. At the boundary warden's earnest plea for a record of his teachings, the sage paused long enough to inscribe a mere 5000 characters on bamboo parchment.

Leaving this with the official he resumed his journey to an unknown destination, and was seen no more.

This small book, the *Tao Te Ching*, is one of the world's great religious classics; zealous Taoists claim that it enshrines the wisdom of the universe. As a result of speculation and commentary on its verses a vast library of Taoist scriptures grew around it. By the 1st century AD it comprised about 60 volumes; by the 7th century the number had increased to 4500. By that time, too, Lao Tze was worshipped as a god; temples were raised in his honour, and his original slender masterpiece was engraved on stone at the capital of every Chinese state.

The teachings of the *Tao Te Ching* are amongst the strangest ever propounded. They are paradoxical, inverse, passive, irrational. Although the term Tao means course or way, Taoism does not point to any particular way and there is no fixed track to be followed. Tao has reality but no form. Like the deep and obscure highways of the sea the waters close behind the moving ship and leave no trace of its passing. Little can be taught: 'The Tao that can be put into words is not the eternal Tao.' It opposes complexity, sophistication, 'cleverness', for these corrupt both mind and spirit.

This idea is well expressed in a famous Chinese story about the clever young fellow who saw a peasant watering his fields by the tedious process of carrying one pitcher at a time from the well, and told him about a mechanical contrivance that would enable him to get his water straight from well to

furrow in a fraction of the time. 'I know o[f] the contrivance,' said the old one, 'but [I] also know that those who use cunning con[-] trivances soon begin to practise cunnin[g] ways. Practising cunning ways their heart[s] become cunning. Those with cunning heart[s] are incapable of being pure in their thoughts[.] Those with corrupted thoughts have rest[-] less and disturbed spirits. And those wh[o] are troubled in spirit are not fit vehicle[s] for the Tao.'

Yielding Is Life

Tao is the uncomplicated essence of what i[s] right. It overflows into everything that i[s] in harmony with it. It is easy, but peopl[e] still prefer the difficult and intricate littl[e] paths, straining to get 'there', when th[e] way 'there' is best found by not makin[g] 'there' your goal. Ambition, fretful desire[,] thirst for fame, striving to be first, are th[e] real hindrances along the way. Take lon[g] strides and your progress is unsure. On tip[-] toe you are unsteady. Grab and it elude[s] you. Action and achievement are limitation[s.] The Tao has no shape but like an uncarve[d] block of wood it holds within itself a[n] infinity of shapes. Give it shape and i[t]

The three great religions of China are Taois[m,] Confucianism and Buddhism: the founder o[f] Taoism was Lao Tze, and Confucius, wh[o] visited him, was overawed by his presenc[e] and his learning *Below* The meeting of Confuciu[s] and Lao Tze *Right* Lao Tze, Buddha and Con[-] fucius, shown tasting saké on a 19th centur[y] Japanese sword guard

becomes fulfilled, formalized and limited. The simple is better than the sophisticated. In the words of the *Tao Te Ching*: 'Relish unflavoured things'. Staying at home is better than wandering: 'The Tao can be known without leaving the house. The further one travels the less one knows.' Silence is better than speech: 'He who knows does not speak; he who speaks does not know.' Beware the distraction of the senses: 'The eyes of a man blind him; his ears make him deaf.' Cultivate less rather than more: 'Power and learning is adding to oneself more and more. Tao is subtracting day by day.' Submission is better than resistance: 'Rigour is death; yielding is life.' Bureaucracy is remorselessly greedy: 'The more government, the still more government.'

Legalism defeats its own purpose: 'As laws increase, crimes increase.'

The *Tao Te Ching* is extremely susceptible to interpretation. When Christian missionaries first discovered the book they were so astonished to find what they thought were resemblances to the teachings of the New Testament, and particularly the Sermon on the Mount, that they called Lao Tze an inspired forerunner of Christ. Some even discovered hints of the doctrine of the Trinity, and found evidence of the Tetragrammaton, the four letters YHVH that make up the name of Jehovah.

Chinese scholars for their part read into the enigmatic verses many strange doctrines, and built up schools of thought and practice on innocuous words and isolated phrases. The expression 'divine man' sparked a search for immortality; 'long life' resulted in the manufacture of elixirs that would enable one to live for centuries; 'taste' inspired a system of dietary observances; 'harmonious infant' laid the foundation for a method of concentration which would create within one's body an embryonic seed that formed the nucleus of another, imperishable body; 'breath retention' started techniques of respiratory mysticism; the 'unknown female' sought the universal life essence in women; 'sex organ' was the beginning of a widespread cult of sexual mysticism.

Taoism actually existed long before Lao Tze, and is sometimes regarded as the primary religion of the Chinese people. One

of its mythical founders was the fabled Yellow Emperor, Huang Ti, who lived about 2600 BC, ten centuries before the Jewish law-giver Moses. In Chinese tradition the Yellow Emperor, like Lao Tze, was reputed to talk at birth. But unlike Lao Tze a great deal of magic was linked with the personal life of the Yellow Emperor, particularly of a sexual kind. Through a combination of the names of these two founders, Taoism is sometimes called the doctrine of Huang Lao, and Taoism in later centuries came to be associated not only with the refined principles of the *Tao Te Ching*, but increasingly with occultism and with the black arts as well.

In the course of time its pantheon came to include ancient deities of sky and mountain,

Buddhist gods, deified emperors, legendary and historical personages, a number of 'immortals', spirits of the stars, constellations, moon and sun, and of all things under the sun. There are guardian spirits of wind and cloud, kitchen and sewer, stone and stove, teats and intestines, tongue and teeth, literary works and account books, doors and hinges.

Most Chinese thaumaturgists have claimed kinship with the cult to add distinction to their particular brand of magic, and Taoism evolved an elaborate hierarchy of priest-magicians, both male and female, who were specialists in various branches of Chinese occultism. They communed with the dead, spoke with the ancestors, flew to heaven or hell as the occasion demanded,

and cast out demons and invoked celestial spirits. They combined the role of medium, oracle, sorcerer and physician.

The Bandits
Taoism has drawn into its orbit all the floating traditions of Chinese magic and sorcery, adding considerably to the bulk of Chinese superstitions and permeating all branches of Chinese occultism. It absorbed the doctrine of the two basic principles that underlie the universe, Yang the active, male and positive force, and Yin the passive, female and negative force (see CHINA). These contrasting but complementary principles lent themselves to further elaboration along sexual lines. Yang and Yin were said to be found in greater concentration in

e Taoist pantheon came to include a
wildering number and variety of gods and
irits, including deified emperors, real or
gendary people, and guardian spirits 'of wind
d cloud, kitchen and sewer, stone and stove,
erary works and account books . . .' *Left*
si Wang Wu, a Taoist deity, walking on the
a: Chinese saucer, 18th century *Right* Bronze
irror of the 3rd century AD, with figures of
oist gods

e human male and female respectively,
it a mutual interchange was beneficial,
d this was effected through sexual inter-
urse in certain special ways, first in normal
rtnership and later in group orgies, so that
e Yang and Yin might be absorbed in
eater variety.

Similarly the various forms of Chinese
vination, including the highly respected
ethod of the I Ching or Book of Change
ee I CHING), were subject to interpre-
tion along Taoist lines. Indigenous schools
medicine and healing, including acupunc-
re or the curing of bodily ills by pricking
e surface of the skin (see ACUPUNCTURE),
milarly claimed a Taoist derivation.
strology or the influence of the heavenly
dies on human affairs; geomancy or the
lection of propitious sites for cities,
mples, palaces, private dwellings and
aves, all developed on lines indicated by
aoist masters on the subject. Alchemy too
olved along Taoist lines. External alchemy
ncerned itself with the manufacture of
ixirs of immortality. Internal alchemy com-
ned breathing with sex techniques in which

C. M. Dixon

Pervading Unity

At the beginning of the present century we find
Taoist religious beliefs and practices still carried
on by numerous and mostly secret sects. Among
these was the society of the 'Pervading-Unity Tao'
(*I-kuan Tao*). This sect believed that the One is
the root of all things and, as a principle,
penetrates through and pervades all existence . . .
Followers of the *I-kuan Tao* were much addicted
to the use of charms, planchette, the practice of
the 'three secrets' of finger signs, and magic
phrases and incantations. They also abstained
from meat, tobacco and alcohol. They worshipped
images of all religions . . .

Werner Eichhorn, in
The Concise Encyclopaedia of Living Faiths

subtle fluids were manufactured by the
body, and were then potentialized and re-
absorbed into the system.

Finally the *Tao Te Ching* provided the
theoretical basis for a number of secret
societies, many of which combined banditry,
sorcery and the precepts of the *Tao Te Ching*
with a shrewd knowledge of military strategy
and tactics, and these societies remained the
bane of Chinese political and social life for
more than 18 centuries. The chiefs of these
societies virtually ruled large areas of China,
and their priest-magicians boasted dominion
over the forces of Nature, and claimed to
be able to divert rivers and command the
lightning.

In 1912 the newly established Chinese
Republic tried to put an end to these outlaw
organizations, but made little progress as
many in their own ranks were themselves
Taoists. But the time of the secret societies
had run out. In 1930 the Red Army stormed
the strongholds of the most enduring of the
great societies, entered the sanctuary in
their mountain stronghold in the province
of Kiang-Si, and smashed all the jars in
which their magicians were said to have
imprisoned the winds.

BENJAMIN WALKER

FURTHER READING: L. Giles, *The Sayings of
Lao Tzu* (John Murray, London, 1928);
R. G. H. Siu, *The Tao of Science* (MIT
Press, 1958); Arthur Waley, *The Way and
Its Power* (Grove Press, 1958); Holmes
Welch, *The Parting of the Way* (Beacon
Press, 1966 reprint).

TARA

OW UPON another time it chanced that
ochaid Airem, the king of Tara, arose upon
certain fair day in the time of summer and
ascended the high ground of Tara to
hold the plain of Breg: beautiful was the
lour of that plain.' As the king looks out
er his domains he sees a splendid warrior
pproaching him, unusual both in his beauty
d in the splendour of his weapons: 'And
ochaid held his peace, for he knew that
ne such had been in Tara on the night
fore, and the gate that led into the enclo-
re had not at that hour been thrown open'
ross and Slover, *Ancient Irish Tales*).
he majestic warrior is in fact the god Midir
ming to claim his wife Etain who, in her
ate of rebirth countless years later, is now
arried to the king of Tara.

This is the Tara of the ancient Irish tales,
e seat of the High Kings of Ireland, and the
cus of much mythological tradition and
tual practice. Here the supernatural is con-
antly present, and the tales frequently
ake the visitation of some god or goddess
e introduction to some amorous or adven-
rous situation associated with the other-
orld. In the story of the *Adventures of Art
n of Conn*, for example, we learn con-
rning Conn (who subsequently marries a
oddess after the death of his wife) that
Conn the Hundred-Fighter son of Fedlimid
echtmar son of Tuathal Rechtmar . . .
as once at Tara of the kings, the noble
nspicuous dwelling of Ireland, for a period

of nine years, and there was nothing lacking to the men of Ireland during the time of
this king, for indeed, they used to reap
the corn three times in the year.'

According to ancient Irish belief, a good
king, one whose conduct was in complete
accordance with the moral attitudes of his
tribe and whose physical being was entirely
unblemished, brought prosperity and peace
to the land and to the livestock and to the
people; the lord of Tara had to be perfect in
these respects or he was deposed by his followers. All these things we learn from the
rich literary tradition of medieval Ireland
which casts so much light on the darkness of
the Iron Age world.

The Screaming Stone

There is, moreover, another source of
evidence for 'Tara of the Kings' as it was
called, the 'noble conspicuous dwelling'.
This is the archeological record. Excavations of the site have provided convincing
proof of the veracity of the story-tellers
in their descriptions of this powerful royal
seat, and have given concrete reasons for the
recurrent mythological episodes which
characterize references to the place in the
early tales.

Tara is situated on a low hill in County
Meath, 23 miles from Dublin. The remains
consist of various earthworks, and a Neolithic passage grave which was used again
in the Bronze Age; this suggests that the
Iron Age occupants of the site took over a
place which was already hallowed, and

applied their own religious traditions to it.
The Celts venerated divine ancestors, deities
who gave their names to the various tribes,
and several of their sanctuary sites can be
seen to have had religious associations ante-
cedent to their own occupation. At Tara,
then, Celtic traditions were clearly attached
to an existing hilltop shrine, which contained a passage grave with later burials in
the mound which covered it. Just as the
Romans tended to construct their temples
on ground already sanctified by the presence
of native shrines, thereby winning over and
at the same time propitiating the supernatural forces already there (as did the
Christians in respect to pagan shrines),
so we must expect the innovating Celts to
have created their holy places at sites which
had been made sacred by centuries of ritual
and belief. They would thus both conquer
the older forces which were believed to
control the territory, and at the same time
render them quiescent by continuing to
observe religious rites there, but in honour of
their own deities. The fact that the patron
goddess of the great Assembly of Tara was
Tea, who is represented in the tales as
having been kept in captivity, and that two
other powerful goddesses of the early tradition, Etain and Medb, were also closely
associated with Tara, suggests that these
may have had an ancestry much earlier than
the Celtic Iron Age, and linking them with
such deities as the tomb goddesses of the
ancient Mediterranean world.

Little is known, comparatively speaking

Tara's Halls

The harp that once through Tara's halls
   The soul of music shed,
Now hangs as mute on Tara's walls
   As if that soul were fled.
So sleeps the pride of former days,
   So glory's thrill is o'er;
And hearts, that once beat high for praise,
   Now feel that pulse no more.

                   Thomas Moore

. . . the exaggerated pretensions of St Columcille had come almost at once into opposition with the established laws of the land, the law which enjoined death as the penalty for homicide at Tara . . . Of precisely such a nature – only with far worse and far more enduring consequences – was the cursing of Tara by St Ruadhan of Lothra. The great palace where, according to general belief, a hundred and thirty-six pagan and six Christian kings had ruled uninterruptedly, the most august spot in all Ireland, where a 'truce of God' had always reigned during the great triennial assemblies, was now to be given up and deserted at the curse of a tonsured monk. The great Assembly or Féis of Tara, which accustomed the people to the idea of a centre of government and a ruling power, could no more be convened, and a thousand associations and memories which hallowed the office of the High-king were snapped in a moment. It was a blow from which the monarchy of Ireland never recovered, a blow which, by putting an end to the great triennial or septennial conventions of the whole Irish race, weakened the prestige of the central ruler, increased the power of the provincial chieftains, segregated the clans of Ireland from one another, and opened a new road for faction and dissension throughout the entire island.

          Douglas Hyde *A Literary History of Ireland*

of the archeology of this ancient royal seat as yet. There are various features which have been named by antiquarians. The Mound of the Hostages, for example, which has been excavated in recent years, contains the primary passage grave and some 40 Bronze Age burials dating to c 1400 BC. The so-called Royal Enclosure consists of a hilltop enclosure with features which are again suggestive of ritual. It has also been suggested that the Banquet Hall is in fact yet another sacred enclosure of a kind known on the Continent. Other structures associated with the site would also seem to have been of a ritual rather than a domestic character.

Archeology, in conjunction with the vernacular literature, demonstrates that the

Tara of the Kings, in County Meath, the seat of the High Kings of the Irish and 'the noble conspicuous dwelling of Ireland': a magical stone pillar, the Lia-fail, used in the ceremonies accompanying the enthronement of the High King, was said to scream in the presence of the rightful ruler

Celts in general venerated stones of various kinds and that stone pillars in particular were worshipped. At Tara a magical stone pillar, known as the Lia-fail, 'Stone of Fail', was used in the inauguration ceremonies which accompanied the enthronement of the High Kings (see STONES). According to tradition, the stone used to scream when a rightful king was about to be inaugurated. A stone pillar which originally stood near the Mound of the Hostages and today marks an 18th century grave, has been taken to be the Lia-fail; it consists of a pillar of granite some five feet in height. The inauguration and choice of the High Kings was attended by much ritual, and a great bull feast (*tarb feis*) used to be prepared whereby a seer could envisage in a trance the rightful King of Tara.

          ANNE ROSS

FURTHER READING: T. P. Cross and C. H. Slover, *Ancient Irish Tales* (Barnes and Noble, 1969); E. Evans, *Prehistoric and Early Christian Ireland* (Barnes and Noble 1966); A. Ross, *Pagan Celtic Britain* (Columbia Univ. Press, 1967); *Everyday Life of the Pagan Celts* (Batsford, London 1970).

TAROT

The strange and beautiful Tarot cards form a system of communication through symbols, showing the relation between God, man and the universe; the symbols act as stimuli to the imagination and it is for each student to interpret them for himself

THE UNINITIATED usually regard the Tarot as a system of fortune telling using a special pack of fancy cards. But this is the lowest, if not a debased, aspect of a method of communication by symbol which has behind it not only antiquity but esoteric knowledge. It may be described as 'the cosmic method in universal creation or emanation, including its purpose and result'. As practised by the Western user, it is generally associated with the Tree of Life of the Cabala (see CABALA) but it has also affinities with the pyramids of Egypt and with Indian theosophical philosophy. 'Like all ancient cosmic symbols which are but the reduction of natural law to the simplicity necessary for human use, the Tarot is of the utmost practical value in all senses.'

The origins of the Tarot are not clearly defined. A. E. Waite concluded that it had no exoteric history before the 14th century and the oldest examples of Tarot cards probably date from about 1390, while occult tradition places their origin at about 1200 AD. It is said that the gypsies are believed to hold the first set of cards and that they alone hold the secret of its meaning.

According to occultists, the system comes first from the East, probably from Chaldea. After the destruction of the seat of learning in Alexandria, the adepts of all countries converged upon Fez in Morocco and made it the pivot of their esoteric science; since they spoke in many tongues, they decided to create a set of common symbols which all could understand and in which their truths could be pictured. 'As a skeleton for their invention the wise men chose the relatively simple system of numbers and letters afforded by the Qubalah' (S. Mayananda, *The Tarot Today*). The Hebrew alphabet consists of 22 letters and these placed upon the 22 Paths of the Tree of Life gave a combination of bases for correspondences (see PATHS). By this system of a pack of cards containing four suits of 14 cards each and 22 trumps unconnected with the suits and called the Major Arcana, ideas could be exchanged without the necessity of either the spoken or the written word.

The four suits are designated Wands, Cups, Swords and Pentacles, symbolizing amongst other things fire, water, air and earth: in each suit are four court cards: the King, the essential Self, 'Spirit', in man; the Queen, the 'Soul' or inner pattern part of a particular human personality; the Knight, representing the special focusing of energies and a personal sense of selfhood; the Page or Esquire, standing for the Body or personal vehicle. These four court cards correspond also to the four letters of the sacred Name of God in Hebrew theology — *Yod, He, Vau, He* (see NAMES). Yod is represented by the Kings of the four suits, and more especially by the suit of Sceptres or Wands, and it stands for the First Principle — the origin of all things. The first He symbolizes substance, in opposition to essence, and this is represented by the four Queens and by the suit of Cups, the form which contains the Life and the Feminine Principle. Vau which indicates Affinity completes the Trinity, and is pictured by the bond of love and the mystery of union exemplified by the four Knights and the suit of Swords. To stop there would indicate Finality. So the fourth court card, that of the Page or Esquire, represents the second He, marking the transition from the metaphysical to the

According to occult tradition, the Tarot pack was invented by adepts and forms a complete symbolic system. Different packs use varying designs and symbols, but there is a rough general similarity. The pack has four suits — Wands, Cups, Swords and Pentacles (*below*) — of **14** cards each, plus **22** extra cards called trumps or Major Arcana

ACE of WANDS.

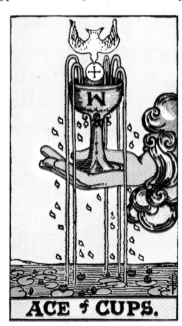
ACE of CUPS.

ACE of SWORDS.

ACE of PENTACLES

THE FOOL.

THE MAGICIAN.

The trumps of the 'Waite' pack, drawn by Pamela Coleman Smith under the direction of A. E. Waite: this is probably the best-known and most often used version of the Tarot pack, though the cards, shown on this and the following pages, vary from the traditional designs of older packs in many respects

material world – God in man made manifest. This is the suit of Pentacles or Coins, the symbol of material gain but also the five-pointed star which leads man from the unreal to the real.

The Tarot in its cabalistic form sets out to show the relation between God, Man and the Universe, and amongst other things it is a symbol of incarnation. It is one of those immemorial systems which were destined to convey this abstruse fact to mankind in a form that could be appreciated even by almost submerged awareness. Oswald Wirth says that a symbol is designed precisely to awaken in our consciousness the memory of that which we have already known. In other words, the use of the Tarot evokes the associations which we have already formed in the past. In *Le Symbolisme Hermetique* he states that 'a symbol can always be studied from an infinite number of points of view and each thinker has the right to discover in the symbol a new meaning corresponding to the logic of his own conception. Symbols are intended to arouse a thought by means of suggestion and thus cause the truth which lies hidden in our consciousness to reveal itself.'

P. D. Ouspensky (see OUSPENSKY) postulates that only a symbol can deliver man from the slavery of words and formulae and allow him to attain to the possibilities of thinking freely: '. . . occult knowledge cannot be transmitted either orally or in writing

The Tarot in its cabalistic form sets out to show the relation between God, Man and the Universe; amongst other things it is a symbol of incarnation

It can only be acquired by deep meditation.'

Tarota or *Taro-Rota* means the Wheel of the Law and the Law of the Wheel, and is a widespread symbol of universal life; the same idea is found in Western symbology in the phrase 'spinning of the Web'.

Dance of Life

There are various methods of using the Tarot cards; reference has already been made to placing them upon the Tree of Life, they can be paired as opposites or complementaries, or they may be set out in a circle or wheel representing the universe.

There are no standard pictures on the packs of Tarot cards. While the pictures are basically the same the presentation may vary. There is one known as the Marseilles or French pack which is probably the oldest in design and can be found reproduced in many books; generally speaking, the designs are crude and not well drawn. Manly P. Hall produced a pack drawn by Augustus Knapp but this is no longer on the market. Paul Foster Case, founder of the Builders of the Adytum, had a pack drawn by Miss Jessie Burns Parke which was very similar to the one usually referred to as the 'Waite' pack, drawn by Miss Pamela Coleman Smith under the direction of A. E. Waite; this, in turn, is generally held to be based on the Oswald Wirth symbolism, though it has

been considered that in certain details Dr Waite expressed his personal ideas of symbolism rather than the traditional esoteric ones. There is no reason why any interested student of the Tarot should not make his own pack, provided that he is prepared to undertake the necessary study to incorporate the correct symbols. Instructions for interpreting the meanings of the cards may be found either in booklets sold with the packs, or in the books on the Tarot written by authorities.

While there is an interpretation for each one of the 14 cards in each suit, either right way up or reversed, the ordinary person is chiefly concerned with the Major Arcana, the trumps, since these are the only cards used in dealing with the Tree of Life or with the system of the Wheel.

There are 21 numbers on the cards, and a zero. This is the attribute of the Fool and its position has been the subject of much discussion. Where does one place 0 and what is its significance? Taking the cards in numerical order it would seem clear that 0 should precede 1, yet Papus, one of the best known and most authoritative writers on the Tarot, places it between 20 and 21, and takes it to refer to the Animal Kingdom, that is the Kingdom of Instinct and not of Mind. If it precedes 1 the subsequent cards will fall sensibly upon their paths on the

Tree, ending with the card called the Universe on the final path leading to Earth – the Plane of Matter. Israel Regardie says 'O must precede 1. This is the most logical place for it'.

If the method of the Wheel is worked 0 will be placed in the centre as the hub; the remaining 21 cards will fall naturally into three segments of seven apiece, and when studied their mutual correspondence, either complementary, fulfilling or opposing, will be clear. There is a legend that once upon a time a man made a magical table and placed on it statuettes of the major trumps modelled as small golden figures. By his own great knowledge of the mysteries he was able to set the figures in motion and they wove in and out of the figures of the Dance of Life, so that he could see the pattern of evolution. But it was not given either to that adept or to his disciples to be able to move the 22nd figure – that of 0 or the Fool; for if the Fool joins in the dance the world is completed and there is an end to all things as we know them.

In this case the Fool represents the mystery of the Divine Love; when that is understood and he takes his place among the dancers there will be no more sorrow and no more misunderstanding, for the former things will have passed away. It will be the Golden Age in reality; we shall see ourselves in proper relation to God and man; we shall

THE HIGH PRIESTESS

THE EMPRESS.

THE EMPEROR.

THE HIEROPHANT

THE LOVERS.

THE CHARIOT.

STRENGTH.

THE HERMIT.

indeed be united with the Highest and therefore there will be nothing left for which to struggle.

The trumps of the Major Arcana, their sequence and their general meaning are:

0. **The Fool.** The picture is of a young man, a bundle over his shoulder, a dog at his heels, gaily treading a cliff edge with no regard for where his steps are leading him. To those who have begun to perceive the esoteric meaning of the cards, this carefree attitude is significant of the man who has followed the Divine Law and become as a little child. In German the title of the card is *Der Sille*, which means the Holy or Innocent one.

1. **The Magician.** In exoteric packs this card is sometimes labelled 'The Juggler'; in the Marseilles and other French packs it is called *Le Bateleur*, which means 'the holder of a small farm or estate' in Old French; no previous origin of the word is known, but it could be that the card is intended to represent a lesser Sun. The man in the picture has a figure eight shaped device over his head, a lemniscate, the sign of Universal Life. One of his hands points upwards and

the other down, while before him lies a table on which are displayed the four suits of the Tarot pack.

2. **The High Priestess.** She sits between two pillars in the place of Equilibrium; partially veiled, a book upon her knees, she is typified in the Book of Wisdom and in the mystical poets; she is the feminine aspect, the reflection of God. In Egypt she represents the Isis of Nature whose veil must not be raised by the profane.

3. **The Empress.** This shows a fine woman with flowing hair; she wears a crown with 12 points, signifying the diffusion of the First Principle in the same way that the 12 signs of the zodiac are disseminated and yet form a perfect whole. The card signifies the basis of Reality.

4. **The Emperor.** He represents the positive or active form of the Empress; he wields a sceptre which has always been taken as an attribute of the progenitor.

5. **The Pope or Hierophant.** This is the complementary opposite of the High Priestess, who is the instructress of the initiates to whom she imparts occult knowledge. The Hierophant gives this

knowledge to ordinary people in a practical and oral form that they can understand.

6. **The Lovers.** This card represents on one hand the dual nature of man: when the child is first conceived its sex is not determined; the potentials of both sexes are carried by every embryo and one sex is finally assumed in the material world. But the lovers also symbolize the most powerful of all the emotions; love properly expressed brings unity with the beloved, so that this dual card is both an analysis and a synthesis.

7. **The Chariot.** This portrays the man who has vanquished the elementary forces. It is the final card of the first seven into which the 21 numbered trumps are divided when they become a triad in the Wheel system; on the Tree of Life in the Hebrew version the card corresponds with the Hebrew letter *Zayin*, which signifies Victory in All Worlds.

8. **Justice.** This card stands for equilibrium in all worlds and in all forms. Occult science has been taught in word and in deed; the sword and the balance are the reward of a man's acts, whether they be black or white. As a man sows, so shall he

TEMPERANCE.

THE DEVIL.

THE TOWER.

THE STAR.

WHEEL of FORTUNE.

JUSTICE.

THE HANGED MAN.

DEATH.

eap. (In the Waite pack, illustrated here, nd in several later ones, cards 8 and 11 are ansposed.)

9. *The Hermit.* This card sometimes ictures an old man and sometimes a young ne. If he is old he is thought to be the man ged in years who yet has a young heart; if e is a young man, he is one who has already earned to walk in the right way. He wears he cloak of protection, carries the lamp of risdom and is supported by the staff of ighteousness. His quality is prudence, and ome packs will give the card this name ather than that of the Hermit. His signifi- ance is silence regarding the Inner Knowledge.

10. *The Wheel of Fortune or the Wheel f Life.* This card does not denote anything n the way of chance but is the symbol of the ternal action of time, the continuous rota- ion of the aeons, the mutable laws each ecurring in turn and then resting in Equilibrium.

11. *Strength.* This is the strength of the oung girl closing the mouth of the lion; bove her head is the lemniscate — the sign f spiritual life and virility. Here is the

counterpart of the young child in the cocka- trice's den; she is Sir Galahad in opposition: 'my strength is as the strength of ten, because my heart is pure'. Galahad the boy knight is as sexless as this maiden.

12. *The Hanged Man.* This most curious of all cards has been given different inter- pretations by different writers but it is generally accepted that it stands for Equilibrated Power. In the Hebrew alphabet the letter *Mem* accompanies this figure on the path of the Tree and is one of the three 'mother letters', standing for water. In all occult matters the element of water signifies a change of plane or of consciousness. This man has come far enough on the road to find absolute submission to the Will Divine.

13. *Death.* Death is the culmination of life in the exoteric sense; in the esoteric meaning it is the passing from one stage of progress to the next. Death has been termed the Negative of Realization, the universal link between material and spiritual. Nearly all versions of this card are based upon a skeleton, and include the very ancient phallic symbol of the sickle or curved blade.

14. *Temperance.* Here man is individual- ized. The water of life is being poured out and he has the power to accept or reject it for himself.

15. *The Devil.* This is a card which has puzzled many people but if it be looked at carefully it will be seen to represent No 1, the Magician, in reverse. The power is now misused. The right hand, the hand of power, points sometimes downwards and sometimes upwards, and those he has taken in bondage are in chains at his feet. The card is sometimes referred to as Pan, unbridled Nature, and his lighted torch is the symbol of destruction. He is to be feared and to be conquered. To allow him to gain the mastery is to allow Matter to overcome Spirit.

16. *The Tower Struck by Lightning.* This card is usually said to be symbolic of the Fall of man; here is the Tower of Babel; man is being hurled into materialism; as he pro- ceeds down the Tree of Life he becomes more man and less God. But it must be noted that in two French versions this card is con- sidered to be a divine happening; one refers to it as 'The Fire of Heaven' and the other as 'The House of God'.

THE MOON.

THE SUN.

JUDGEMENT.

THE WORLD.

17. **The Star.** This picture represents the Word in action in Nature. The butterfly or ibis symbol is a sign that the spirit is not lost though man may have far to go; the spirit will survive and the Fall is not irreparable.

18. **The Moon.** Here again is comfort for the soul in involution. The material world is only a reflection; man can descend no lower, and the Spirit is now immersed in Matter from which it must eventually start to climb again. Yet other writers have other ideas. S. Mayananda says, 'The picture presented by this Trump is a terrible travesty of what should be shown, or rather it is but the negative half. It seems to have been dictated by sorcerers or the Church in whose teaching the "world" is merely an evil condition to escape from to "Heaven".' And an Indian writer, Govinda, says of this card 'the symbolism of the elements moves on many planes'.

19. **The Sun.** This picture represents the first of the elemental kingdoms beginning its slow progress by development back to God. Spirit is renewed in a different form; man is freshened for his evolutionary climb and the mineral kingdom is slowly individualizing.

20. **Judgement.** Life is progressing a little further up the stairway, for this trump governs the evolutionary development of the vegetable kingdom.

21. **The Universe.** Here in this last card the macrocosm and the microcosm have met. Here the Earth of matter is represented in the four quarters – the four Worlds – and here the four animals of the Apocalypse and

There are almost as many interpretations of the Tarot as there are interpreters, and the meanings attributed to each card vary with the understanding of the student *Above* The Tarot may be used for fortune telling, although occultists generally regard this as the lowest use to which the cards can be put; during a reading the client shuffles and cuts the cards of the Major Arcana (*left*); these are then returned to the reader, who spreads them into a fan (*right*) from which the client selects seven cards which are placed clockwise on the table *Below* The cards of the Major Arcana laid out according to the system of the Wheel; the Fool is placed in the centre as the hub, and the student of the Tarot then meditates upon the significance of the cards, either complementary, fulfilling or opposing

of the vision of Ezekiel are depicted. It is the reconstruction of the synthesis of all and the figure of the androgyne is lightly veiled as with the Lovers, sex is undefined. This represents in one form God in man at the foot of the middle pillar of the Tree of Life.

These are the major trumps of the Tarot pack. Only one suggestion of meaning can be given by any one person in a limited space; and it must be remembered that there are meanings to each trump according to the understanding of each student, and that they are intended to act as stimuli to the imagination. Each and every writer on the Tarot will have something different to say, will develop another aspect; all anyone can do is to suggest an approach. This is a system of universal communication by symbol and therefore it must be sufficiently fluid to allow each man to use it as an expression of his ideas on the Absolute. The more that is read about the Tarot; the more the cards are meditated upon, the greater will be the flow of understanding and the wider the comprehension.

(See also CARDS; WALDENSES.)

CHRISTINE HARTLEY

FURTHER READING: P. F. Case, *The Tarot* (Macoy, 1947); Gareth Knight, *Practical Guide to Quabalistic Symbolism* (Weiser); S. Mayananda, *The Tarot Today* (Weiser); Papus, *Tarot of the Bohemians* (Weiser); A E. Waite, *The Holy Kabbalah* (Wehman); *The Pictorial Key to the Tarot* (Wehman).

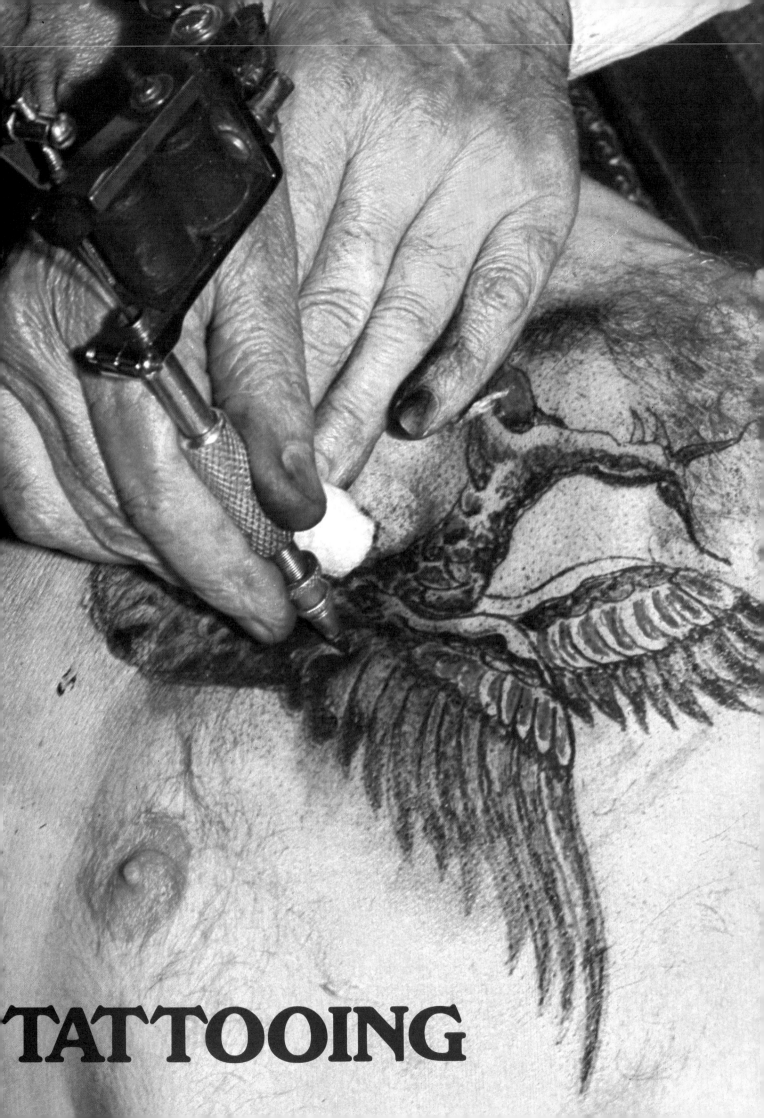

TATTOOING

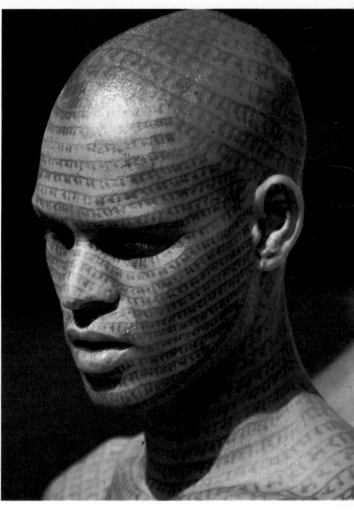

John Bulmer/Uniphoto

Among the Polynesians of the Marquesas every part of the body, face, trunk and limbs had to be tattooed; even lips, eyelids, gums and skull were not excluded

Elaborate decoration of the face and body satisfies an almost universal human drive; in many primitive societies tattooing and cicatrization have ritual importance as part of an initiation rite, and marks on the body often emphasize an individual's achievements or social status

THE·URGE TO ENHANCE the beauty of the human body by artificial means is worldwide, but the techniques of doing so differ from culture to culture and age to age. Among peoples who do not wear clothes, or whose clothing is sparse, efforts at altering the body's natural appearance concentrate on the decoration of the actual surface of the skin. The most prevalent methods of achieving this may be classified as painting, tattooing and cicatrization.

Painting includes all types of decoration in which coloured substances are applied to the skin without causing permanent discoloration. Tattooing consists of pricking pigment into the skin in such a way as to produce, under a smooth surface, a permanent pattern, usually of black or blue. This may be done in two ways. A small chisel or adze-like implement can be used to produce grooves in the skin, into which pigment is rubbed; or a needle and thread covered with soot may be drawn under the skin. In some cases the desired design is painted or imprinted on the skin with a stamp before the tattooer sets to work.

Cicatrization, which involves the artificial creation of scars, is effected by scratching, cutting, piercing or burning the skin. The wounds may be allowed to heal naturally, forming plain scars which are usually slightly depressed, or they may be aggravated so that they form deep gashes. Raised scars may be produced by continued and extremely painful irritation which results in the proliferation of regenerative tissue.

All these methods of changing the appearance of the skin are widespread, but the most extreme forms of cicatrization are confined mainly to the dark-skinned peoples of Africa, Australia and Melanesia.

The word 'tattoo', sometimes spelt 'tatu', was introduced to the Western world by Captain Cook, and is derived from the Tahitian term *tatau*, which is used to describe the marking or puncturing of the

During tattooing pigment is pricked into the skin so that a permanent pattern is produced under a smooth surface *Previous page* A tattooist at work in London *Facing page* Patterns formed by tattooing vary in different parts of the world; plain stripes are imprinted on the face, neck and shoulders of a New Guinea woman (*far left*) while a formalized design (*left*) covers an Indian's shaven head *Right* Selection of implements used for tattooing and marking the flesh includes (*back row, left to right*) a skin-marker from Guyana, tattooing instruments from New Zealand, Borneo and Japan, and (*front*) implement used in making Hindu caste-marks and tattooing tools from Burma

Horniman Museum

skin for ornamental purposes. Although tattooing in its most elaborate form was found among the Polynesians of such islands as the Marquesas and New Zealand, the technique was well known to the ancient civilizations of the Near East and the Mediterranean countries.

The pre-dynastic tombs of Egypt (c 3500 BC) contained clay figurines which bear marks suggesting tattoos, and the Egyptians of the New Kingdom (1567–1085 BC) tattooed their breasts and arms with the names and symbols of deities. In more recent times the practice has been common in many parts of Egypt, reflecting a persistence of the custom throughout more than 5000 years. Today its purpose is mainly curative, and tattooing is used for such ailments as headache, toothache, weak eyesight and possession. There are suggestions that it is a sign of sexual maturity, and it is also used to enhance sex-appeal.

In Iraq tattooing is believed to increase a woman's fertility, and her chances of becoming pregnant. It is also used for protective purposes. A woman who has had several children who have died will try to save the next by having it tattooed, for the practice is held to confer a long and vigorous life.

In Europe tattooing was known to Greek and Latin writers of the classical period. Herodotus mentions that Thracian women were tattooed as a sign of noble status, while Pliny refers to Dracian and Sarmatian men being tattooed. The custom was also current among several tribes of ancient Gaul, but was not practised by the Greeks and Romans. It seems to have disappeared from all parts of medieval Europe. The revival of tattooing among certain classes, such as sailors, may be the result of contacts with Asian and African countries where it was widespread, and often practised by professionals whose services were available to European travellers. It was common among the pre-Columbian indigenous population of the West Indies, Mexico, Central America and South America. Other areas where there is a high frequency of tattooing are Polynesia, including New Zealand, Melanesia, Micronesia, Indonesia, Malaysia and Burma. It is practised to a lesser extent in India and Tibet. Although it was common in ancient China it soon ceased to be used as

decoration and survived only as a distinctive mark. Today elaborate tattoos are found mainly among primitive peoples.

In traditional Maori society (see MAORI) men of aristocratic families had their entire faces tattooed, the patterns consisting of intricate designs of curved lines which formed spirals and arabesques and emphasized the nose and chin. Each chief was tattooed with the design peculiar to his family or tribe, while the figures marked on the faces of dependants and retainers were the same in form as those by which the chief was distinguished, although they were less elaborate. During the operation of tattooing a Maori chief had to be fed through a special funnel, for he was not allowed to touch his food, and a strict taboo prevented him from communicating with anyone not in the same condition. The pattern imprinted on the faces of Maori women was much simpler than that tattooed on the men, and covered mainly the upper lip and the chin. It was a disgrace for a woman not to have her mouth tattooed, for red lips were thought to be shameful. The operation was performed as soon as a girl had reached puberty. A girl's tattoo was also a sign of her maturity in Tahiti.

The most extensive tattooing found anywhere in the world was that common among the Polynesians of the Marquesas Islands. There every part of the body, face, trunk and limbs had to be tattooed, and even lips, eyelids, gums and skull were not excluded. The tattoo was applied in several stages, each taking three to six months. It was rare

for a tattoo to be completed before a man reached the 30th year of his life. The women were not as extensively tattooed. The designs and motifs in Polynesian tattoo patterns are largely the same as those used in the decoration of implements and boats; it seems that they are chiefly ornamental.

In Polynesia it is commonly believed that tattooing originated among the gods, and a similar idea is current among the Ainus, in the northern part of the Japanese archipelago. Their women are tattooed on their lips and arms in order to keep away the demons of disease, who believe them to be the wives of gods, since the gods are tattooed in the same manner.

Tattooing is an essential part of an initiation rite among the inhabitants of the Indonesian island of Mentawei, and no man who has not undergone it is allowed to marry. The tattooing is done with the aid of two little sticks, on one of which is a vertical needle. This tool is used by tapping it with the other stick to make small punctures in the skin, into which the colouring matter, the darkened sap of sugarcane, is inserted. The design starts with a convex bow running from the chin to the shoulders, and lines are also made over the breast to the pit of the stomach. The hips, arms, legs and fingers are tattooed. A man's upper legs are always tattooed just before marriage. The calves of the legs, the backs of the hands, and the sides of the body are the last areas to be decorated. Formerly this was always done at the time of a special religious ceremony involving the

n some Naga tribes great ritual and ocial importance is attached to the attooing of girls; the operation has he character of a 'rite of passage'

ft Fantastic animals tattooed on the mum-fied arm of a Siberian chief who lived in the h century BC Below Designs on a sailor's ns and chest; many seamen have themselves tooed, as a mark of virility and heroic venture Below right Intricate tattoo, typical the elaborate designs that may still be seen modern Japan

rification of the participants and the crifice of animals. This particular rite s performed to nullify the evil influence blood shed when someone was stabbed side the village or killed by a crocodile. A ecial porch was constructed to prevent the od that flowed from the tattooing, and ich was intended to 'cover the blood of e dead man', from falling on the ground.

Every village has its own pattern of tattooing. After a headhunting expedition the victorious warriors were traditionally allowed to have the beheaded man's image tattooed on their bodies.

The custom of using tattoos to register martial deeds is widespread. Among the mountain tribes of the Philippines, such as the Kalingas, successful headhunters were entitled to cover their chests, and in some cases also their backs, with elaborate patterns. Even women who participated in headhunting expeditions as carriers were marked with a special sign. But not all tattooing has a symbolic character, and Kalinga women cover their necks and arms with intricate designs made from lines as a form of decoration.

The Naga tribes of the Assam-Burma borderland (see NAGAS) also tattoo the bodies, and in some cases the faces, of men who have been successful in headhunting raids. The Kanyak Nagas, in particular, cover the faces of warriors with an extensive pattern of curved broad lines, giving them a fierce expression. The tattoos on their chests consist of geometric patterns combined with small figures of men which represent enemies killed in war. However, tattooing is not confined to men and in some Naga tribes great ritual and social importance is attached to the tattooing of girls. For them the operation has the character of a 'rite of passage', symbolizing the transition from one stage of life to another.

The tattoo of an Ao Naga woman consists

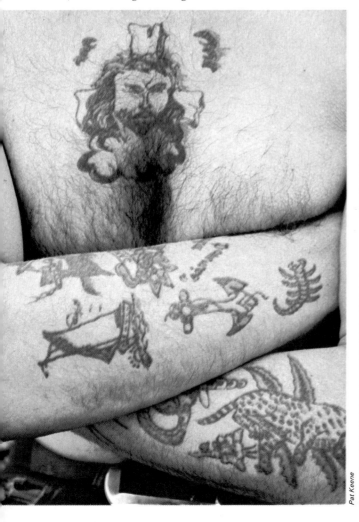

Pat Keene

John Hillelson Agency

Strength from the Forest

With regard to preferences among the women as to where they give birth, it varies. But there is unanimity that if there is any difficulty at all, then the right thing to do is to go off away from the camp and into the forest, which will 'help'. The forest appears quite clearly as helper and protector in the vine and wooden medicines and charms, and in the scarification that will take place at the first sign of sickness. Even with adults this is done: the skin is cut in a number of small slits with an arrow, and some of the flesh is gouged out. The ashes prepared from forest woods and plants are made into a paste with spittle and rubbed into the wounds. When the skin grows back, the black ash is still visible beneath, and is regarded as a source of the strength and health and happiness that derive from the forest . . . Insofar as this strength is conveyed by washing the baby with the juice of forest vines, tattooing it with forest ashes and binding it with forest symbols, this may be regarded as sympathetic magic. But it is better regarded as the beginning of a lifetime of close intimacy between the Mbuti and the forest . . .

Colin M. Turnbull *Wayward Servants: The Two Worlds of the African Pygmies*

roughly of four vertical lines on the chin, a chain of lozenges from the throat to the bottom of the breast-bone, inverted V's on the front of the shoulders and the stomach, solid squares on the wrists, an arrow pattern on the knee and lozenges on the lower part of the leg. It usually takes five years to complete this elaborate ornamentation. When a girl is about ten or 11 years old her legs are tattooed up to the bottom of the calf; the next year her chin, chest and the front of her shoulders are completed; in the third year the pattern on the calf is done, and in the fourth year the knees are tattooed; in the final year her wrists and stomach are ornamented. All the girls of the same age are tattooed in the same year, although in small villages there may not be enough girls to make it worth while calling a tattooer every year. In this case some of them may have reached marriageable age before their tattoo has been completed. Once a girl is married the only addition that may be made is on the wrists, and there are numerous women whose tattoo pattern has never been completed.

The tattooing is carried out in the jungle near the village by old women, and no male may be present. The pattern is marked on the skin with a piece of wood dipped in colouring matter, and the girl is held firmly to the ground while the marked-out design is punctured all over with an adze-like instrument to which a little bunch of cane-thorns is attached. The black colouring matter is applied once again after the blood has been washed off. The process is exceedingly painful, and if a girl struggles and screams overmuch a fowl is sacrificed close by to appease any evil spirit that may be increasing her pain. The punctures sometimes become infected resulting in bad sores, and a girl may occasionally lose a leg. However, considering the lack of precautions against infection, the proportion of septic cases is small.

Passport to Heaven

The Baigas, a primitive tribe of middle India, also regard tattoos as greatly enhancing feminine beauty, and aesthetic considerations are foremost in their attitude to the practice. That they are inextricably linked with the function of tattoo marks as a powerful sexual stimulant is partly indicated by the fact that a girl's arms and breasts are not tattooed until she is adolescent, nor her legs until her marriage. Tattooing seems to play a role in the skin-eroticism that is a strong sexual agent in Baiga love-making. Women themselves take great pride in their marks, mainly no doubt, because they know it increases their attractiveness to their men. A woman's husband is forbidden to watch her being tattooed, and for two days afterwards she is treated as though she were menstruating. Her body is then covered with turmeric and oil, and she bathes. A triangular decoration on the forehead is generally made when a girl is about five years old, and on the breast is the figure of a peacock or of a basket, done when the girl reaches puberty. At the time of marriage, or later, a pattern is applied to the back of the hands and lines of dots are tattooed on the thighs.

Among the Muria Gonds of the middle Indian highlands, tattooing is used mainly for feminine adornment. The day when she is tattooed is an important moment in the life of a young Muria girl, a real step towards maturity. It is desirable that girls should be tattooed before marriage, and if possible before they are betrothed. The marks also appear to be a kind of passport to heaven. According to a Muria saying, 'the god of heaven will punish a girl who dies without being tattooed, but if she brings him beautiful drawings from the terrestrial regions, he will keep her with him and look after her'. The tattooing is done by women of a special caste, and a myth relates how a goddess performed the operation on a woman of that caste at the beginning of time, and then instructed her in the art of tattooing. The method followed today is still the same as that described in the myth. Lamp-black, charcoal and pounded incense are mixed with castor oil and then burnt in a potsherd over a fire. The resulting black deposit is used as colouring matter which is pricked into the girl's skin with needles.

Some Indian tribes ascribe protective qualities to tattoo marks, particularly if they represent symbols of family or guardian deities. But in other cases they are curative; tattooing over a tumour is supposed to relieve it, for instance, and applied to the belly it will cure colic. Some Gonds tattoo the figure of a horse on the front of their thighs, and of a saddle between the knee and thigh, to represent the horse god who can make their thighs as strong as those of a horse; or they mark each upper arm with the image of Hanuman, the monkey god who is a symbol of strength; this is believed to enable a man to carry unusually heavy weights. Cicatrization is not unknown among the tribal people of India, although it is not used as extensively as in Africa and Australia. The Oraons of Bihar brand young boys in five or six places on one arm with a piece of burning cloth before admitting them to the bachelors' hall, and Gonds brand their joints with burning wood in the belief that this will make them supple for dancing.

Tattooing is also widespread among the Indians of the tropical zone of South America. The usual tattoo of the Apiacá Indians consisted of three lines extending from each ear to the nose, mouth and chin. At the age of 14 a boy's face-tattoo was completed with a rectangle around the mouth, indicating that the wearer was allowed to eat human flesh. The designs on the body illustrated a man's deeds in war and hunting. They included crude representations of animals, fish, men and women applied to the arms and legs. Among the tribes of the Xingu region a person's social importance was indicated by the width of the vertical stripe running down the middle of the face. A chief's face was tattooed all over, and gave the impression of being totally black.

While in most societies tattooing is done mainly for aesthetic purposes, it may also fulfil a protective function. The women of certain Arab communities of Morocco, for instance, have small crosses or other designs tattooed on their cheeks or the tips of their noses to avert the Evil Eye.

Cicatrization is widespread among the dark-skinned races of Africa, and the scars

Body painting may be practised for religious or ceremonial reasons, or it may be purely decorative *Above right* **A tribesman, his face painted white in order to intimidate the enemy and a child (far right), his face decorated with paint** *Right* **A woman in ceremonial costume. All these examples of body painting are from New Guinea** *Far right* **A young girl's sexuality is emphasized by the formal pattern painted on her body** *Following page* **New Guinea tribesmen; their bodies are covered in mud as a sign of mourning**

Axel Poignant

Axel Poignant

Axel Poignant

Carl Perutz

Harald Schulz

Harald Schulz

which are produced artificially on the face as well as other parts of the body, often serve as distinctive marks by which members of a tribe or clan can be recognized (see MUTILATION). In many tribes the operation forms part of the initiation rites of boys and girls, and is therefore a sign that social maturity has been attained. Similar practices occurred among many of the aboriginal tribes of Australia, and also among the indigenous and now extinct inhabitants of Tasmania. The scars, which usually cover the chest and abdomen and sometimes also the shoulders and arms, were produced by cutting the skin with sharp shells or stone-blades and by rubbing clay or sand into the wounds to delay the healing process. The scars are partly decorative and partly indicative of social situations. For instance, bereaved persons may inflict scarification on themselves to express their sorrow over the death of a relative. As in Africa the operation is also performed during the initiation rites through which boys attain the status of fully privileged members of the tribe (see INITIATION).

Paint for Beauty and Status
In the course of these rites and other religious ceremonies, the Australian aborigines change their appearance by painting their faces and whole bodies in a variety of fantastic patterns. The only colours available are red, yellow, white and black, and these are applied in broad bands and stripes. The aborigines often use their own blood, which they draw from their veins, as a basis for the paint.

Body painting is also widespread among the tribesmen of New Guinea and other islands of Melanesia, where, in addition to wearing masks, it transforms the appearance of men who represent ghosts and ancestor spirits when performing the ritual dances which form part of initiation rites and agricultural ceremonies. But the face and body are also painted for cosmetic reasons, and Melanesians make a clear distinction between decorative painting, which enhances their beauty, and the custom of smothering themselves in soot to extinguish all their attractions as a sign of mourning.

The Indians of South America, many of whom wore no clothes before they came in contact with Europeans, make extensive use of paint to adorn body and face. The most

The artificial creation of scars, cicatrization is caused by cutting, scratching, burning or piercing the skin; the wounds may be allowed to heal naturally, or they may be aggravated so that a raised scar is produced *Above left* and *Above* A Brazilian Indian undergoes a form of cicatrization in which vertical lines are scratched into his leg *Above right* Aborigine woman: the cicatrix strengthens her breasts and is also decorative

common pigments are red and blueish-black, both of which are derived from locally available vegetable substances. Some of these pigments remain indelible for ten days or more, and travellers often confused these apparently permanent painted patterns with tattoos. Among the Indians of the Uapes-Caqueta region, body painting is widely practised by both sexes, elaborate designs being produced by a roller dye. Women paint the undersurface of the jaw and throat blue to achieve a curious sculptured effect for ceremonial occasions, and smear their faces with red pigment to ward off danger on working days. Their backs are crudely spattered with blue pigment, but care is taken with painted designs on the legs, thighs, breasts and face (see COSTUME).

Elaborate painted designs were also common among the Tupi Indians. The combination of arabesques, frets, undulating lines, and other motifs differed so greatly in the various groups that a person's tribal affiliation could be immediately discerned. The design was named after an animal, the markings of which were supposed to have served as a model.

The custom of decorating the body, either permanently or temporarily, appears to exist in primitive and more advanced societies throughout the world. Tattooing and cicatrization are the most common types of permanent decoration, and though similar methods are used in widely separated countries it can hardly be assumed that the wide distribution of such

techniques is entirely due to diffusion. Specific styles, such as the elaborate tattoo patterns of Polynesia and the Philippines, which cover the whole body and represent an art form comparable to painting or sculpture, are certainly associated with a definable cultural tradition, but the actual technique of inserting pigment into the skin must have arisen independently in various parts of the world.

There can be little doubt that artificial modifications in the appearance of the body by tattooing, cicatrization and painting developed in early prehistoric times, but tangible evidence is limited by the impermanence of human flesh and the substances used. Tattooing has, however, been found on mummified corpses from tombs of the first millennium BC in the Altai region of central Asia, but such discoveries are rare; for the most part evidence is provided by stamps of baked clay which were used to apply paint to the skin, and earthen palettes used in the preparation of paint for cosmetic purposes. These palettes have been found on various Neolithic sites as well as among the ruins of higher civilizations. It seems that the modern practice of elaborate cosmetic make-up satisfies an almost universal human drive, and has its antecedents in the earliest civilizations accessible to archeological research.

Aesthetic considerations may be the most frequent, and are often the dominant, motives behind the practice of tattooing; but they are usually by no means the only reasons for the importance which many societies attach to body marks. Among peoples who lack a system of writing, tattoos and patterns painted on the body are a convenient means of recording and publicizing information about an individual's activities and achievements, and they may serve a similar purpose in societies where there are no distinctive clothes, uniforms or badges of rank to emphasize the status or social condition of persons and groups. However, their role as identifying labels becomes obsolete where more precise and sophisticated symbols are available to indicate the rank of individuals or the identity of groups.

C. VON FÜRER-HAIMENDORF
FURTHER READING: W. D. Hambly, *History of Tattooing* (Singing Tree Press, 1969 reprint).

Tau
Last letter of the Hebrew alphabet, and so connected with the end of the world and believed to be the sign with which the righteous would be marked, to protect them in the last days; as a result, a T-shaped cross, or St Anthony's cross, became a protective device against evil.
See CROSS; TALISMANS.

Taurobolium
Rite in the Mysteries of Cybele and Attis; the initiate descended into a pit and was drenched in the blood of a bull which was slaughtered above him; after this the initiate was regarded as 'reborn'.
See BAPTISM.

TAURUS

THE SECOND sign of the zodiac, Taurus the Bull was identified by the Greeks with Zeus's transformation into a bull when he abducted Europa; to the Babylonians he was the heavenly bull whose rising marked the beginning of spring.

Taurus is ruled by Venus, and people born under this sign are governed by their affections; they will go out of their way to avoid ill feeling. Modest, they do not seek popularity. Because he is associated with the earth, Taurus has been described as hefty, clodhopping, obstinate, lazy and the opposite of intellectual. However, these adjectives are no longer thought to apply to the constellation. The following description, by the 1st century AD Roman astrologer Manilius, has similarly been superseded:

Dull honest Taurus to manure the field
Strong Taurus bears, by him the Grounds
    are till'd:
No gaudy things he breeds, no prize
    for worth,
But blesseth Earth, and brings her
    Labour forth.

According to modern astrologers, although Taurus is not ambitious his rewards are the fruit of his toil, and not the result of getting others to work for him. Valens, a classical writer of the 2nd century AD, says: 'Those born will be good handicraftmen, hard-working, good at keeping things, fond of pleasure and music, and generous: but some of them will be labourers, planters, and builders. And if the benefics (that is, Jupiter and Venus) aspect the ascendant, or the ruler is well placed, they become high priests or athletic trainers, and are awarded wreaths and purple robes, statues and busts, and are given charge of sacred rites and become notable and famous.'

This is the origin of the association that Taurus is supposed to have with money. In

The Babylonians associated Taurus with the heavenly bull whose rising marked the coming of spring. People born under this sign of the zodiac are said to be good-natured and reliable; fond of pleasure, they are nevertheless hard workers, often scholars or philosophers and often extremely creative: illustration from *Stars and Marvels of the East,* a 12th century English manuscript

Bodleian Library Colour Filmstrip

fact, this sign actually symbolizes not money but real wealth, the result of the material forces of production. However, music is also a Taurean art, and people born under Taurus are competent musicians and singers. The influence of Venus means that the Taurean is fond of pleasure, generous and more than usually amorous. The bull is naturally highly sexed, but his attitude to sex is uncomplicated and he does not need to be stimulated by artificial glamour. Taurus's keynote is devotion, to a person, an ideal or simply to his work. His love is deep, lasting and undemanding. Humble by nature, he feels that he has no right to ask anything for himself.

Faithful Friend
Because he is ruled by Venus there is nothing heavy or unimaginative about Taurus. Although sensitive and keen-witted, the Taurean is not afraid of hard work or dirt or the unpleasant aspects of life, but accepts them as part of living. He enjoys beauty, however, and tries to avoid ugliness.

Emotionally truthful, the person born under Taurus is good-natured, reliable and a faithful friend. But he is inclined to brood, and needs encouragement. If religious, he is not necessarily conventional in his beliefs even though he is strong in faith and devotion. The Taurean gift for profound study makes scholars, philosophers and artists, and people born under this sign excel at work that requires patience.

THOMAS TAYLOR

THE FIRST TRANSLATOR of Plato's work into English was Thomas Taylor the Platonist (1758–1835). His edition, published in 1804, includes nine dialogues by Floyer Sydenham (who had died in a debtors' prison). Taylor's edition includes long introductory essays, and extensive notes, with long extracts from the Commentaries of Proclus. He also translated much of Plotinus, founder of the Neoplatonist school of philosophy, and the principal works of his successors, Porphyry, Iamblichus, the Emperor Julian, Sallust and Proclus, besides the Chaldean Oracles, the Orphic Hymns and the works of Aristotle, and many minor works. To all these he added long introductory essays and notes; of his own writings, the most important is his *Dissertation on the Eleusinian and Bacchic Mysteries.*

His translations have been superseded; his English style has at all times been criticized; according to Coleridge he translated Proclus from 'difficult Greek into incomprehensible English'. S. Mackenna's translation of Plotinus is, as a work of literature, superior to Taylor's; in philosophic exactness of rendering this is not always so: he himself wrote that 'in perusing the works of these great men, the reader must not expect the sublimest truths to be explained in a familiar manner, and adapted, like many modern publications, *to the meanest capacities'.* G. R. S. Mead (whose own work on Orpheus is but an expansion of Taylor's preface to the Mystical Hymns of Orpheus) called him 'a wonderful genius and profound philosopher'; 'what was true of his critics then is true of his critics today: though they may know more Greek, he knew more Plato . . . Taylor was more than a scholar, he was a philosopher in the Platonic sense of the word.'

Taylor himself recorded that his interest in the Platonic philosophy came through mathematics; his first work (published when he was 23) was a mathematical essay; and in 1816 he published *Theoretic Arithmetic,* based upon the Pythagorean philosophy of number; a work which retains its value to the present time. But his first significant publication – one of the seminal works of the Romantic movement – was the anonymous translation of Plotinus *On the Beautiful* in 1787. This paraphrase translation of the epitome of the aesthetics of Plotinus lies at the root of that doctrine of the imagination as the formative principle of all art which Blake and Coleridge independently formulated. This little book may well be the common source of their similar ideas. Wordsworth too must have read it, for the theme of 'the inward eye' of the mind, as well as the phrase itself, comes from this tractate with its impassioned introduction and epilogue in which the young Taylor summoned his contemporaries to a revolutionary return to tradition: 'Let us then boldly enlist ourselves under the banners of Plotinus, and, by his assistance, vigorously repel the encroachments of error, plunge her dominions into the abyss of forgetfulness, and disperse the darkness of her baneful night. For, indeed, there never was a period which required so much philosophic exertion; or such vehement contention from the lovers of truth. On all sides nothing of philosophy remains but the name, and this has become the subject of the vilest prostitution: since it is not only engrossed by the Naturalist, Chemist, and Anatomist, but is usurped by the mechanic, in ever trifling invention and made subservient to the lucre of traffic and merchandise.'

For Taylor erudition was not an end but a means 'to diffuse the salutary light of genuine philosophy', which was for him '. . . that sublime theology which was first obscurely promulgated by Orpheus, Pythagoras and Plato, and was afterwards perspicuously unfolded by their legitimate disciples; a theology which, however it may be involved in oblivion in *barbarous*, and derided in *impious* ages, will again flourish for very extended periods, through all the infinite revolutions of time'. That Taylor took seriously the ideas of the Platonists and hoped to see these ideas carried into effect, was, to the 'pedants' and 'verbal critics' with whom he carried on a lifelong battle, intolerable. According to the *Encyclopaedia Britannica*, 'His efforts were unfavourably – almost contemptuously – received'. For this the chief reason was undoubtedly the extreme antipathy of the age of deism and pragmatism to the Platonic philosophy as such. Taylor's works nevertheless proved seminal for the three most significant intellectual revivals of the 19th century, in England, America and Ireland.

The texts Taylor placed in the hands of the Romantic poets were the same that Ficino, founder of the Platonic academy of Florence in the 15th century, had made accessible to the Florentine painters, and their transforming effect was the same. As a translator and exponent of the Platonic philosophy Taylor must be seen in the context of that renaissance at the end of the 18th century of which the Romantic movement in poetry is only the most discernible aspect. The Greek revival had its beginnings in the visual arts, with such works as Stuart and Revett's *Antiquities of Athens and Ionia*; in the publicity that was given to the Portland Vase by the Wedgwood replicas made at the suggestion of Flaxman, the sculptor; and with work brought to England by collectors, notably Lord Elgin. Taylor must be seen in this context, as providing the Platonic texts and the exposition of Greek theology which accompanied this rediscovery of ancient Greece. He gave, in 1787 or 1788 a series of lectures on the Platonic philosophy at the house of Flaxman; and it is likely that among those present was Flaxman's friend William Blake. The substance of these lectures is probably to be found embedded in the several long essays included in Taylor's *The Philosophical and Mathematical Commentaries of Proclus* (1788-89). In the second volume of this work is included *A History of the Restoration of the Platonic Theology by the Latter Platonists* an impassioned discourse upon the Neoplatonic philosophers.

This essay is a manifesto; and on the title page of the first volume (dedicated 'To the Sacred Majesty of Truth') is a quotation from Isaac D'Israeli's *Curiosities of Literature*: 'Mr. T. Taylor, the Platonic Philosopher and *The Modern Plethon*, consonant to that philosophy, professes polytheism.' Taylor's polytheism was of course of a philosophic kind; his profession was perhaps made in order to add greater force to his rejection of Christianity, and his challenge to the monopoly of 'the classics' by Anglican clerics who alone could hold Fellowships at the colleges of Oxford and Cambridge.

Taylor was educated at St Paul's School; his father was a Dissenter, and Oxford and Cambridge were therefore closed to him. His father intended him to go to Aberdeen University, but he made instead a rash (but apparently very happy) early marriage, and so never went to any university, working instead in a series of ill-paid posts. Nevertheless his reputation extended to France; and the Platonic Marquis de Valady stayed for a time in Taylor's house before returning to France, there to be guillotined under the Terror. Another lodger under Taylor's roof was Mary Wollstonecraft, one of the first champions of the rights of women, who described the philosopher's study as 'the abode of peace'.

Taylor's studies were pursued in such spare time as his employment allowed; he was for some years assistant secretary to the Royal Society for the Promotion of Arts, Industries and Commerce, whose President, the Duke of Norfolk, subscribed to the whole edition of his Plato. In later years

National Gallery of Canada, Ottawa

Left Portrait of Thomas Taylor by Sir Thomas Lawrence; described as 'a wonderful genius and profound philosopher', Taylor exposed himself to satire because of his professions of polytheism. According to rumour he sacrificed a bull to Jupiter, and honoured other gods in equally appropriate rites **Right** Taylor's Neoplatonism influenced the poetry and paintings of William Blake, and his translation of Plotinus *On the Beautiful* may have been the source of Blake's belief that imagination is the formative principle of all art: *When the Morning Stars Sang Together*, one of a series of illustrations to the biblical book of Job by William Blake

he found a patron, William Meredith, but it is his early works – those published before 1800 – which had the greatest impact upon his contemporaries. These were welcomed by the young Romantics for precisely those elements for which they were anathematized by the *Edinburgh Review*, Horace Walpole, and 'the black-coated gentlemen' of Oxford. The strong Neoplatonic element in Blake comes from Taylor; his works were among the 'darling studies' of Coleridge as a schoolboy; traces of Wordsworth's reading of his translations of Plotinus are to be discerned in many images and verbal echoes. Shelley possessed a copy of his Plato; and his friend Thomas Love Peacock was one of Taylor's circle of friends in later years.

By his open professions of polytheism Taylor willingly exposed himself to satire; according to rumour he sacrificed a bull to Jupiter in his house at Walworth, and

honoured the other gods in no less appropriate rites. This was of course pure invention; but an episode in which the young Taylor started a fire at the Freemason's Hall while demonstrating the principle of the Perpetual Lamp of antiquity, is fact. That Taylor was a striking personality even in a generation of eccentrics is evident from his appearance in Isaac D'Israeli's novel *Vaurien*, as 'the modern Pletho'; and, many years later, as 'Mr Mystic' in Thomas Love Peacock's *Melincourt*. Coleridge refers to him as 'the English Pagan'; and he was in his lifetime always known, as he remains to the present time, as 'Taylor the Platonist'.

Taylor's 'polytheism' (or rather, his exposition of the symbolic language of Greek mythology) was for the Romantic poets the main source of the revival of mythological poetry which distinguishes their work. Blake's polytheism is contained within a

As a translator and exponent of the Platonic philosophy, Thomas Taylor must be seen in the context of his time, a period when there was a great revival of interest in ancient Greece and its works: part of the Parthenon frieze, one of the most famous of Greek antiquities, which was brought to England at the beginning of the 19th century

Christian framework; both Blake and Coleridge gave modern guise to their gods and daemons; though Coleridge's *Ancient Mariner* evidently derives in part from Taylor's writings on Odysseus as symbolically understood by Porphyry and Plotinus.

Shelley and Keats revived the Greek pantheon, but in a living way made possible by Taylor's presentation of the gods as the ever-active divine energies of the cosmos. The most important of Taylor's works on the interpretation of Greek mythology are his

Dissertation on the Eleusinian and Bacchic Mysteries; *The Mystical Initiations, or Hymns of Orpheus*; Porphyry's *Cave of the Nymphs*; Apuleius' *Fable of Cupid and Psyche*, and his dissertation on daemons; Sallust's *On the Gods and the World*; and an Introduction to *The Republic*, books 2 and 3, *Containing an Apology for the Fables of Homer*. The great merit of Taylor's expositions is their fidelity to the tradition from which they derive. Bacon had set the fashion in euhemerist interpretation (referring myths to a historical basis), so congenial to the 18th century English mentality; Jacob Bryant (author of the *New System of Mythology*) and Bishop Warburton interpreted the Greeks in terms of a religion alien to them; whereas Taylor unfolded the Greek mythology in terms of the Orphic theology (see ORPHEUS) and Platonic metaphysics.

Through the enthusiasm of Ralph Waldo Emerson and Bronson Alcott the works of Thomas Taylor crossed the Atlantic to become one of the main sources of the inspiration of the Transcendentalist movement, that 'new declaration of independence made on behalf of literature and art and philosophy'.

When in 1842 Bronson Alcott visited England, he paid Taylor the compliment of collecting, with Charles Lane, a library which included as many of Taylor's books as they could find; of the 214 titles which were taken to America for the library of their 'new Eden' at 'Fruitlands' in Harvard, Massachusetts, 16 bore the name of Thomas Taylor as translator, editor or author.

In England there was little interest in Taylor from the time of his death until the beginning of the Theosophical movement (see THEOSOPHY). Through the movement Taylor became known to George Russell (the poet A.E.) and to W. B. Yeats. A.E. called Taylor 'the uncrowned king'; as Emerson had described him as 'a better man of imagination, a better poet, or perhaps I should say a better feeder to a poet, than any man between Milton and Wordsworth'. William E. A. Axon, who published in *The Library* (1890) a bibliography and memoir of Taylor wrote: 'He was an enthusiast, and only an enthusiast could have done his work. His translations represent a side of Greek thought that but for him would be unrepresented in English literature.'

KATHLEEN RAINE

FURTHER READING: *Selected Writings of Thomas Taylor the Platonist*, with an Introduction by Kathleen Raine, an essay on Taylor in America by G. M. Harper, and a bibliography (Princeton University Press, 1969).

TEA-LEAF READING

ALTHOUGH TELLING FORTUNES by consulting the patterns formed by tea-leaves on the base and sides of a cup is often regarded as drawing-room entertainment, it is not purely an amusement. The tea-leaves can act as a medium through which the clairvoyance of the reader is stimulated so that he or she is able to reveal truths that would otherwise remain hidden; or the figures formed by the leaves may be believed to reflect patterns that exist in the astral.

The method used in tea-leaf reading is time-honoured and simple. The client inverts her cup, turning it round three times; she places it on the saucer and then taps the bottom three times with her left index finger. The clairvoyant, who is in a light trance, picks the cup up and turns it round so that the leaves can be inspected.

All tea-leaf readers have their preferred methods of interpreting the patterns made by the leaves, and only some general indication of their meaning is given here:

Chain of small leaves: A journey, travel; if two larger leaves are in close proximity, the excursion is mental and not physical.
Serpentine chain of small leaves: a visit to the mountains; if two larger leaves are in close proximity, there will be ups and downs in daily life; inability to settle down.
Three small leaves close to one leaf: A man.
Two leaves close to a small leaf: A woman.
Group of small leaves in a triangular pattern: A child or children.

Heart: Love; a heart broken or crossed by a chain of leaves represents a broken love-affair or a divorce.
Triangle: Emotional involvement; jealousy; rivalry. If pointing downwards this shape indicates a *ménage à trois*, if upwards, ambition and success are suggested.
Square: Several different possibilities are suggested by this formation; it may mean that the person concerned is well-established, conservative and a solid character. But it can also imply a need for protection, or the client's failure to excel in his career.
Star: Great success; a sign of genius; spiritual enlightenment. However, if it falls on or near a heart formation, the passions may be crushed and replaced by a life of asceticism.

The appearance of more complicated symbols or geometric signs needs profound study; because of their rarity they are extremely significant.

Many leaves spread all over the cup: A rich or confused character; extravagance; negligence; generosity.
Very few leaves in the cup: Clarity; direct action in the future. However, this also indicates poverty in emotional life, and if the leaves seem to arrange themselves in a provocative way they must be read with great care so that they offset the poverty of the all-over pattern.

Cup-Tossing, a 19th century engraving: tea-leaf reading is a homely branch of the old art of geomancy, the reading of omens in the patterns formed by earth, sand, pebbles or shells scattered on the ground

Cross: This means that the client is at a crossroads in life, and that a personal sacrifice may be necessary. If this pattern is in conjunction with one large leaf, it can signify death. However, care and tact should be exercised in making such an interpretation, and it should be remembered that the possible death is not necessarily that of the client. Other leaves close by will ward off danger, and show a remedy for whatever ill is likely to befall him.
Circle: Marriage; a close partnership; fame. A good omen.
Circle with a cross on it: Enforced confinement, possibly in a hospital, prison, or other institution.
Two parallel lines of leaves: A propitious journey; dreams that will come true; a long and happy life. Reinforcement of all else seen in the cup.
Dots: Letters; messages; thoughts.
Stars: Good luck.
Dashes: Surprises.
Flowers: Joy; an engagement and marriage.
Fruit: Good fortune; children.
Daisy: Simple happiness.
Gun or dagger: Danger; strife.
Scythe: A good harvest; a death warning.
Musical instruments: Good company.
Scales: Justice; success at law.
Ladder: Increasing success.
Key: Secrets revealed; knowledge.
House: Stability.
Bottle: Excess; flirtation at a party.
Envelope: News.
Fan: An indiscreet love-affair.
Teapot or kettle: Good cheer; contentment.
Pair of scissors: Angry words.
Hammer: Hard work.

There are other general indications:
Time is represented by the different levels of the cup. The rim is the present, and below this lies the near future, while patterns formed on the base refer to events that are many years ahead.
Place is indicated by the parts of the cup in which the leaves settle. Those nearest the handle tell of events that affect the home; the leaves on the sides suggest distance according to their proximity to the handle, and the ones on the base show the place of birth, nationality and hidden nature of the client.
Letters of the alphabet represent the initials of people concerned in the reading; the nearer they are to the handle, the closer their relationship to the client.
Clear symbols are lucky, with the exception of those that represent illness or death. *Faint symbols* tend to be unlucky, suggesting a weak character or lack of purpose.

In occult lore the bowl of the cup corresponds to the dome of the sky, and the leaves to the stars, and there is therefore said to be a connection between tea-leaf reading and astrology. There are also correspondences between the cup, the sky and the palm of the hand, and tea-leaf reading is linked with palmistry as well as with the stars. Other correspondences, such as the link between the leaves and the moles on the body and the bumps on the head have also been observed.
(See also DIVINATION; GEOMANCY.)

BASIL IVAN RAKOCZ

Mansell Collection

Marxist and 'hyper-Catholic', Teilhard de Chardin believed that the human race is still evolving; his vision was of humanity as a union of free persons propelled towards the God 'ahead', the point of convergence at which mankind is to find its consummation and meaning

TEILHARD DE CHARDIN

BORN ON 1 May 1881 at Sarcenat near Clermont-Ferrand in the Auvergne, France, Pierre Teilhard de Chardin died of a heart attack in New York on Easter Sunday, 10 April 1955. In 1901 he took his first vows as a Jesuit and remained within the order until his death. But Teilhard was not only a priest but also a scientist – a paleontologist – of some distinction. Before his death he enjoyed a considerable reputation in his chosen field and in 1948 was offered a chair in Prehistory at the Collège de France. This offer he had to decline because his Jesuit superiors in Rome would not allow him to publish his most famous book, *The Phenomenon of Man*. For Teilhard had ideas of his own, and these did not correspond to the official Roman orthodoxy of the day. Hence his superiors considered it more 'prudent' that he should spend most of his life working 'in the field', mostly in China, while the last four years of his life were spent in the United States where the impact of his ideas was less likely to be felt than in France where he was already well known. Right up to his death, however, he was not allowed to publish anything except papers of a purely scientific nature within his own speciality, but fortunately he had the prudence to entrust his manuscripts to a friend and not long after his death *The Phenomenon of Man* was published in the original French, the English translation appearing with a warmly sympathetic introduction by Sir Julian Huxley, in 1959.

The Soul of the World

The publication of *The Phenomenon of Man* created something of a sensation. The worlds of both science and theology were split down the middle in their attitude towards the 'phenomenon' of Teilhard. Some scientists denounced him as insufficiently grounded in biology, while others took up his ideas with enthusiasm. The theologians were also split, the orthodox remaining obdurately antagonistic while the liberals hailed his totally new approach to Christianity as a real breakthrough in that it seemed to make Christianity once again relevant to the modern world. Rome severely discouraged the reading of his works since they had been published without its permission under the auspices of a committee that was largely scientific and not by any means entirely Christian. Then came Pope John XXIII and the Second Vatican Council, and the rock of Peter, monolithic and unmoving since the Council of Trent in the 15th century, lurched forward with unforeseen and unforeseeable speed.

Teilhard was dead; but at last his ideas received a sympathetic hearing from the great majority of his fellow churchmen.

Posthumously he had his reward, for the contradictions of his life reflected the integrity and completeness of his thought. Within the Church he was the apostle, prophet and mystic of a purposeful progress, and yet, despite constant setbacks, despite what often seemed petty and timorous persecution, he remained not only a loyal son of the Roman Catholic Church but also faithful to his vows of absolute obedience to the Society of Jesus and the pope. His non-Catholic friends could not understand why he did not break with such pusillanimous lack of understanding. But his own philosophy of life, and vision of the future, made it impossible for him to break away from what he saw as the one 'axis' of cohesion in a world in travail. He had been attacked as a theologian, as a scientist, and as a philosopher, but basically he was none of these things. True, he *was* a scientist but his science was the prehistoric past of this planet, whereas his real and absorbing interest was the goal towards which evolution was, in his opinion, guiding and

'One of those human beings who could not be pigeon-holed into any obvious category', Teilhard de Chardin was a mystic, visionary and prophet; because his ideas did not correspond to the official Roman orthodoxy of the day, it was considered 'prudent' that he should spend most of his life working in the field, mainly in China. Although he was only allowed to publish scientific papers, he entrusted his manuscripts to a friend and his most famous book *The Phenomenon of Man* appeared in French not long after his death

pushing not only Earth, but the whole universe. As a theologian and philosopher he was never more than an amateur and he knew it. He was one of those awkward human beings who could not be pigeon-holed into any obvious category: he was a mystic, a visionary, and a prophet.

Basically he saw the salvation of the world in terms of a real reconciliation between science and religion, a situation in which religion would be able to re-interpret itself in terms of evolution, and in which science itself would be 'tinged with mysticism and charged with faith', in terms of a 'synthesis of the (Christian) God "above", with the (Marxist) God "ahead"'. In scientific terms he saw the world as evolving to ever-higher stages of 'complexity-consciousness', for, quite rightly, he saw that there was no reason to suppose that evolution had suddenly come to a halt with the emergence of self-conscious man. The very troubles of our times were a sign that the human race was undergoing a new 'mutation', a new qualitative change which would result in a new and higher form of consciousness in which the individual consciousness would be transcended in some form of collective consciousness. The precursors of this were the modern totalitarian movements. During the Second World War, most of which he spent in China where he was out of touch with the ghastly realities of the European situation, he refused to see the conflicting powers as black-and-white alternatives. Nazism, insofar as it was a cohesive and progressive force, he considered as an advance on what had gone before, although he was well aware that ultimately it could only lead to an 'ant-hill' civilization, which would be an evil parody of his own vision of the 'totalization' of humanity as a union of free persons animated and propelled forward by what he had once called the 'Soul of the World' towards a unique point of convergence. He was later to call this point 'Omega', that is, God or Christ as the ultimate term of human evolution and history.

The Cosmic Christ

At a time when the Vatican under Pius XII was fulminating against international Communism as the chief enemy, Teilhard saw in it the shape of things to come. In China where he had seen it at first-hand and had witnessed the vast human energies it had been able to unleash, he was convinced that here was a power working along the very 'axis' of evolution, which no earthly force could stop. Yet he saw that the new 'totalized' society could never be wholly valid unless it were underpinned by love. 'The world cannot endure, advance, or realize itself,' he wrote, 'without the action of a power that is a species of love. This is why, much as I sympathize with the "totalitarian" faith of popular fronts, I am forced to acknowledge that their *impersonal* forms of ideal "Humanity", "Society", (*a fortiori* the "Race" or "Empire of fascist doctrines") without soul or "face", are going to nip the Evolution that they want to promote and save in the bud.' What Teilhard had been anticipating actually came to pass for an all too brief period in Czechoslovakia, when

'Communism with a human face' became a living reality.

Despite the divisive tendencies that seemed to be tearing this world to pieces during two World Wars and their aftermath, he remained incurably optimistic; for he had an unshakable faith in Christ and the Catholic Church, which he liked to speak of in biological terms as the Christian 'phylum' (in biology a 'phylum' is a main division of the animal or vegetable kingdom).

But what kind of Christ did Teilhard worship? His was not Christ as preached by the 'orthodoxy' of the Roman bureaucrats but the cosmic Christ preached by St Paul in his letter to the Colossians in whom 'were created all things in heaven and earth' and who 'holds all things in unity'. As to the Roman Catholic Church (and Teilhard, far from denying his Catholic faith, described himself as 'hyper-Catholic'), according to this same letter of St Paul 'the Church is his body, and he its head'; and 'in this body lives the fulness of divinity, and in him you too find your own fulfilment, in the one who is the head of every Sovereignty and Power.' All this was vitally real to Teilhard, and this was the 'gospel' of which he felt himself to be the prophet.

'Spirit of the Earth'

In his vision the Church was not just a divinely appointed organization designated to save individual souls through a more or less mechanical administration of the sacraments. Rather, it was a living organism – a single phylum – which had to be saved in

its totality, for he could not conceive of the salvation of the part except in the context of the salvation of the whole. Nor was his God simply 'our Father which art in Heaven,' but the God 'ahead', the point of convergence at which the human race, through the instrumentality of the Church, was to find its consummation and meaning. This vision presented itself to Teilhard with irresistible force when he was serving as a stretcher-bearer in the First World War; and it never left him till his dying day.

In his vision there were two ingredients always present. Christ as the point of convergence in the future and his own almost physical awareness of the 'Spirit of the earth' – an awareness of the 'holiness' of matter and the 'essence' of the world that had 'hit' him when he was still a child and from which his 'whole internal life had sprung and grown . . . a personal psychological experience: nothing more, but also nothing less.'

A Paroxysm of Love

Teilhard was a pantheist and he knew it; but according to him there were two types of pantheism. These were what he describes as Hindu pantheism – the pantheism of diffusion and dissolution of all individual personality into an indeterminate whole – and a pantheism of 'centration' in which personality, so far from being obliterated, is heightened and clarified through love and centred on to the cosmic Christ who is the point to which all creation (or at least all of it that can be saved) is destined by evolution itself to converge. The 'oriental' pantheism

of diffusion, which he had himself experienced time and again, is a blissful experience all right, but it is nonetheless essentiall retrograde, a step back into a state of 'co consciousness' before self-consciousnes was born. The new mysticism neithe abolishes personality nor sinks back into th beatific peace of undifferentiated oneness but throws itself in a paroxysm of love int him who is both the source and goal of al personality and the collective fulfilmen of all personalities.

Teilhard was both a mystic and a Marx ist. He looks forward to the Marxist 'associa tion in which the free development of eacl will be the condition for the free develop ment of all' and to a state of cosmic aware ness which will be suffused by love, and concentrated on and towards that ultimat unity to which evolution is driving us and which is the true goal of Christianity and th Catholic Church – Christ Omega, the cosmi fulfilment of mankind. This is the gospe according to Pierre Teilhard de Chardin humanist, Marxist, mystic, and 'hyper Catholic.'

R. C. ZAEHNEI

FURTHER READING: Pierre Teilhard d Chardin, *Hymn of the Universe* (1964) *Le Milieu Divin* (1960) and *The Phenom enon of Man* (1959) are published b Harper and Row; *Letters to Two Friend 1926–1952* (World Publishing, 1969). Se also: C. Cuénot, *Teilhard de Chardir* (Helicon, 1965); Robert Speaight, *Teilhar de Chardin* (Harper and Row, 1968).

Telekinesis

Paranormally caused movement of objects: examples include the fall of a picture at someone's death, the flight of the Communion wafer to the recipient's mouth, and the movement of furniture or flinging of stones or crockery in poltergeist cases; teleportation, or apportation, is the mysterious conveyance of objects into closed rooms.
See MEDIUMS; POLTERGEISTS; PSYCHOKINESIS; SPONTANEOUS PSI EXPERIENCES; STIGMATA.

Telepathy

Communication between one mind and another without the use of speech, gesture or any of the normal methods of communicating; thought transference; 'the direct experience of another person's mental state'; a type of extra-sensory perception.
See EXTRA-SENSORY PERCEPTION; SPONTANEOUS PSI EXPERIENCES.

A practical and down-to-earth mystic, Teresa of Avila at the same time attained lofty heights of spiritual experience; on the one hand, an able administrator and on the other, a saint who showed the way to the ultimate fusion of the soul's being with God

TERESA OF AVILA

RECOGNIZED AS ONE of the greatest Christian mystics, Teresa de Cepeda y Ahumada, in religion Teresa of Jesus, will always be known as Teresa of Avila, from the Castilian town in which she was born on 28 March 1515 and where she spent most of her 67 years until her death on 4 October 1582.

She was one of ten children – mostly boys – and when her father's second wife died in 1528, Teresa became something of an anxiety to her father, who finally put her in a boarding school, which she had to leave after 18 months owing to ill-health. He opposed her wish to become a nun, but at the age of 20 she eventually entered the Carmelite convent of the Incarnation in Avila.

The Carmelite Order, which originated in Palestine at the foot of the mountain from which it takes its name, had been, in intention, a body of hermits dedicated to extreme austerity. The extension of the hold of the Moslems in the Levant in the 13th century made life increasingly difficult, and the members of the order left Carmel for Cyprus, France, England and Spain. Progressive

mitigation of the primitive rule became th accepted thing, and the convent of the Incar nation was lax in its observance and worldl in its spirit. Teresa was to reproach hersel in later years for her own unfaithfulness, ye we know that during the 18 years she spen in that first convent, she seems to have ha authentic mystical experiences. As the resul of one of these, a vision of Christ in hi Passion, she experienced a 'conversion' an began to lead a stricter life. In the yea 1560, together with a small group of like minded nuns, she decided to found a con vent of strict observance, and in Augus 1562 she left the Incarnation for the ne house, dedicated to St Joseph, also in Avila There she was to spend what she later des cribed as the happiest years of her lif from 1562 to 1567. It was at this time that she wrote the first version of her *Life* and also her *Way of Perfection*.

In 1567 she was ordered by the general of the Carmelite Order, then on a visit to Spain, to make other foundations. The remaining 15 years of her life were largely spent in travelling, negotiating, working with her own hands – she was, a contemporary declares, the best cook in the order. For, whilst she enjoyed the most remarkable and lofty mystical experiences, she always kept her feet on the ground. 'The Lord walks amongst the saucepans', was a famous saying of hers. In all, she was personally responsible for setting up 19 establishments, including two for men. She was helped in her work by a Carmelite friar, Fr Jerome Gracian. But her chief support in the closing years of her life came from an even greater exponent of mystical theology, John of the Cross (see JOHN).

The seal was set on her life's work when, in 1581, the distinction between the 'calced' or shod, and 'discalced' or shoeless Carmelites, as the relaxed parent body and the stricter reformed order were respectively known, was officially recognized by their separation into two orders, with separate governing bodies. She died in the following year, at Alba, one of her many foundations.

'Suborned with a Sardine'

The first important work from her pen was the *Life*, written between 1562 and 1565. It falls into four main divisions: an account of her early years, down to her 'conversion' to a life of perfection; a treatise on prayer; an account of her spiritual experiences, graces and temptations after her conversion; and the story of the foundation of St Joseph and some account of further experiences. To be grouped with the *Life* are the *Relations* which, from time to time, she wrote for the benefit of her confessors and spiritual directors. We should bear in mind that there was in Spain at the time much suspicion of those who claimed to have had special revelations, and Teresa was always anxious lest she should be deluded. Equally, her spiritual directors needed reassurance about their remarkable penitent.

The Way of Perfection, probably written in the year 1565, and rewritten before 1571, was intended as a guidebook for her nuns at St Joseph. The first part is a treatise on the ascetical preparation necessary for the aspirant to the heights of mystical experience, together with some account of 'mental prayer', the preliminary to true mystical prayer. The latter is treated, in the second part of the work, in the shape of a comentary on the Lord's Prayer.

The Interior Castle, written in 1577 and revised three years later, is universally recognized as her greatest achievement. It treats of the progress of the soul from the earliest imperfect stage to the final achievement of the mystic marriage. The 'castle' is pictured as a fabulously rich building, consisting of seven 'mansions' or apartments, the seventh and central one being the dwelling place of the Blessed Trinity, residing in the depths of the soul. Thus the mystic way is a turning away from outward reality to enter 'into oneself', there to find oneself in the embrace of God.

The Foundations, written at intervals during the last nine years of her life, is basically an account of the travels, negotiations, adventures and difficulties that attended the work of setting up the different convents of the reformed order. But it also contains much practical and spiritual advice to her nuns and to their superiors.

Letters, written throughout her life, give us an invaluable picture of the woman of affairs, the negotiator, the mother, the friend, remaining a complete human being even in the times of her great mystical experiences. They bear the stamp of a remarkable personality the warmth of whose heart is equalled, it would seem, only by the range of her interests and the solidity of her common sense.

Like all mystics, who see the end of human existence as a union with God, Teresa used language which implied a disregard of, if not a positive contempt for, the ephemeral realities of this world. Since this seems to be

The Carmelite convent of the Incarnation in which Teresa of Avila spent 18 years was worldly in spirit and lax in its observance, and she later reproached herself for her unfaithfulness during this period. However, she seems to have had authentic mystical experiences while at the convent, and as a result of one of these, in which she had a vision of Christ in his Passion, she was 'converted' and began to lead a stricter life: *The Ecstasy of St Teresa* by Cignaroli

Mansell Collection

a basic element in all types of mystical doctrine, it calls for a further study. It must be recognized that such an attitude of mind, even if it is often expressed in absolute terms, can be justified only as an appreciation of relative values. In any human situation, certain values, pleasures, satisfactions, have to be sacrificed for the sake of a more pressing, more important demand. We have seen that, in everyday affairs, Teresa was eminently practical; we know that she was immensely affectionate and sensitive; she had her natural preferences, as when she said: 'It must be my nature – I could be suborned with a sardine!'; she constantly exhorted her nuns to accept their daily, concrete responsibilities. If, then, she was fond of saying *todo es nada*, 'everything is nothing', she meant this in the sense that everything derives its value and its significance from its relationship to God, its creator. Apart from him – if such an expression has any meaning – 'everything' is worthless and meaningless.

In her description of the total process leading to final mystical union, she distinguishes two main stages – the stage in which the emphasis is primarily on human effort, and the stage where all the work is seen as done by the spirit of God. In a famous passage in her *Life*, she compares the soul to an orchard, in need of water. At first this water is laboriously drawn from a well by hand. Then, the labour is lightened by the use of a *noria* (windlass), and water pipes. Yet more effective is the irrigation of the soil by streams, but best of all is the beneficent rain of God.

The approach to God, the way of perfection, is to be achieved, then, first by the ascetical effort which 'detaches' the soul from created reality so that it may come to a clearer vision of the Creator. Such detachment, not merely from possessions but from the sort of 'natural' affection which is a kind of self-seeking, will pave the way for true charity, a total love of the other for the sake of the other. Humility, the recognition of our own insignificance before God, is seen as another kind of detachment – from comfort, health, even life, to say nothing of reputation.

Concurrently with this ascetical effort must go the cultivation of 'mental prayer', the use of imagination and intellect about the things of God. As distinct from 'contemplation' or what Teresa calls 'supernatural' prayer, this first stage is due primarily to our own striving. In general, she would lump together the asceticism and the kind of prayer that goes with it as forming our contribution, our active progress towards the stage when God 'takes over' and the soul becomes 'passive'. In the imagery of *The Interior Castle*, the first three 'mansions' represent the first stage of the soul's journey.

When the soul enters the fourth mansion, it is coming under the influence of those graces which become more and more powerful as the soul submits more and more to their influence. From a state of recollection, in which the aspirant finds less and less savour in the sort of human conversation which merely dissipates the mind, God brings the soul to the prayer of 'quiet', in which the faculties of imagination and intellect become almost completely suspended. It is, one may suggest, as though the specific qualities of the individual human personality are surrendering to the power of God. Yet, as Teresa insists, the personality does not thereby become weakened or impoverished. On the contrary, the effects of this kind of prayer are an increased liberty of spirit, a growing sense of the Infinite and 'a great mastery of earthly realities'.

The final stages of the mystic way are the steps leading to the ultimate fusion of the soul's being with the Godhead. In Teresa's analysis there are three successive experiences to be undergone. Using the analogy of marriage, she speaks first of the meeting, the introduction of the spouses. The soul is being prepared for betrothal and marriage by a minute conformity of its will with the will of God the Beloved. In the prayer of (infused) 'union', the understanding and the will become united with the Godhead, in such a way that the human being no longer understands or wills anything otherwise than as God sees and wills. During this phase, too, the soul undergoes the purification of the senses. Yet the pain of this purification, and the purification of the spirit which follows, are essential experiences in that fullness of union which, daringly described in language reminiscent of sexual ecstasy, is at once intolerably painful yet incomparably delightful. But, in the very heart and centre of the 'castle', where the mystical marriage is at last celebrated, the encounter is such that the soul, now totally forgetful of itself, lives only for God. Life is desired solely as an opportunity of serving him. A foretaste of eternal bliss, this full union represents the highest favour that God can bestow on a human soul. Perfection is achieved.

T. CORBISHLEY

FURTHER READING: A. Peers ed, *The Complete Works of St Teresa of Jesus* 3 vols (Sheed and Ward, 1946); *Letters of St Teresa* (Burns & Oates, London, 1951). See also: Marcelle Auclair, *St Teresa of Avila* (Doubleday); R. Hoornaert, *Saint Teresa in Her Writings* (Sheed and Ward, 1931); Kate O'Brien, *Teresa of Avila* (Max Parrish 1951).

Tetragrammaton

The four Hebrew letters of the name of God in the Old Testament, spoken as Jehovah or Yahweh; regarded with profound awe it was rarely pronounced, and in the ordinary services in the synagogue the names Adonai or Elohim were substituted for it; it passed into European magic as one of the major 'names of power'.
See NAMES.

Theogony

Birth of the gods, an account, myth or theory of the origin, generation and line of descent of the gods; specifically, Hesiod's poem on the genealogy of the Greek gods.
See CREATION MYTHS; CRONUS.

The Theosophical Society does not identify itself with any particular religion, but has been described as 'a philanthropic society in that it attempts to promote a love of mankind and it is religious in that it demonstrates a spiritual background to existence'

THEOSOPHY

THE GERMAN ORIENTALIST Friedrich Max Müller (1823–1900) defined theosophy as 'expressing the highest conception of God within the reach of the human mind, and the perception of the eternal oneness of human and divine nature.' The emphasis is on the intuitive, inner nature of the knowledge, something not experienced through facts open to ordinary intelligence.

It is an ancient conception, particularly in India, where the philosophical schools of Vedanta and Sankhya, and the Yoga *Upanishads* teach it. At Alexandria the philosopher Philo Judaeus (1st century AD) joined the ideas of Plato with Judaism in a theosophic system. It persisted in the Cabala and Neoplatonism, and adherents of the system appear down through the centuries. Paracelsus, Giordano Bruno, Jacob Boehme, Emmanuel Swedenborg, John Tauler and Meister Eckhardt – all taught the essential basis of theosophy (see BOEHME; BRUNO; CABALA; ECKHARDT; NEOPLATONISM; PARACELSUS; SWEDENBORG).

In modern times the name is associated with the system set out in the 19th century in her books by H. P. Blavatsky (see BLAVATSKY). She stated that she had received these doctrines from Indian teachers or masters who had reached a higher plane of being and of spiritual development. Her experiences and witness to occult feats made her salon a magnet for a wide variety of people, who usually found her in possession of out-of-the-way facts in their own special subjects. The Theosophical Society, which she founded in conjunction with Henry S. Olcott and W. Q. Judge, exercised an influence on many notable people, either by its books, or by recruiting them as members. A copy of Blavatsky's *The Voice of the Silence* was on Lord Tennyson's bedside table when he died. Sir William Crookes, chemist and psychic researcher (see CROOKES), was a member; so were Thomas Alva Edison, the inventor, and W. B. Yeats, the poet (see YEATS). Lord Crawford, the astronomer, was a frequent visitor in London, and the student Mahatma Gandhi made his first acquaintance with the *Gita* among the theosophists. Rudolf Steiner, editor of Goethe and founder of Anthroposophy, was for a time at the head of the German section of the Society (see STEINER).

Annie Besant (see BESANT) was criticized for her political activity in India, but she explained, in 1929: 'What I say of the Inner Government of the World I speak from personal knowledge, for I have studied and practised Raja Yoga steadily during 40 years. . . . the Freedom of India within the great Federation of Free Nations linked by the British Crown is a condition essential to the Great Plan which must ultimately succeed.'

On her death in 1933 the Vice-President A. P. Warrington, took charge, and appointed in his own post C. Jinarajadasa a well-loved and accomplished lecturer and author. There were two nominees for President, and some acrimony because a letter had been made public in which Mrs Besant had remarked to the recipient, Dr George S. Arundale, that he was to be her successor. The other nominee, Ernest Wood (Sanskrit scholar and former secretary to C. W. Leadbeater, who had been closely associated with Annie Besant) objected to this and himself circularized the membership. However, out of a 72 per cent vote he secured only 4825 votes against Dr Arundale's 15,604.

In 1934 Dr Arundale stated what he called the marks theosophy makes upon the chart of Life: '(1) Life is essentially one and universal; (2) Life is within a great evolutionary process whereby an infinitude of life-units move from lowliest unconsciousness through innumerable stages of unfolding to heights of self-consciousness; (3) This irresistible movement is under beneficent and immutable law, order and purpose; (4) That all good and ill fortune individual or collective are signs of this evolutionary principle at work; (5) Each life-unit can hasten or retard the pace of its own evolutionary process, through understanding or through ignorance.'

Dr Arundale married an Indian lady

hrimati Rukmini Devi, who did important ork in the revival of the classical Indian ance, Indian art, and the education of omen. As President he did not travel as idely and frequently as others, but that was artly owing to the Second World War. He id give a great deal of attention to the ovement in Australia, with good results. is books on special subjects like *Nirvana, undalini, You* (some critics said it should e '*Me*') and *Mount Everest, its Spiritual ignificance,* were intended to stimulate the ntuition of the reader. This applied still ore strongly to his large book on symolism, *The Lotus Fire,* which most people und too difficult.

iddu Krishnamurti

a the early 1900s some European male sidents of the Theosophical Society's eadquarters used to swim of a morning the Adyar river. Two young Indian others used to watch them and then were ven swimming lessons. C. W. Leadbeater ad noticed the exceptional aura of the older oy, and it occurred to him that it would interesting to look at the previous lives an ordinary Indian boy like this and see hat his history was. The boys were two of rather large family who lived in the village the estate, sons of a minor local official, Narayaniah. Ernest Wood claimed to ave suggested to Leadbeater that he look the past lives of Krishnamurti and Nityananda, and that this was done with the ther's permission. Wood's idea was that ost Indians he knew abhorred the suggeson that they might be reborn in the West, d he wondered if experience in different ces was the general rule. Leadbeater found his surprise that the boy had had previous es of great significance, and he comented, 'surely he is not here by accident'.

An offer was made to the father that Mrs esant would undertake the future educan and development of Krishnamurti and tyananda, and he signed a statement fore witnesses that he had no objection the boys being taken to England to conue their education. However, pressure m orthodox Hindu friends and relatives ade the father change his mind, and he ed for the restoration of the boys; and the urt ruled that they should be returned to e father by May, 1913. Mrs Besant pealed first to the High Court, Madras,

where she lost, and then to the Privy Council in London. There the case was reviewed with the welfare of the boys as the first priority. The boys had stated that they wished the benefits of an English education and did not wish to return to India. The Council over-ruled the two previous decisions, allowing the father, if he so wished, to make application in England for restoration regarding the guardianship, custody and maintenance of his children.

In 1910 Dr G. S. Arundale had formed among the boys of the Central Hindu College a private association called 'The Order of the Rising Sun of India'. He meant it to include those of his pupils who believed that the coming of a great Teacher was near. This Order was opened to the public in 1911, at the instance of Mrs Besant, and shortly afterwards she altered its name to 'The Order of the Star in the East', and put Krishnamurti at its head. The Order brought out a magazine called *The Herald of the Star,* and through sympathetic members of the Theosophical Society it spread rapidly in many countries. Other members strongly opposed its intrusion upon the time and resources of its followers.

Much newspaper publicity was focused upon Krishnamurti, whom they concluded to be a 'Messiah'. This effectively prevented him being sent to an English university, as it seemed certain his life would be made intolerable. His first venture into print was while still a boy, a booklet in simple English titled *At the Feet of the Master,* in which he recorded the instructions said to have been given him in sleep by an adept. Later he tried to express his mystical feelings in collections of poems, and wrote editorials for the magazine of the Order.

In the middle and late 1920s large gatherings of Star members took place yearly, camping in the grounds of Castle Eerde, belonging to Baron van Pallandt, near Ommen, in Holland. At the time of the first Camp, an unusual and severe cyclone

Founded by H. P. Blavatsky, in conjunction with Henry S. Olcott and W. Q. Judge, the Theosophical Society influenced many eminent figures including Mahatma Gandhi, the inventor Thomas Edison and W. B. Yeats *Below left* Mme Blavatsky, and (*left to right*) Dr G. S. Arundale, C. Jinarajadasa and N. Sri Ram, successive presidents of the Society

tore across that part of the Low Countries, and strangely seemed to bifurcate and pass on either side of the tented camp. The local villagers were much impressed in favour of the Star by this phenomenon. These gatherings with ritual camp-fires in the evening were like elderly versions of a Scout jamboree. According to Lady Emily Lutyens, on 10 August 1925 Dr Arundale brought through from his overnight experience the names of ten of the '12 apostles' of the new religious impulse that was to come through Krishnaji, as he was called.

However, Krishnamurti became increasingly impatient of being associated with theosophists. He had his own individual outlook and message. In 1929 he dissolved the Order of the Star in the East, and returned Castle Eerde and its grounds to Baron van Pallandt, who had wanted him, or a group on his behalf, to take it over. In the following years he made his base at Ojai in California, and there and elsewhere held seminars of talks and question and answer meetings. Many books, revised from these occasions, were published. He became a friend of Aldous Huxley and other original thinkers. From time to time he has visited Europe and India.

In 1927 he had a profound experience, and on 2 August he said: 'I could not have said last year, as I can say now, that I am the Teacher; for had I said it then it would have been insincere, it would have been untrue. But now I can say it. I have become one with the Beloved, I have been made simple. As I have changed, as I have found my end, which is the end for all . . . and because I have affection – and without affection you cannot attain the end . . . because I have suffered and seen and found all, naturally it is my duty . . . my pleasure, my dharma, to give it to those who have not . . . I am not going to be bound by anyone; I am going on my way, because that is the only way. I have found what I wanted. I have been united with my Beloved, and my Beloved and I will wander together the face of the earth.'

One cannot but agree with the English theosophist T. H. Redfern when he says: 'The strange and puzzling thing is that although his work has turned out much different from what was expected of him, yet Bishop Leadbeater, using his psychic faculties "picked a winner" in a lad of about

12, described by Professor Wood as "a very frail little boy, extremely weak . . . He was bullied and beaten to such an extent that it seemed the boy might fade away from this life and die."'

On the death of Dr Arundale in 1945, C. Jinarajadasa, or 'Brother Raja' as he was affectionately called in theosophical circles, became President of the Society and so remained until 1953. He took his degree at St John's, Cambridge, and later studied languages so that he could lecture in French, Italian, Spanish and Portuguese. He continually pressed for the introduction of Beauty and Art into theosophical work. He branched out in original directions; interviewed Mussolini in 1923; inspired the formation of a Muslim League to study the relation between Islam and theosophy; and devised a Ritual of the Mystic Star. Apart from his many excellent books, students of theosophy hold him in high esteem for his care of the headquarters archives, and the editing and publication of many documents which would otherwise have slipped into oblivion.

The successor to C. Jinarajadasa was N. Sri Ram. He was assistant editor of Mrs Besant's paper *New India* from 1923 to 1933, and was also her private secretary. In 1937 he was made Treasurer of the Theosophical Society. His lectures and writings are logically structured and full of a limpid wisdom. In spite of his years he is an active and continual traveller, and inspires the national sections by his quiet emphasis on the truly spiritual and unselfish solutions to world problems. His tenure of office has seen the completion and opening at Adyar of a fine new library building, which in addition to printed books, houses a very valuable collection of palm-leaf manuscripts. Recently a new building has been erected for the printing and publishing department, with a bust of its founder, Annie Besant, in the forecourt. The North American membership has been generous in its support of these projects.

Blueprint of Evolution

The important divergence of viewpoint between modern theosophy and current scientific thought is that the former insists that the evolutionary plan, both in the material and the non-physical worlds, pre-exists in blueprint form in the Universal Creative Mind. It cannot be substantially interfered with by man or angel. The supposed chance emergence of an organizing force which we call life, owing to the juxtaposition of certain chemicals, water, and sunlight, is regarded by theosophists as confusing the predetermined suitable conditions for life manifesting, with the cause of life so manifesting.

Theosophy harks back to Pythagoras (see PYTHAGORAS), and indeed to ancient India, in underlining number as a guide to understanding the scheme of things. There is One Supreme, the Logos or Word, expressing itself in a triple mode or Trinity. Seven distinctive streams of energy from the One pour out into 12 areas of expression. Creation is a continuous, or rather cyclically recurring, process throughout the Universe.

The widespread variety of stages in cyclic development occurring among suns, planets, supermen, men, animals, and lower kingdoms, permits the maximum economy of energy by using the mutual aid and interaction between the older and younger lives. For example, man in his extraction and manufacture of metals for his own use is speeding the development of the minerals. The failures and backward units of one cycle become the wise and stable shining lights of another or later cycle.

Self-conscious man, in theosophical theory, is the product of an extraordinarily long evolution, not only as to his body, but as to his thinking and emotional consciousness. The innermost unit of consciousness is divine in origin – 'the One willed to become Many' – but the bridging sheaths, through which that unit or monad can contact the physical world, have been taken over by him from some animal which reached the peak of animal consciousness. Then a long pilgrimage of incarnations is required to develop the means to become self-conscious at the highest levels, and ultimately conscious of unity with the One. These lives or incarnations are linked and moulded by the operation of the law of adjustment, or Karma (see KARMA). This law continually tends to balance outgoing forces. Energy continuously expended towards an objective must bring success if it lies in the realm of the possible. But it can produce an imbalance in the individual, and a back-surge of unexpected results if it is selfishly motivated.

Shrimati Rukmini Devi; the wife of Dr G. S. Arundale, she played an important part in the revival of the classical Indian dance, Indian art, and the education of women

C. Nelson Stewart

The prehistory of mankind goes back, the theosophical system, not tens of thousands, but millions of years. Seven great human types will develop during the earth present cycle of activity, and we are already well through the fifth type. But there a natural phenomena which shut off th great races from each other – ice age subsidence into the ocean, earthquakes an volcanic storms. These catastrophic even are initiated and controlled by non-huma intelligences under the command of th Planetary Logos. Hence the last word do not lie with man, who thinks he is no powerful enough to devastate his home space.

Later theosophists have published wh they claim to be life-stories and inciden recovered by clairvoyance from th 'memory of Nature'. Something similar done by what are called object-readers psychometrists in regard to more rece events. One extraordinary compilation Annie Besant and C. W. Leadbeater pu ports to describe in detail the infra-structu of many of the chemical atoms and mo cules. So far no bridge has been foun between their diagrams and models and t mathematically-based arrangements of t physicists. They tell us that the ultima physical atom is built in a spiralling vort of about 14,000 million bubbles in *koilo* Koilon, it seems, is what fills space. In th study of the building bricks of matter it interesting to hear that the atoms themselv alter in their capacity to respond to vibr tions as the cycles proceed. And it must admitted that these seers stumbled up isotopes before the scientists did.

An early Vice-President like A. P. Sinne thought membership should be sought the upper classes, and their acceptance the ideas would filter down to the low orders. When Annie Besant was at h peak as a travelling lecturer, the membe ship probably reached its highest leve When the post-Revolutionary spread Russian power took place, the countri dominated were unable to mainta theosophical societies. To some exte counterbalancing the loss, many ne centres opened in South American countri as a result of tours by C. Jinarajadasa, w was able to lecture in Spanish and Port guese. In 1925, when the Order of the St in the East was flourishing world-wide, membership exceeded 100,000 or mo than twice that of the Theosophical Societ The Theosophical membership figures (wi some returns awaited) given in the Gener Report for 1966 were 26,487 in 49 cou tries. The three largest totals were Indi 7664; United States of America, 405 and England, 2252.

C. NELSON STEWA

FURTHER READING: H. P. Blavatsky, *T Secret Doctrine* (Theosophical Publishi House, 1968, abridged edn); *Key Theosophy* (T. P. H., reprint); W. Q. Jud; *The Ocean of Theosophy* (T. P. H., reprin Mary Lutyens ed, *The Krishnamurti Read* (Penguin, 1970); Victor A. Endersby, *T Hall of Magic Mirrors* (Carlton Pre 1969).